Literary Criticism and Cultural Theory

Edited by
William E. Cain
Professor of English
Wellesley College

A Routledge Series

Literary Criticism and Cultural Theory
William E. Cain, *General Editor*

WILDERNESS CITY
The Post World War II American Urban Novel from Algren to Wideman
Ted L. Clontz

THE IMPERIAL QUEST AND MODERN MEMORY FROM CONRAD TO GREENE
J. M. Rawa

THE ETHICS OF EXILE
Colonialism in the Fictions of Charles Brockden Brown and J. M. Coetzee
Timothy Francis Strode

THE ROMANTIC SUBLIME AND MIDDLE-CLASS SUBJECTIVITY IN THE VICTORIAN NOVEL
Stephen Hancock

VITAL CONTACT
Downclassing Journeys in American Literature from Herman Melville to Richard Wright
Patrick Chura

COSMOPOLITAN FICTIONS
Ethics, Politics, and Global Change in the Works of Kazuo Ishiguro, Michael Ondaatje, Jamaica Kincaid, and J. M. Coetzee
Katherine Stanton

OUTSIDER CITIZENS
The Remaking of Postwar Identity in Wright, Beauvoir, and Baldwin
Sarah Relyea

AN ETHICS OF BECOMING
Configurations of Feminine Subjectivity in Jane Austen, Charlotte Brontë, and George Eliot
Sonjeong Cho

NARRATIVE DESIRE AND HISTORICAL REPARATIONS
A. S. Byatt, Ian McEwan, Salman Rushdie
Tim S. Gauthier

NIHILISM AND THE SUBLIME POSTMODERN
The (Hi)Story of a Difficult Relationship from Romanticism to Postmodernism
Will Slocombe

DEPRESSION GLASS
Documentary Photography and the Medium of the Camera Eye in Charles Reznikoff, George Oppen, and William Carlos Williams
Monique Claire Vescia

FATAL NEWS
Reading and Information Overload in Early Eighteenth-Century Literature
Katherine E. Ellison

NEGOTIATING COPYRIGHT
Authorship and the Discourse of Literary Property Rights in Nineteenth-Century America
Martin T. Buinicki

"FOREIGN BODIES"
Trauma, Corporeality, and Textuality in Contemporary American Culture
Laura Di Prete

OVERHEARD VOICES
Address and Subjectivity in Postmodern American Poetry
Ann Keniston

MUSEUM MEDIATIONS
Reframing Ekphrasis in Contemporary American Poetry
Barbara K. Fischer

THE POLITICS OF MELANCHOLY FROM SPENSER TO MILTON
Adam H. Kitzes

THE POLITICS OF MELANCHOLY
FROM SPENSER TO MILTON

Adam H. Kitzes

Routledge
New York & London

Published in 2006 by
Routledge
Taylor & Francis Group
270 Madison Avenue
New York, NY 10016

Published in Great Britain by
Routledge
Taylor & Francis Group
2 Park Square
Milton Park, Abingdon
Oxon OX14 4RN

© 2006 by Taylor & Francis Group, LLC
Routledge is an imprint of Taylor & Francis Group

Transferred to Digital Printing 2009

International Standard Book Number-10: 0-415-97628-6 (Hardcover)
International Standard Book Number-13: 978-0-415-97628-2 (Hardcover)
Library of Congress Card Number 2005031467

No part of this book may be reprinted, reproduced, transmitted, or utilized in any form by any electronic, mechanical, or other means, now known or hereafter invented, including photocopying, microfilming, and recording, or in any information storage or retrieval system, without written permission from the publishers.

Trademark Notice: Product or corporate names may be trademarks or registered trademarks, and are used only for identification and explanation without intent to infringe.

Library of Congress Cataloging-in-Publication Data

Kitzes, Adam H., 1971-
　　The politics of melancholy from Spenser to Milton / by Adam H. Kitzes.
　　　　p. cm. -- (Literary criticism and cultural theory)
　　Includes bibliographical references (p.) and index.
　　ISBN 0-415-97628-6
　　1. English literature--Early modern, 1500-1700--History and criticism. 2. Melancholy in literature.
3. Politics and literature--Great Britain--History--16th century. 4. Politics and literature--Great Britain--History--17th century. I. Title. II. Series.

PR428.M4K58 2006
820.9'353--dc22   2005031467

ISBN10: 0-415-97628-6 (hbk)
ISBN10: 0-415-80291-1 (pbk)

ISBN13: 978-0-415-97628-2 (hbk)
ISBN13: 978-0-415-80291-8 (pbk)

Taylor & Francis Group
is the Academic Division of Informa plc.

Visit the Taylor & Francis Web site at
http://www.taylorandfrancis.com

and the Routledge Web site at
http://www.routledge-ny.com

Publisher's Note
The publisher has gone to great lengths to ensure the quality of this reprint but points out that some imperfections in the original may be apparent.

For My Parents

Contents

Acknowledgments — ix

Introduction
Black Humor — 1

Section I
The Production of Melancholy as a Discourse — 25

Chapter One
Melancholy and the Possibility of Nationhood in Bright and Spenser — 27

Chapter Two
"Reason is Fled to Beasts": Malcontents and Animals in the "Humour" Plays of Jonson and Shakespeare — 59

Chapter Three
Civil Dissension and its Malcontents, or States of Melancholy — 85

Section II
Melancholy and the Question of Government — 103

Chapter Four
"And Yet I am My Own Executioner": Rumor, Suicide, and Textual Authority in John Donne's *Devotions* — 105

Chapter Five
Robert Burton and the "Language" of Melancholy — 123

Section III
The Distractions of the Times   151

Chapter Six
The Distractions of the Times: Ideologies of Madness and
Disease During the Civil War and Interregnum   153

Chapter Seven
"Tell us the Sum": Milton's Accounts of Melancholy and Madness
in the 1670s   175

Notes   197

Bibliography   233

Index   255

Acknowledgments

This project began as a dissertation entitled, "'This River Leads to Saturn': The Paradoxes of Melancholy and the Early Modern State:" The dissertation was completed in 2003 at University of Wisconsin-Madison, under the direction of Heather Dubrow, who painstakingly read and re-read sections, offered suggestions for revision, and provided the encouragement I needed to see the project through in a timely fashion. Jacques Lezra, David Loewenstein, and Susanne Wofford served on the committee, generously offering both their time and their attention to help refine the overall shape of the project. In addition to the supervision and suggestions for revisions that the committee members offered, numerous colleagues offered support in the form of advice, feisty conversations, and complaints. These included David Ainsworth, Jason Cohen, Amy Cort, Bob Darcy, Jonathan Ewell, Cora Fox, Jon Fowler, Thomas Herron, Braden Hosch Rebecca Lemon, James Mardock, Jim Neighbors, Elizabeth Rivlin, Matthias Rudolf, Jeff Theis, Henry Turner and Andrew Weiner.

During subsequent years, many others have in order to help realize *The Politics of Melancholy* in its current form. I am especially grateful to the members of the NEH Seminar, held at the Folger Shakespeare Library in the summer of 2003, entitled "Sites of Stress From Reformation to Revolution." The conversations that took place in the Folger basement could not have been more lively, and many of the new developments between dissertation and book have their source in that "site of stress." I am also grateful to my colleagues at the University of Missouri, who expressed an interest in my work, who read sections, and who offered their own fresh insights. These included Bill Kerwin, Ellie Ragland, and David Read. Most important, I would like to thank my family, without whom none of this would have been possible.

Introduction
Black Humor

"Thus millions are miserable, melancholy, discontent, by their own conceit; when thousands would think themselves happy, had they but a piece of their happiness. Which discontent or melancholy occasions more murmuring amongst us, than ever there was among those Israelites in the wilderness; an unthankfulness able to make or keep them poor and miserable, and that everlastingly."

—Richard Younge, *The Prevention of Poverty, Together with the Cure of Melancholy, Alias Discontent.*

"Me been two, tree, fore day studying and turning over all de Autors to find cure for your distemper. Me read Galen, Hippocrates, Sennertus Fuchsius and twenty more, and break me Brane vit de study, and now you spoil all vit de Caudle—cram—cram—cram—. . . Maistress Priscilla, you be de very learned Voman—but you be troubled also very much vid de Melancholly, I can prove dat—and all de House is troubled vid de Melancholly, and all de Varld is troubled vid de melancholly."

—Dr. Quibus, *The Factious Citizen, or, The Melancholy Visioner.*

"From this Complexion are *Poets,* and the more highly pretending *Enthusiasts:* Betwixt whom this is the great difference, That a *Poet* is an *enthusiast in jest,* and an *Enthusiast* is a *Poet in good earnest;* Melancholy prevailing so much with him, that he takes his no better then *Poeticall* fits and figments for divine Inspiration and reall Truth."

—Henry More, *Enthusiasmus Triumphatus: Or, A Brief Discourse of The Nature, Causes, Kinds, and Cure of Enthusiasm*

The title of this book makes clear enough what its topic consists of; that does not necessarily mean, however, that it answers all questions concerning what it is actually about. To begin with, in exactly *what* sense can melancholy be understood as a matter of politics in sixteenth and seventeenth century England? After all, in its original sense, the word refers alternately to a physiological substance—one of the four humors, as described in Hippocratic medicine[1]—or to the disorder believed to have been brought about by an excessive amount of that same substance. If the so-called melancholy disposition has outlasted the physiological system that gave rise to it in the first place, that fact owes more to poets who are given to lament such things as "beauty, a beauty that must die," than to statesmen or (lasso!) policymakers. Even in contemporary psychology, the term feels like a decidedly out of date manner of speaking about depression (a point we will return to later). Melancholy thus has its place in physiology, psychology, and poetry, and by no means is it immediately obvious that it lends itself to political matters as well.

Meanwhile, other questions emerge. Even if "politics of melancholy" is accepted from the outset, what justifies a political study in a period that has been more or less defined by two *poets* (poets who did enjoy careers in public office, but who saw their ambitions as literary above all)? Finally, why another study on melancholy at all; in what sense do questions about melancholy remain unanswered, and exactly what does another book about melancholy suggest about the state of scholarship at the beginning of the twenty-first century?[2] The following pages represent both my effort to provide answers to these concerns, as well as to provide a more detailed description of what the remaining chapters set out to accomplish.

Straightforward as it may appear, the phrase "politics of melancholy" serves a number of purposes; that being the case, I begin by discussing in what senses I use it here. To the extent that this project has its origins in a single event, one might say that it began with the re-discovery of a series of interregnum and Restoration texts. Among them were included several pamphlets and sermons in which the authors made explicit links between melancholy and a set of publicly disruptive conditions, all of which (taken together) suggested that the disease was not only a personal affair, but a matter of concern for the commonwealth as a whole. These included, among others, Richard Younge's contention that widespread poverty was contributing to an excessive amount of discontent throughout the Protectorate.[3] On a different level, there appeared a series of pamphlets concerning the question of religious enthusiasm—one of the more threatening assaults on traditional church authority, and in turn the subject of one of the more cantankerous debates during the 1650s. Among those who objected to self-proclaimed enthusiasts on the traditional grounds that the Bible explicitly warns against false prophets, a few writers included the additional claim that such blasphemers were afflicted with melancholy.[4] Finally, there turned up an anonymous city comedy, apparently staged during the 1690s, entitled, "The Melancholy Visioner, or The Factious Citizen."[5] The play was a spoof about Quakers—a family of self-proclaimed messiahs who, despite the recent settlement, continued to conspire to bring down as many institutions of authority as they could name. Also in the playwright's sights was the profession of medical know-it-alls who tried to link religious and social misconduct with the medical condition of melancholy. Thus midway through the play, when the Quaker daughter proves herself to be too much for others to handle, enters a Dutch doctor (Caius), who is two parts watered down Burton, one part Commedia dell'Arte buffoon, and one part broken English, (in the manner of what Thomas Middleton used to stage in his city comedies). By the time the doctor is finished, audiences cannot help but realize that he is in fact part of the problem. Meanwhile, they may be entitled to wonder whether the problem itself is the remnant of a cultural crisis that, for inexplicable reasons, refuses to come to an end.

Sadly, while this play does receive extensive analysis or criticism in the chapters that follow—a shortcoming that I concede—nevertheless, the issues it raises figure in the background. For at the outset, and on a much larger scale, this project undertakes to something that happens both in the spoof and in the sorts of materials it ostensibly holds up to ridicule. Namely, certain forms of misconduct and turmoil—sometimes violent in its manifestations—come to be characterized as symptoms of melancholy. And indeed it is from this play that the following questions come to mind: in what ways did writers from the early modern period understand melancholy explicitly in the context of political affairs; more specifically, in what ways did writers use melancholy in order to account for political turmoil, including disobedience and religious enthusiasm, but also extending to faction, rebellion, and civil war?

For in fact, when we examine the tremendous and diverse body of writing about melancholy, written between 1580 and 1700—this would include literary texts, books on physiology or "health," spiritual guidebooks, sermons, treatments for melancholy (often taking the form of jest books), even political speeches—we discover in sometimes surprising fashion that while it certainly wasn't the only way to account for political turmoil, nevertheless it was one definite way. More important, it could perform a considerable number of tasks, depending on who was using it. Thus the word "melancholy" could, in turn, describe a symptom of or cause for discontent, be it social, economic, or otherwise. It could also describe, alternately, the causes and symptoms of civil war, and all the more so when it was used in conjunction with such related terms as madness, frenzy, distractions, and furor.[6] Perhaps most intriguingly, many writers used it to account for various forms of publicly disruptive religious conduct, such as religious enthusiasm and lay prophecy; and if this is intriguing, it is not only because it represents a clear attempt to pathologize politically subversive conduct, but more importantly because both the pathology and the general theory of the humors on which it was based had come to be as questionable as the behavior that such writers purported to describe. As this survey already suggests, during the historical period that has been dubbed "the age of melancholy" by literary historians, the condition could be used to account for a considerable variety of potentially disruptive political action.

All of this may sound counterintuitive, for as it is commonly understood melancholy describes a condition that has little to do with any activity whatsoever, let alone such public activity. The conventional melancholic tended to be associated with quietude and seclusion; if melancholics had an anthem, it would have been "O sweet woods, the delight of solitariness." To be sure, one precedent did exist: the link between melancholy and statesmanship appeared in a classical text, known as the *Problems,* commonly believed to have been written by Aristotle (though more likely by his student Theophrastus).[7] As that text posed the question: "Why is it that philosophers, statesmen and politicians all have a melancholy temperament, so much so that it often appears as though they are afflicted with the disease itself?" Significantly, though, as some of its most astute commentators have observed, the Renaissance readers who revived the *Problems* were much more responsive to its emphasis on the contemplative life.[8] If Marsilio Ficino drew inspiration from the passage, it was not in order to create better statesman, but rather to encourage his own readers to seek better wisdom, and to seek it carefully (for as Ficino knew, melancholy was not without its dangers). As we shall observe in chapter one, this claim holds true for English writers who undertook to write about the disease in the late 1500s, during what might be considered the introduction of melancholy into early modern English discourse. Finally, among genealogies of mental pathology, melancholy has frequently been taken as something of an historical midpoint between acedia (sloth) and the contemporary illness known as depression. Freud's remarks are among the most memorable (if not the most original), when he characterizes it as a peculiar form of grief, or a mourning that exceeds the value of the object ostensibly lost.[9] One might just as well think of the young Nietzsche, who associated melancholy with—of all things—too much attention to historical detail, at the expense of life itself.[10] Given the prevailing tendency to regard melancholy as one of the more extreme rejections of the active world, it is a bit surprising to realize that, for early modern England, this was not always the case.

In many ways, in fact, early modern England may have been particularly well-suited to connect melancholy with political turmoil. To begin with, the interest in melancholy took place in the context of renewed interest in the classical theory of the "body-politic." This concept had posited an analogy between the individual human body and the collective "body" that political organizations consisted of. More than a mere literary topos, the notion of the body politic could give rise to an extraordinary and diverse set of rules concerning good government. In John Huarte's *Examination of Men's Wits,* for instance, the author lays out a system for assigning individual members of society to various prescribed public positions which, in turn, corresponded to the bodily functions they were supposed to resemble. (This totalitarian vision was in fact a revival of the portrait of public organization as it is found in Plato's *Republic.*) Alternately, a book like Thomas Wright's *Passions of the Minde in Generall* could describe the respective functions of human faculties in ways that suggested that our bodies were effectively well fortified, yet vulnerable institutions, always on the lookout either for attack or defense. While they put it to different purposes, both writers took for granted that they could not only use the analogy but extend it to as many particulars as they saw fit.

As the subsequent chapters will discuss more extensively, the analogy between a healthy body and healthy state could perform the additional task of indicating that all parts intuitively understood their respective positions within a predetermined hierarchy, while simultaneously remaining united under the collective purpose of health and sustenance. By the same token, political disorder could be regarded as unnatural as trying to see with one's foot, to modify an example that appears in the *Homily Against Disobedience and Wylful Rebellion.* Such rhetoric was not new to early modern political theorists, though it appears to have taken on renewed significance, especially as the Tudor and early Stuart monarchs sought to consolidate power under their own governance, and thus reshape the political structure of the nation along more centralized lines. (It did not hurt that King James was particularly fond of the analogy, and that he repeatedly envisioned the role of a good monarch as roughly the equivalent to a good physician. I do not think it is entirely a coincidence that Donne's most eloquent meditations on melancholy and rebellion, as well as Burton's *Anatomy* were composed late in his reign.) As the following chapters also discuss, however, this renewed interest was accompanied by a series of imaginative transformations, particularly as conceptualizations about state power, as well as the physical body itself underwent significant re-evaluations. It is difficult to sustain an analogy between body and state when new forays into anatomy, on the one hand,

and equally revolutionary discoveries about the nature of power, on the other, begin to challenge long held beliefs about what these respective entities were in the first place. Rather than sustain a traditional hierarchical model of government based on a principle of health as stability and harmony, then, the renewed interest in the body-politic topos signaled growing concerns with respect to questions of what political "health" might consist of. Paradoxically, the renewed interest in political health occurred during a period when its traditional expressions proved untenable on both theoretical and practical levels.

To be sure, early modern England was concerned with a considerable number of illnesses; many of them were far more deadly than melancholy (and to that extent their concern hardly needs explaining). Thus the fact that melancholy itself took on widespread interest might also be understood as a sign that certain principles of cultural unity were undergoing scrutiny. For in many ways, melancholy signaled a cultural divide, particularly during those moments when it was considered *fashionable*. Chapters one and two discuss the ways in which the publication of major treatises about melancholy during the late sixteenth century expressed a tension between certain philosophical systems associated with continental learning (Ficino, notably, but also Bruno) and the theological interests of the reformed English church. In other words, it examines what it may have meant for writers like Timothy Bright or Edmund Spenser to take an interest in melancholy while simultaneously dedicating themselves to a program of militant and proto-nationalistic Protestantism. On still another level, I consider what it may have meant for conventionalized representations of malcontents to be associated so frequently with travel, and particularly with travel to Italy. Why *did* so many stage characters return to their respective homes, only to find themselves so terribly, yet so predictably disappointed in their peers and traditional mores? To simply say that melancholy represented a form of rebellious self-assertion seems, in some ways, not to answer these questions sufficiently. Rather, as I argue, the interest in melancholy was spurred, at least in part, by a concern over the very principles of uniformity and collective membership that defined official political spaces. Indeed, to write about melancholy could (and frequently did) expose many of the internal inconsistencies that marked such a project of defining the political domain as such in the first place.

The collective body of literary texts, medical treatises and spiritual guidebooks gave rise to a diverse array of melancholy types, which in turn intersected with a fairly complex set of political concerns. Put another way, not all melancholics were alike, and it is part of the purpose of this study to examine these differences. To that end I reconsider a popular expression of melancholy from the period, and a type that has already enjoyed considerable attention from previous literary studies, namely the malcontent.[11] The melancholy malcontent was a recognizable stock figure in drama by as early as 1580;[12] when he was not represented on stage he appeared in verse satire, a form that enabled him to stand at some distance from his intended audience.[13] As a type, he generated both terror and ridicule among his peers—the surest sign of cultural anxiety, for in the end the malcontent figure did harbor a legitimate complaint that his own talents had been thwarted by an unequal social system that seemed designed specifically to keep the likes of him from fulfilling their true potential. In addition to this stock character, as this study shows, we can include such instances as the following: Spenser's translations of Du Bellay's "Complaints," in which he compares the civil wars of Rome to an uprising of the humors, or his depiction of rebellion as a form of melancholy illness, such as he does in the Castle of Alma episode of *The Faerie Queene;* John Donne's sermons and meditations on illness, which seem inconceivable without reference to melancholy and madness; and an abstraction of the disease as the key for understanding corruption and civil uprisings, such as Burton presents it in the opening pages of his *Anatomy of Melancholy*. Most important, in order to reinforce that the melancholic was more than simply a popular fictional type whose fortunes went the way of the public theater, chapter six focuses on the disorder in connection with the events of the civil war and interregnum period. Dissension between Parliament and the crown, and the ascendance of the Roundheads, followed by the emergence of various radical religious sects in the 1650s, sparked a tremendous number of pamphlets, sermons, ballads and speeches about melancholy, along with its counterparts, such as frenzy, madness, distraction and delusion. Clearly understood as a disease rather than an enabling condition, it became a convenient way to account for political conflicts in all spheres. As we shall also observe in chapter six, pamphlet writers invoked an astonishing number of terms in order to characterize the public disorders that England underwent during these decades—indeed, section three takes its title "The Distractions of the Times" from a popular phrase that linked civil war with mental illness in a particularly effective manner. In other words, melancholy becomes a component of a larger discursive system that sought to frame political turbulence under a broad spectrum of conditions that were coming to be defined as "madness."

The notion that any society's definition of madness is marked by political conflict has become, if not a commonplace, then a belief shared by many. On one level, to identify certain forms of behavior as symptoms of madness frequently amounts to an expression of power in its most brute forms; and diagnosing certain members of a society with pathological afflictions can be a way of silencing their complaints, invalidating whatever grievances they happen to hold. Thus, for instance, one person's mania could be another person's intense dissatisfaction with the distribution of property. (And certainly, no less an authority than Paul himself sanctioned certain types of folly precisely because they exposed the true folly of worldly wisdom.) On a perhaps more complex level, the discursive strategies that seek to identify madness, and to distinguish it from ostensibly "rational" states of mind, are themselves contaminated by ideological presuppositions, to which they must necessarily remain blind. Merely to categorize the mental lives of human beings in terms of madness and sanity is already to engage in a process that advances certain forms of knowledge as expressions of power. When this project emerged, a number of crucial studies, not only of melancholy but of madness more generally in early modern England had already made considerable headway in advancing each of these positions.[14] Winfried Schleiner's *Melancholy, Genius, and Utopia*, for instance, is instrumental in terms of differentiating different systems of belief that, in turn, gave rise to radically different conceptions of melancholy. As Schleiner suggests, these differences were not merely theoretical, but in fact were the expressions of very real political disputes among those who participated in representing the human mind. Specifically, he refers to the problem of lay prophecy and divination:

> The gift of divination, which as we shall see has a wide range of meaning in the Renaissance and which in the most prominent texts was attributed to melancholics (or at least to some melancholics), became the crucial topic that divided Renaissance thinkers. For with that topic melancholy became relevant to theology and thus to politics.[15]

Indeed, my own study has benefited considerably both from research which has demonstrated the ways in which the concept of madness was contested by various writers. Meanwhile, my research draws from the work of writers like Roy Porter, Fiona Godlee, Clement Hawes, and several others, each of whom respectively examines the ways in which the developing category of madness served the interests of the politically dominant classes.[16] According to some of these critical assessments, the history of madness can be re-written as the history of marginalization. This holds true particularly for the interregnum, when writers came to use melancholy as a device for countering religious radicalism, specifically (though not exclusively) the Quaker movement. In working with these premises, I regard melancholy as a function of ideology, inasmuch as it was employed as a demystifying term that had the peculiar tendency to occlude as much as it brought to light.

As important as the conflicting opinions and beliefs that differentiated writers from each other, this project often attends to internalized differences *within* specific writers, rather than to the disputes between one writer (or group of writers) and another. For as will become clear in the chapters that follow, melancholy performed multiple, inconsistent tasks for individual writers. Such inconsistencies may have been the result of changes to a writer's way of what Debora Shuger describes as "conflicts as much within individuals as between sects or parties, conflicts that seemed to have less to do with formulated doctrines . . . than with barely articulated assumptions and feelings about how the pieces of the world fit together, about what counts as fitting."[17] In either case, while such internal inconsistencies may prevent us from drawing conclusions about a particular writer's beliefs about a topic, they also throw into doubt such projects that interpret melancholy in early modern literature according to the "prevailing" medical knowledge about the condition during the period. There is no physiological or theological context against which literary texts can be read securely, but rather all texts whether literary or otherwise were concerned with the question of what melancholy *could* mean. To write about melancholy was effectively to bring it forth, and to that extent, all writing about melancholy was, if not poetic, then at least "poietic."

As I argue then, one of the curious features that many of the writers I discuss share, is that to write about melancholy becomes, in part, an attempt to discover just *what* it is. For in a deeply troubling way, it could be as elusive as it was ubiquitous and as hard to define as it was plain for anyone with eyes to see.[18] To that end my approach is heavily informed by the major iconographical studies that appeared in the first half of the twentieth century.[19] It is important to stress, here, that a version of my position can already be found in the book *Saturn and Melancholy*. This collaborative study by Klibansky, Saxl and Panofsky, (as well as Panofsky's study of Albrecht Dürer, which offers an abridged account), has more or less determined the way contemporary critics understand the history of melancholy in the Renaissance. As they argue, the concept of melancholy (and its attendant deity/zodiacal sign Saturn) underwent a substantial "philosophical rehabilitation" during the late fifteenth and early sixteenth centuries.[20] At the hands of Marsilio Ficino in particular, the pseudo-Aristotelian doctrine of the melancholy genius was revived and worked into a larger philosophy of inspiration; and if this new philosophy did not altogether supplant the prevailing medieval assumptions that melancholy was a component of sloth or *acedia* (insofar as it was a matter of concern at all), it did create a substantial cult of genius throughout the continent. Most importantly for the Warburg critics, the restoration of genial melancholy single-handedly transformed the notion of the artist from craftsman to isolated, deeply disturbed individual who lives beyond the trappings of the conventional social world. In short, this artistic type—among whom were included Michelangelo, Raphael, and Tasso on the continent, Donne and Shakespeare in England—embodied all the characteristics of eccentric genius that so much criticism of subsequent years has rejected as ideological mystification. The artist/genius who represented the culmination of this philosophical revival was, of course, Dürer, whose *Melancolia I* embodies not only the Ficinian philosophical ideal, but a truly massive collection of medieval attitudes toward melancholy as sin as well. In Panofsky's words:

> Blasphemous toward Dürer as it may sound—those homespun images must be counted among the ancestry of his famous engraving. Primitive though they are, they supplied its basic compositional formula, as well as the general idea of gloomy inertia. In both cases a woman, prominently placed in the foreground, is accompanied in a diagonal grouping by a less important representative of the opposite sex, and in both cases the essential characteristic of the main figure is her inaction.[21]

Of course what matters to Panofsky is not the source of Dürer's engraving, but the way he transforms it to correspond with Ficino's revival of melancholy inspiration. To be both genius and sinner at once—to walk atop the mountains at the cost of a stable ground—this was the truest and most precarious manifestation of melancholy that one could hope to attain.[22]

Rather than develop as a single coherent set of beliefs though, Renaissance melancholy was the conglomeration—really, the lumping together—of several different strands of thinking, not all of which were entirely compatible with one another. To that end, a clear link develops between melancholy and iconography, so much so that the very discipline of iconography can be seen as the response to an overwhelming array of symptoms, pseudo-symptoms and idiosyncrasies, all of which somehow needed to be organized. As it is put in *Saturn and Melancholy*:

> What was needed was not so much a full or even a profound picture as one that was clearly defined. Men wished to know how the choleric, the sanguine or the melancholy type could infallibly be recognized, at what times each had to be particularly careful, and in what manner he had to combat the dangers of his particular disposition.[23]

Small wonder, then, that iconography and melancholy should go hand in hand—almost as though the relative stillness of the melancholic in itself signaled a willingness to accept one's role *qua* figure.

As desirable as a clear portrait of melancholy may have seemed, it was precisely this over-determination that both produced the initial need for an iconography and threatened to dissolve it into a cacophony of disconnected ideas and statements.[24] In the search for a coherent picture of melancholy, cases that might be classified as marginal or borderline become increasingly difficult to account for. This has troubling implications for the authors of *Saturn and Melancholy*. On occasion, the conclusions they draw seem downright bizarre, such as in the case with Petrarch. To the extent that they deal with Petrarch at all—which is not very much, in fact—they do their best to show that, while he anticipates "a world yet to come," he is not an authentic melancholy figure after all:

> The same poet who describes so joyfully his own poetic ecstasies was yet familiar with that state of empty depression and dull grief which made him "see all life in black," and with a sadness which drove him from company to solitude, and from solitude to company once more . . . But he is still far from describing this sadness—which, to quote Lessing, gives his poems a "voluptuous melancholy" as "melancholy" itself. Rather he calls it by the medieval name of "acedia," which, however, as he uses it, seems to hover half-way between sin and disease.[25]

Given the dimensions of lyric poetry in the sixteenth and seventeenth centuries, particularly the trend known as Petrarchism, we must wonder what, after all, is behind this distinction. At its worst, it seems far-fetched. At its best, it points to a subtle methodological restriction which, though understandable, nevertheless ends up closing off the very cases that made iconography necessary (and that it therefore benefits most to leave open), namely the cases that resist the theoretical schema we have developed in retrospect.[26]

My point here is not to find fault with the above critical assessment of Petrarch, but rather to acknowledge just how difficult can be the problems that emerge in the most basic attempts to define melancholy. In fact, this is a problem shared both by modern critics and the texts they study. For my part, I address this issue by examining many literary texts in which characters exhibit some of the traditional characteristics of melancholy without going so far as to present themselves as actual malcontents—characters such as Shakespeare's Brutus, Milton's Samson, and perhaps the John Donne of later years. Unlike more traditionally recognizable characters such as Hamlet, Jaques, or Malevole, these characters have been viewed as melancholy only occasionally by contemporary critics; but such diagnoses depend on importing contextual knowledge that may or may not be appropriate for the occasion. Rather than prove or disprove whether these characters are melancholic though, I examine the limitations of the term as an explanatory device in their respective cases, particularly as it intersects with political conflict.

As will become clear in the following chapters, one of the recurring concerns among the writers I discuss is a need to represent melancholy in static terms. Consequently, the mere acknowledgment of temporality frequently comes across as a problem to be staved off, particularly insofar as it compromises their ability to define the subject they are writing about. Burton's choice of the term "anatomy" for his study of melancholy was hardly an accident. To anatomize is to work with a corpse, and with the corpse comes the assurance that the subject will not unexpectedly change positions. For similar reasons, several of the writers whom I discuss make recourse to Orpheus, a figure who plays a prominent role in the sections on Spenser and Burton (and who is in the background for the sections on *Julius Caesar* and *Samson Agonistes*). What makes Orpheus such an important figure in discussions of melancholy is not only his resemblance to the pseudo-Aristotelian genius figure; as a singer, he possesses the unique ability to stop the flow of rivers, even to halt time itself, as allegorical interpretations of the legend maintained.[27] So too does his death and dismemberment, his floating in pieces down the river while his head continues to sing, indicate his ultimate surrender to Heraclitian temporality. Finally, as the following chapters will suggest, in many ways melancholy amounts to the sudden recognition that one cannot simply step out of the trappings of immediate circumstances—we cannot comprehend the shape of the world from a mountain-top, as Burton's Democritus Jr. invites his readers to do. Such recognition does not come without a tremendous price, as the characters I discuss demonstrate, particularly during their moments of crisis. As will become evident throughout the course of this book, to be melancholic (particularly in the political arena) is to pursue a sense of justice and order that one must acknowledge cannot exist except within the confines of one's own imagination.

Given the nature of this project, I rely less directly on psychoanalytic theory, in its original formulation, in the many subsequent revisions from within the field itself, or in the many subsequent critiques that have emerged in the wake of feminism, new historicism, and deconstruction. There is, however, one important exception. In the course of studying the relation between melancholy and political turmoil, I do make use of related psychoanalytic studies that discuss the relation between melancholy and aggression. Certain aspects of psychoanalytic theory are particularly helpful in pointing us to a connection between aggression and self-reproach, and this connection is a useful starting point for articulating the role melancholy plays in political affairs. It is useful to reconsider the ambivalent hatred/love with which Freud characterizes the melancholy patient; as he argues in "Mourning and Melancholia," the self-loathing of the melancholy patient, often exaggerated, nevertheless just as often seems an appropriate gesture of hatred toward "someone whom the patient loves or has loved or should love."[28] In fact, when Freud identifies what finally constitutes melancholia, the political undertones that had been present throughout the essay suddenly become explicit:

> Their complaints are really 'plaints' in the old sense of the word . . . All this is possible only because the reactions expressed in their behaviour still proceed from a mental constellation of revolt which has then, by a certain process, passed over into the crushed state of melancholia.[29]

If there is a connection between a psychic state normally associated with sluggishness, isolation and inactivity, and the most violent assertions of power imaginable, it is that melancholy is always only a step or two away from this revolt against external oppressive forces. For Freud, melancholy is hatred with a conscience. In subsequent generations of psychoanalytic theory, among writers as distinct as Melanie Klein and Julia Kristeva, melancholy has become associated with an infantile aggression that is fully cannibalistic in nature. Kristeva describes the dynamic of hatred and aggression in melancholy patients, where it becomes apparent that what the patient wants to destroy is the hated other:

> According to classic psychoanalytic theory . . . depression, like mourning, conceals an aggressiveness toward the lost object, thus revealing the ambivalence of the depressed person with respect to the object of mourning. "I love that object," is what that person seems to say about the lost object, "but even more so I hate it; because I love it, and in order not to lose it, I imbed it in myself; but because I hate it, that other within myself is a bad self, I am bad, I am non-existent, I shall kill myself." The complaint against oneself would therefor be a complaint against another, and putting oneself to death but a tragic disguise for massacring an other.[30]

It is the infant's pre-Oedipal relation to the maternal breast, in short, that becomes the defining moment in cannibalistic aggression. By extension, I argue, based upon these descriptions of self-reproach there will be apparent enough reasons for certain individuals to redirect their internal grief toward other, more "palatable" objects.[31]

This is not to say that my approach will consist exclusively of linking early modern melancholy to twentieth century psychoanalysis at the expense of other possibilities. Some texts lend themselves better than others to the sorts of readings that a properly psychoanalytic hypothesis suggests. In fact, while the bond between melancholy and aggression may play a role in framing a politics of melancholy, in the long run I rely on early modern theories of the *humors* and of the *body politic,* many of which were often shrewd enough in pointing out what was repressed among their own worlds. In particular, I focus on texts where these two doctrines intersect. Many of the texts I examine are themselves deeply concerned with the relation between the constitution of the healthy body and the creation of healthy commonwealths, frequently linking various forms of revolt to various sorts of illness; rather than tie them back to a Freudian or post-Freudian solution, I explore the way these writers themselves tried to express this relation. And as it turns out, many suggest a model for what might be called the "melancholy of politics," a condition which includes the following components: the awareness that the elements that create the political commonwealth turn out to be the very elements that bring about its ruin, so that paradoxically rebellion, sedition, and illness become indistinguishable from the "healthy" body politic; the awareness that the very terminology available to express this condition might itself be insufficient; and the suspicion that an insufficient way to describe the body politic might have something to do with its inevitable collapse. If melancholy had such a tremendous impact on Elizabethan and Stuart England, and if it had its deepest impact on those parts of society which, for one reason or another, faced disenfranchisement, perhaps the most compelling explanation is that it became a vehicle to address the inadequacies in the very language of political experience. To write about melancholy was thus not merely a way to vocalize discontent with society; in many cases, the cases that are of interest to this project, it was to call into question whether discontent could even be expressed.

Each of the following chapters attends to a specific aspect of this problem. *The Politics of Melancholy* is organized into three sections. Section one, "The Production of Melancholy as a Discourse," reevaluates the work of several writers who introduced melancholy into late Elizabethan literary and social milieus. During approximately the last twenty five years of the sixteenth century the status of melancholy in England changed from virtually irrelevant to tremendously important; and by the time Queen Elizabeth died melancholy had penetrated virtually all aspects of the arts, to say nothing of medicine and theology. Literary and cultural historians have offered a number of explanations to account for this sudden and remarkable transformation. Among them, it was an unexpected consequence of the new vogue for learning—or more precisely, an unprecedented upsurge in public education, itself brought on by the need to create an intellectual population capable of explaining the new policies of the Church of England. As more individuals came to perceive themselves as educated, or at least educated in the linguistic arts, the pseudo-Aristotelian doctrine of melancholy would have appealed for its erudite qualities alone; so much the better that that document claimed melancholy made for great intellectuals when properly harnessed.

Meanwhile, with the increase in intellectuals came an increase in *alienated* intellectuals, as more and more talented individuals confronted fewer and fewer opportunities to realize those talents professionally.[32] Again, the language and iconography of melancholy provided suitable terms to complain about thwarted, or unrecognized genius. To take only two examples (both related in some manner to lyric): Petrarchan love poetry became a coded way to express both rhetorical talent and alienation, thus becoming, implicitly, the vehicle for announcing unwarranted political marginality; similarly, poetic complaints could give rise to that notorious political phenomenon, namely the ruin of kingdoms and empires. (Spenser, for instance, translated a number of complaints that lamented the destruction of Rome.) As a corollary, the complaint could give rise to the oddity of a political subject whose membership within an identifiable state has been reduced to incessant mourning. (Incidentally, this condition is not the same thing as exile, for an exile depends on the existence of the state in order to attain his status as such; by contrast, the melancholic literally has no place to return to.)

The fascination with melancholy also seems to have emerged in a political climate that was already rife with other various forms of political discontent. It seems more than coincidence that the so-called vogue of melancholy emerged when Queen Elizabeth began to face serious challenges to her authority, some of which were significant enough to raise doubts about her command. These included the Jesuit infiltration of the 1580s, the Irish rebellions and subsequent Spanish war toward the end of the same decade, and the series of spectacular coup attempts whose own failures owed as much to their planners' shortsightedness as to the Queen's political acumen. While Queen Elizabeth did ultimately enjoy remarkable longevity, and while her popularity in death gained considerable momentum, her successes were determined more by her ability to withstand discontent than its absence during her reign.

Finally, as if melancholy alone were not enough to provide a vehicle for expressing discontent, it had the additional advantages of being associated with foreignness, and pre-Reformation foreignness at that. Indeed, to some extent melancholy was associated with travel, and to that extent the very disposition of the melancholic not only expressed discontent with one's domestic conventions, but fascination with various continental lifestyles. While Lawrence Babb may well have been correct to call it an "Elizabethan" malady, it was a malady which, in significant ways, tugged at the very notion of what it meant to be a member of Elizabethan England in the first place. It is this subject that Section One explores in greater detail.

Three underlying premises are at work in the three chapters that comprise this section. First, the explosion of melancholy did not entail passive reception of an already established continental tradition; in fact, one of the crucial operations at work in many of the major texts from the period was an engagement with familiar continental traditions in order to give shape to post-Reformation English national identity. The relation between, say, Ficino and Bright and Spenser (both of whom are considered in Chapter One) was not based on continuity. But neither was it entirely discontinuous, and therein lies its importance. For writing about melancholy became one device for interrogated to what extent familiar cultural forms continued to apply in a nation that sought to distinguish itself as a vanguard in—among other areas—church reform. Second, the Elizabethan texts on melancholy gave rise to questions about membership within a political community, and they did so in ways that official documents such as the Oaths of Supremacy and Allegiance simply were not designed to do. In the chapters that follow melancholy intersects with various questions about the conditions that determine nationhood. These include: who are its members, and based on what qualities; what are the respective rights and obligations of members, on what are they based, and how are they articulated; and how shall the political body be preserved, particularly in cases when usurpers threaten to undermine its stability?

To some extent the arguments in these chapters run against the grain by selecting topics that were not always easily recognizable markers of national identity. But it is in noting this fact that the third premise becomes more apparent. Melancholy enabled writers, whether deliberately or by accident, to examine the conditions of nationhood in ways that more ostensibly political texts tended to ignore; and it is precisely this that gives melancholy its peculiar advantage as a political topic. While they account for a wide perspective, they also include more detailed readings of several passages from Spenser's poetry, Jonson's *Every Man Out of His Humour,* and Shakespeare's *As You Like It* and *Julius Caesar.*

Section Two, "Melancholy and the Question of Government," focuses on the 1620s, when many writers returned to melancholy in order to interrogate the foundations of political institutions, as well as to raise doubts about whether stable governments could indeed be sustained over time. In the course of this section, I shift from examining literary characters who exhibit characteristics of melancholy toward individuals who make it a primary concern of theirs in their writing. Separate chapters focus on John Donne's spiritual autobiography, *Devotions Upon Emergent Occasions,* and Robert Burton's *Anatomy of Melancholy.* In addition, it examines these two texts in relation to some of the broader. political and ecclesiastical conflicts that were unfolding during their professional careers.

Of all the writers considered in this study, Donne is the one figure who not only makes a career out of his melancholy, but who most consistently identifies the disease metaphorically as a form of rebellion. Indeed, for Donne, who tended to think in terms of analogies whenever he thought of anything, the physical symptoms of melancholy had their counterpart in political discontent that ranged from murmuring (the verbal discontent which warns rulers that more hostile expressions are on the way) to outright rebellion. Chapter Four focuses almost entirely on the spiritual autobiography he published near the end of his life, the *Devotions Upon Emergent Occasions.* The *Devotions* deserves special consideration in part because of its recent critical reception, but even more because of its use of melancholy as a key term toward understanding the process of rebellion. Recent critical attention has given considerable weight to the political imagery that Donne scatters throughout the text, even to the point of suggesting that at a certain level the *Devotions* functions as a sort of oblique intervention into political affairs, rather than the spiritual meditation it purports to be. As I argue in the chapter, such an approach not only has distorted the overall significance of the treatise, it has more fundamentally misunderstood the ways in which it could be taken as a political engagement. Thus while previous critics have argued that Donne was offering political advice to the king and heir apparent, I suggest that Donne's political concerns were more formal, revolving around the question of whether and how political authority operates. In the course of his meditations, Donne touches upon the problem of rumor—which is, as the text indicates, the equivalent of melancholy vapor on a political scale—in order to address the problems that political authority faces in its effort to maintain itself.

To the extent that we can read Donne's *Devotions* as a statement about politics at all, we must depend on inference and (admittedly) speculation. By contrast, Burton is far more explicit about discussing political corruption and internal contradiction, as well as pointing out the role that melancholy plays in the ruin of civil institutions. As I argue in chapter five, Burton quite emphatically advocates a doctrine of political reform, while paradoxically accepting its impossibility—in the best and worst senses, Burton's political objectives are utopian. Both positions stem from his notion of what melancholy is, which he sees as a condition that leads to the decay of otherwise good and healthy governments *and* an all encompassing condition that breaks down whatever boundaries a society sets up in order to distinguish normal from pathological. This conflict is reflected in recent critical assessments of Burton, which tend to read the *Anatomy* in one of two ways. First, as the first in a series of statements that contribute to the pathologization of hitherto non-pathological activities—most famously, Burton begins the historical revolt against religious enthusiasm. Second, as a postmodern achievement *avant a lettre,* insofar as its prose style, which depends on various forms of *amplificatio* and *digressio,* ultimately leads to the breakdown of all master discourses, including the one that attempts to distinguish pathological from normal behavior.

The chapter on Burton concentrates on two sections from the *Anatomy,* which read as commentaries on one another: the Prefatory "Democritus Jr. to the Reader" and the quasi-conclusion on "Religious Melancholy." In each section, Burton tries to resolve the above contradictions in two ways: first, by invoking a "poetical" utopia, which simultaneously recalls the Orphic achievements that Spenser had dwelled on and re-frames the question of political healthiness as an exclusively textual matter; and later, by accepting what might best be described as the tyranny of the *status quo,* specifically the policies of the Church of England. In his section on religious melancholy, Burton appears to acknowledge that the church's authority stands on tenuous grounds; in fact, he is only about a step or two away from accepting that it amounts to a tyrannical institution. Nevertheless, by reaffirming its policy, specifically its policy concerning predestination, he appears to back away from a potentially dissident position in favor of a more expedient solution. Whether Burton learns to stop worrying and love the church because doing so helps him accomplish his own objectives—after all, dwelling on questions of predestination only leads to despair—or whether, more formally, he has come to understand that there is no institution that is not in some way illegitimate never becomes clear. Instead, Burton's survey leads to the more troubling hypothesis that it is impossible to distinguish criticism of public institutions as a form of melancholy madness from a fullfledged participation in that same madness, albeit from another point of view.

Any study of the political dimensions of early modern madness must address the turbulent decades of civil war and interregnum, when assertions of madness became pervasive, if not universal. To that end, Section Three, "The Distractions of the Times," concentrates on the turbulent decades of civil war and revolution, decades which witnessed a virtual explosion of pamphlet literature that invoked humor theory, several versions of madness, and melancholy, in order to account for the nation's political unrest. Such questions became particularly resonant during the 1650s, following the defeat of the Leveller army at Burford, when more radical religious sects (such as the Quakers or Fifth Monarchists) and pseudo-sects (such as the Ranters) began to emerge. (If the propaganda that their opponents produced is a reliable measure, these religious groups were a source of extreme public fear and anxiety.) As critics have argued, the most significant development was a fundamental shift in the public's perception of religious radicalism—what had formerly been viewed as a theological matter increasingly became a psychological one, and Bedlam hospital took over the role of containing (and silencing) these radical voices. To put it succinctly for now, the Age of Reason replaced the Age of Enthusiasm.[33] My own approach argues for a much more uneven picture, particularly uneven on the question of whether enthusiasm is a symptom of melancholy. Turning to Meric Casaubon and Henry More—two writers who are incorrectly associated with each other as pioneers in the so-called revolt against enthusiasm—I argue that seventeenth century writers were divided over the question of whether to interpret enthusiasm on physiological grounds or not. Enthusiasm becomes, alternatively, a radically unknowable condition, one that cannot be explained—even to the person who experiences it—or, more simply (and less persuasively) the symptom of an illness.

The final chapter consists of a reading of Milton's closet drama, *Samson Agonistes* as an attempt to recreate religious prophecy and enthusiasm on the basis of an as yet emerging conceptualization of 'experience.' Through this term, which appears several times in the text, Milton hopes to work around the radical doubt to which the question of divine inspiration had been subjected. While Milton may have moved beyond the arguments pertaining to melancholy and religious enthusiasm that dated back at to the mid-sixteenth century, he introduces a problem that had been implicit all along—that of acting within a climate where the grounds for making correct decisions are unavailable.

The one stock figure who is most conspicuously absent from this project happens also to be the most well-known—the love-sick lyricist who prefers the solitary reveries of the wilderness to the public world (and the helpless captive audience who is doomed to hear the endless expression of such "grief in solitude"). While I refer briefly to such figures as Colin Clout and the young John Donne who sat for the famous Lothian portrait, I do not focus on the Petrarchan lover—a glaring omission, especially when one considers how deeply Petrarch himself longed for a resurrection of the ancient Roman republic. The omission of the Petrarchan lyricist has nothing to do with its inaccessibility to political readings. On the contrary, critics like John King and David Norbrook have shown that shifts in poetic diction from the Edwardian period to the Elizabethan reign can be connected to specific power struggles within the culture.[34] Thus, as Norbrook argues, the development of a courtly lyric sensibility that contrasted with the "rude and rustic" verse that had been popular earlier in the century, itself corresponded to a widespread demand for a more docile courtly environment.[35] In the end though, if this omission seems glaring for some readers, I hope to make up for it both by examining texts and documents that hitherto have been unexplored—or have not been explored as texts about melancholy—as well as by offering a new approach to the question of what made melancholy such a popular vehicle for the expression of political complaint in the first place.

If it can be put in such a peculiar way, this book suffers from the benefits of good timing. One of the remarkable features of melancholy is its remarkable staying power, its seeming permanent ability to capture the interests of people even when the scientific underpinnings that gave rise to its existence no longer exist; the theory of the humors, along with the notion of the universe being composed along a four element structure, no longer obtains, yet it is still possible to write about melancholy as though it were clear what it referred to. More important, many of the major studies of melancholy have appeared at moments when the subject would otherwise appear to have been exhausted. Without wishing to lay claim to the status of this book, it is important to acknowledge that at the very least, interest in the topic among literary scholars has grown considerably over recent years. During the final decade of the twentieth century, and continuing through the first decade of the twenty-first, new studies about melancholy have emerged in virtually all areas of literary research, betokening an interest in the condition not seen since the decades following the first world war. While literary studies have touched on virtually all historical periods, scholarly research has concentrated heavily on the era currently designated as "early modern"—Keats' Odes notwithstanding, it is still the period between the late sixteenth and seventeenth century that earns the dubious distinction for being the "age of melancholy." The revival, or perhaps persistence, of a concern with melancholy today can be attributed to a number of underlying factors. With a renewed interest in the history of medicine, fostered both by Foucault's genealogical studies and a widespread critique of psychoanalytic "character studies" for being insufficiently conscientious of historical methodologies, literary critics have turned to the various psychological models that really were, at one time, believed to describe human psychological phenomena. These models included, among others, a classical humoral tradition inherited from Galen and Hippocrates, the emergence of new medicinal treatments developed by Paracelsus, and the rise of what might be termed a "drug industry."

Meanwhile, the renewed interest in melancholy is paralleled in contemporary medicine by a tremendous increase in pharmacological treatments for depression (to say nothing of their relative success in curing those afflicted). Curiously though, while there may be a faint resemblance between classical theories of melancholy as an imbalance of the humors and contemporary theories of depression as an aberration in the proper functioning of neurotransmitters, the revival of melancholy within psychoanalysis seems to stem from altogether different motives. As Julia Kristeva suggests, for instance, traditional studies of melancholia retain importance precisely because they point to the limitations among overly physiological models. In *Black Sun,* she writes, "At the current stage of attempts to think out the two channels—psychic and biological—of affects, it is again possible to formulate the question of *language's* central importance to human beings" (*emphasis added*).[36] If there is an answer to the question, why study melancholy today, the answer lies at least in part with the recognition that the certainty we feel today, with regard to our bodies as objects of research, by no means guarantees that we will feel that same certainty in another time to come. At the very least, the historical interest in melancholy is a reminder of a problem that physicians of the period undoubtedly had to confront, namely that our bodies are as much the *products* of our models for investigation as they are its objects.

On occasion, contemporary inquiries into melancholy have betrayed a curious nostalgia—one is tempted to call it inconsolable mourning—for a traditional notion of subjectivity believed to be lost, overcome, or simply consigned to the long list of outdated historical concepts (phrenology, mesmerism, ESP). Thus, if Kristeva worries that exaggerated attention to depression as a strictly chemical matter risks losing our understanding of that body's experience of being rooted in language and the play of the signifier, by contrast, a writer like Michael Vincent Miller simply wears his heart on his sleeve. In his prefatory remarks to Jacques Hassoun's recent study, *The Cruelty of Depression: On Melancholy,* Miller explains the author's preferred term "melancholy" over the far more clinical term "depression." After rejecting the "current overuse of the word *depression,*" Miller invokes the entire history of Western civilization in a way that smacks of "great tradition" theories. (I quote the entire paragraph):

> The sound of the word *melancholy* has a kind of poignant reach that suggests something beyond what *depression* conveys. *Melancholy* resonates with a sense of secret inner tragedy, of Byronic wounds. It hints at brooding from which one unmistakably suffers yet which also could be, one imagines, the wellspring of poetry or philosophy. One thinks of the pre-Socratic thinker Heraclitus, who was known as the melancholy philosopher, and of Shakespeare's Hamlet, the most melancholy of princes. Aristotle and Montaigne were prominent among those who felt that only melancholics could be philosophers. Kierkegaard, who managed to anticipate almost every modern feeling, gave melancholy an existential setting in his book *Repetition,* defining it as a state in which one lives in the present moment as though the worst future one can dream up has already happened (a notion, in fact, that turns out to be similar in ways to Hassoun's psychoanalytic interpretation). Freud, who invented our therapeutic outlook, joined this esteemed group when he wrote "Mourning and Melancholia," the first attempt to provide a theoretical foundation (as we understand theory, Robert Burton, in the seventeenth century, produced a sprawling work of scholarship, but not exactly a theory, called *The Anatomy of Melancholy*) for what we now diagnose as depression.[37]

To be sure, a certain element of snobbishness has always been implied by the term melancholy. From the moment it was first introduced as a problem in the pseudo-Aristotelian text, melancholy has always been associated with the gifts of the ruling classes, no matter what price of suffering came with it. A similar attitude persisted throughout the Renaissance. Despite its association with disease, the sin of sloth, and the more abhorrent social vices, melancholy underwent a revival during the Renaissance, with a veritable cult of genius springing up around it. As critics of the sixteenth and seventeenth centuries have shown, melancholy had an appeal that related terms such as "madness" or "delusion" did not as easily enjoy. As Michael MacDonald reminds us—quoting John Lyly, an Elizabethan playwright who knew the business of class aspirations about as well as anybody—melancholy was, in all senses, *reserved*.³⁸

In turning to the political dimensions of melancholy, I seek to draw attention to a different, though by no means unrelated notion of subjectivity. To the extent that melancholy and modern notions of subjectivity go hand in hand, it is possible to raise a few questions. Among them: To what extent does being a subject entail being involved in a larger organization of people, particularly when that organization seems to prevent one from affirming too strongly one's own individualism in the first place? To what extent does being a subject involve being a member of a larger organization that one finds oppressive or unworldly, and thus itself in need of change? Finally, to what extent does being a subject involve being a participant in a larger organization whose rules for maintaining itself often take on a certain air of inscrutability of their own?

Section I
The Production of Melancholy as a Discourse

Chapter One
Melancholy and the Possibility of Nationhood in Bright and Spenser

INTRODUCTION

During the final years of the sixteenth century, following the publication of Timothy Bright's *Treatise on Melancholie* in 1586, and the translation of Andre du Laurens' (Laurentius') discourse on melancholy in 1599, the Elizabethan concept of melancholy underwent a radical transformation.[1] What made these publications so crucial was not that they drew attention to a condition hitherto unknown, either to physicians or to poets—from Chaucer's "Knight's Tale" to Thomas Elyot's *Castel of Helth*, there were in fact numerous printed references to melancholy. More fundamentally, both Bright and Laurentius assigned melancholy a genuinely new status: henceforth it would be treated as an object of study in its own right. Whereas earlier medical treatises had described melancholy, both as a substance and as a condition replete with various symptoms (such as a morose and withdrawn disposition, or a tendency to seek out solitude), it was clearly understood that it made up only one humor among the four that comprised the normal animate body. The notion that melancholy deserved special consideration, let alone a full length study, simply had not occurred to English physicians until Bright's *Treatise* undertook precisely that task. And while physicians like Bright and Laurentius may not have been solely responsible for creating what subsequently became known as "The Elizabethan Malady,"[2] it was through such medical treatises that the production of melancholy as a discourse takes on a distinctly new character.

In the process of accounting for these treatises, critics frequently have drawn attention to their literary implications, situating them as the cornerstone for a revival of a classical concept of melancholy. This concept, commonly known as "genial melancholy," was particularly conducive to the theories of poetry, theories which also happened to be emerging at roughly the same point in time. The link between melancholy and three kinds of genius—specifically, poetic, political, and prophetic—dates as far back as the pseudo-Aristotelian *Problems*. As this text maintained, talents in these intellectual arts could indeed be accounted for on materialist grounds; to that end, melancholy functions as a cause for the types of genius under consideration.[3] Just as the pseudo-Aristotelian text had defined melancholy and genius as a cause-effect relationship that ultimately had its fulfillment in the writings and engravings of Ficino and Dürer, so too have contemporary critics regarded Bright and Laurentius as the cultural "context," from which literary descriptions of melancholy both derived and departed.[4] To some extent the assumption seems reasonable enough. Several writers did put forth lengthy treatises devoted to the study of poetry, including Sidney's *Apology*, Puttenham's *Arte of English Poesie*, and Spenser's (presumably lost) *English Poet*.[5] Meanwhile, in the poetry of Sidney, Spenser, and Jonson (whose marked up copy of Puttenham's treatise itself has become the subject of critical interest), melancholy characters figure prominently. The simultaneous emergence of medical and poetic discourses is therefore suggestive, and critics could not help but associate them as two components of a larger cultural project, namely to revive a traditional theory of poetic genius grounded in physiological disorder.[6]

As important as literary historical research into the cultural antecedents of melancholy has been, however, the result often has been a somewhat distorted portrayal of the relation between medical theory and poetic practice. To the extent that Bright and Laurentius have received due attention during the twentieth century, they have appealed to critics who have sought a reliable cultural context, with a mind toward explicating the literary documents that portrayed melancholy characters at the forefront. In this manner a quasi-teleological approach to medical handbooks has predominated in many literary studies of melancholy, as critics read the works of Bright, Laurentius and others almost as though they were written for the sake of their literary counterparts. Meanwhile, literary critical interests in the various non-literary medical "sources" precisely because they would state more explicitly (and transparently) what fictional characters could only demonstrate indirectly.[7] Characters such as Sidney's Philisides, or Shakespeare's Hamlet and Jaques, harbored a fundamental mystery by virtue of their melancholy, which could not but go unexplained. To that end, one thinks of Antonio's opening line to *The Merchant of Venice*, "In sooth, I know not why I am so sad," a line that suggests exasperated defeat in the face of a relentless mystery.[8] By contrast, medical writers who had written with the purpose of explaining the disease objectively, and with articulating clearly what the term in fact referred to, could easily solve the various problems that literary texts would in turn create.

What is most noticeable about early treatises such as Bright's or Laurentius', however, begins with the realization that the classical concepts of genial melancholy that might have indeed contributed to the vatic poetics laid out in Sidney's *Defense of Poesie* and Spenser's *English Poet* receive dutiful acknowledgment at best.[9] While Laurentius refers to the *Problems*, he devotes noticeably little and highly qualified space to its contents in his text. Moreover, Laurentius explicitly notes that the *Problems* had attended to a very specific kind of melancholy only, and not one which did justice to the schemes that had been discovered throughout later generations: "Aristotle in his Problemes sayth, that the melancholike are most wittie and ingenious: but we must looke that we understand this place aright, for there are many sorts of melancholie" (N3). For his part, Bright alludes to Aristotle by the symptoms of the disease as:

> dulnesse of conceit, both by reason the substance of the braine in such personnes is more grosse, and their spirite not so prompt and subtile as is requisite for readie vnderstandinge.[10]

While he does make note of some exceptions, his remarks are noticeably restrained:

> Sometime it falleth out, that melancholie men are found verie wittie, and quickly discerne.[11]

They strike Bright not so much as geniuses, than as prodigies whose strengths are as much the result of happenstance as they are of a sort of stumbling (as the word "falleth" suggests). To the extent that Bright even allows for a fortunate melancholic, he enjoys a contemplative life rather than an active one. Meanwhile, to the extent that Bright shows even an awareness of poetry in any capacity, it is more diagnostic than appreciative in nature:

> It appeareth these humours only assert the organ and corporall part, & nothing come nigh the mind and soule: which in the meane time of these stormes and tempests of passion, these delusions, fears, false terrours and poetical fictions of the braine sitteth quiet and still, nothing altered in faculties, or any part of that divine and impatible disposition, which it obtaineth by the excellencie of creation.[12]

Poetry, in other words, refers to a brain that has lost its grasp on things of the world; and it is hardly a vocation that Bright deems worthy of pursuit. Surprisingly, while all the pieces were available for an Elizabethan turn to a classical (and continental) philosophical tradition, which bolstered the poetic, political, and prophetic arts by means of a rigorously analytical investigation of human physiology, in fact such a turn did not take place after all. In order to account for melancholy's emergence in Elizabethan England then, critical approaches require significant modification.

This is not to say that medical and poetic discourses shared no common interests; rather, it is to indicate that what they shared has not been sufficiently characterized to date. To that end, it is worth noting the extent to which both English physicians and poets drew attention to their basis in vernacular writing. These were not only books written in English; their authors were self-conscious of this fact. As Bright notes in his preface:

> I write it in our mother tong that the benefit (how small soever it be) might be more common, & as the practise of all aunctient philosophers hath ben to write in their owne language their precepts, whether concerning nature, or touching maners of life, to the end their countrey men might reape the benefite with more ease, and seeke rather for sound judgement of vnderstanding, then for vaine ostentation of strange toys: which is also after a sort followed in translations: so I tooke it meetest to impart these some poyntes of Philosophie, & phisick in English to the end our people, as other natiōs do, might acquaint them selues with some part of this kinde, rather then with friuolous discourses, neither profitable to vse, nor delectable to the vertuous and well disposed minde.[13]

As melancholy emerged as an "Elizabethan malady," its description began to take on a distinctively vernacular shape, with concerns about the significance of writing in an English vernacular very much coming into the foreground. Meanwhile, in the course of becoming an English disease, melancholy signaled a larger concern over the development of a specifically nationalist physiological character—a character which Edmund Spenser would express through his well-known request to Gabriel Harvey for "a kingdome of oure owne langauge." For Bright in particular, it proved possible to describe a theory of melancholy that not only distanced itself from the classical theory of inspiration, but that responded to the specific demands that emerged in the course of writing to a specifically English audience. Perhaps this distance can in part be attributed to ambivalence, if not outright rejection of the fifteenth century continental revival of melancholy, as presented most famously by Ficino. But more fundamentally, these traditional concerns simply were unimportant. For Bright, to write about health was to demonstrate that health was in fact a matter of defining a specifically national ethos. Indeed, the provenance of nationalist sentiments extended so far as to suggest that, even in disease, the characteristics marked off by these political boundaries not only could be detected, but actually required due attention as part of the curing process.

The very idea that health and illness corresponds to characteristics defined largely by national boundaries seems questionable, even counterintuitive. The fact that Bright makes the link so explicitly thus invites further examination. As the following section will argue, at stake for Bright are two questions: to what extent can we identify a body on physiological grounds, and therefore separate from the cultural institutions which give it significance in our daily affairs; just as important, though, to what extent can we identify nationhood as the reflection of a physiological condition, as opposed to a political construction forged by other bonds? By no means were these questions simple and straightforward during the Elizabethan period, when the very notion of nationhood was beginning to emerge as a widespread concern among English writers.[14] As the following examination of the *Treatise of Melancholie* will indicate, while Bright understood his project to speak to a specifically English audience, he was in turn marked by a profound uncertainty about what the composition of that audience consisted of. Reading the *Treatise* in the context of Bright's other publications of the period, it will become clear that this uncertainty was not limited to his study of melancholy alone; rather, underlying the bulk of his work was a consistent set of doubts about the composition of Englishness. Later sections of this chapter will in turn examine select passages from Spenser's poetry. Although it is not likely that Spenser read Bright, much less borrowed his ideas about melancholy from him, it will become clear that Spenser's references to melancholy display strikingly similar concerns about the constitution of nationhood. As will also become clear through this comparative examination, Bright and Spenser come to very different conclusions. While the *Treatise on Melancholie* belongs to a larger project concerned specifically with the construction of a nation-based conceptualization of health, Spenser's references to melancholy ultimately will cast the very notion of defining an English nation—if not nationhood altogether—on the basis of language as a paradoxical, if not impossible, endeavor.

A SHORTHAND ACCOUNT OF TIMOTHY BRIGHT

As a professional writer, Timothy Bright sought to bridge the natural sciences, specifically medicine, with an emphatically nationalistic and Anglo-centric political agenda. For Bright, practicing medicine went hand in hand with promoting both the Elizabethan monarchy and a highly revised English language as a potentially dominant vernacular within an emerging commercial setting. The relation between Bright's scientific discoveries and his political ambitions is made explicitly in one of his earliest publications, entitled, *A Treatise: Wherein is declared the sufficience of English Medicines, for cure of all diseases, cured with Medicine.*[15] As the title suggests, Bright's purpose is to demonstrate that the unique characteristics of illness in England require correspondingly unique treatments, using medicines that grow domestically. Physicians ought to avoid foreign markets for medicinal cures and look toward a domestic market instead. Specifically, he mentions India, Arabia, and Spain as the primary sources of trouble for English doctors, a gesture which suggests that Bright's agenda had more to do with Reformation biases than with medicine itself. In the course of expressing what could have remained a strictly pragmatic rationale, however, he makes the following assertion: something like an essentially English complexion can be identified, described, and differentiated from the complexions of nations whose political and religious characters were in direct conflict with England's. As he puts it,

> Our English bodies, through the nature of the region, our kinde of dyet and nourishment, our custome of life, are greatly diuers from those of straunge nations, whereby aryseth great varietie of humours, and excrementes in our bodies from theirs, and so the causes of diseases rising vpon breach of diet (the diet being of an other sort) must needes be vnlike, whervpon although their humours be in kind, and in a generalitie agreable to ours, as bloode, choler, flegme, melancholie, & such like, yet rising vpon other matter then the same in vs, & otherwise framed by a farre other state of body, by reason of a diuerse kind of life, the medicines which helpe them must needes hurt vs, not finding the like cause to striue with: and this no doubt is the cause, why we are not able to beare such dose of quantities of their Medicines, as those nations are, to whome they be natiue.[16]

To be sure, Bright does concede that certain similarities do exist. For instance, he admits that the four humors can be found in all human beings. Nevertheless, he maintains that important physical differences do in fact correspond with national boundaries. As he writes,

> Who hath not horror of the torments which both the Hellebores bring to the body? Yet saith Paulus Aegineta in his seuenth Booke, and fourth

> Chapter, the blacke Helleborus purgeth yellow choler from the whole body, without paine: which can not be verified of our bodyes, howe so euer it be in theirs, and therefore we feare to minister the pouder thereof in any sort, but the steeping onely of the barkes of the rootes, from twentie graines to fixite, they being bolde to take a whole dramme thereof in sustance, which is more then treble the quantitie, for one dose.[17]

When administering remedies for melancholy or choler according to traditional medical authorities, physicians found themselves confronting the ailing body's stubborn resistance—doubtless, to the disappointment of all concerned parties. However, if traditional beliefs about hellebore in fact proved not valid, the discrepancy could thenceforth be explained on physiological grounds. It was not that previous doctors had been wrong; it was rather that their books were written for people with radically different physiological complexions.

If Bright's ambitions as a physician included developing a medical program with explicitly nationalist overtones, his ideals as a linguist were somewhat more complicated. By far, Bright's most important contribution to the study of languages—and perhaps his most important contribution to the practical arts in general—consisted of his 1588 treatise on shorthand, *Characterie an Arte of Shorte, Swifte, and Secrete Writing by Character*. As his dedicatory epistle to Queen Elizabeth makes clear, Bright wished to revive the ancient Roman practice of shorthand for the sake of political and commercial efficiency. A conventional language with relatively fewer characters to work with would, in turn, create a professional environment unencumbered by ambiguity or literary excesses. In its entirety, the opening paragraph reads as follows:

> Cicero did account it worthie his labor, and no les profitable to the Roman common weale (Most gratious Soueraigne,) to inuent a speedie kinde of wryting by Character, as Plutarch reporteth in the life of Cato the yonger. This inuention was increased by Seneca: that the number of Characters grue to 7000. Whether through iniurie of time, or that men gaue it ouer for tediousnes of learning, nothing remaineth extant of Ciceros inuention at this day. Upon consideration of the great vse of such a kinde of writing, I haue inuented the like: of fewe Characters, short, & easie, euery Character answering a word: My inuention meere English, without precept, or imitation of any. The vses are diuerse: Short, that a swifte hande may therewith write Orations, or publike

actions of speech, uttered as becometh the grauitie of such actions, verbatim. Secrete, as no kinde of wryting like. And herein (besides other properties) excelling the writing by letters, and Alphabet, in that, Nations of strange languages, may hereby communicate their meaning together in writing, though of sundrie tonges. It is reported of the people of China, that they haue no other kinde, and so traffike together many Prouinces of that kingdom, ignorant one of an others speech. Their Characters are very long, and harde to make, that a dousen of mine, may be written as soone as one of theirs: Besides, they wanting an Alphabet, fal into an infinite number, which is a thing that greatlie chargeth memory, and may discourage the learner.[18]

If Bright hopes to succeed where others have fallen short, it will be possible to measure his success quantitatively—for to develop a successful shorthand, it is necessary to develop precisely the number of characters that would reduce the amount of time to carry out daily transactions without itself becoming more cumbersome than the very linguistic conventions it was designed to replace all along.

At first blush, Bright had in mind something like a universal language freed from the deficiencies of ordinary speech, the most common forms being ambiguous syntax or unintended wordplay. The work itself consists of several sets of indexes that contain various words, along with their corresponding shorthand symbols. Such a system is not only swift; it is orderly, almost to the point of rigidity. To that end, the shorthand project responded to an increasing concern over a standardized national language—one which would unite the several provinces, create an intellectual elite, and establish a clear ethos that could, in turn, be distributed to anyone who could read. Meanwhile, it anticipates the desires for purely symbolic languages developed by seventeenth century philosophers with the express interest in improving the art of understanding. While similar ideals may have lurked in the back of Bright's mind, nevertheless the system that he devises would be better characterized as a universal *English* language. In fact in the pages that actually present the shorthand characters themselves, it becomes clear that what Bright produces is not a language per se; it is a code, and a code based entirely on English words. As a code the shorthand system enjoys a feature common to all codes, namely a cover of secrecy, or a distinction of those who can follow it from those who must break it. (While Bright keeps relatively quiet about the virtues of a shorthand system as a potential secret code, subsequent writers would articulate the virtue more explicitly.[19]) Finally, as he quietly suggests with his allusions to Cicero and Cato—respectively, the most famous rhetorician and the most famous philosopher of the entire pre-Christian Roman civilization—a contemporary work on shorthand would itself be beset with nagging questions about the nature of the commonwealth's own political character. In the case of both authors, the overriding concern lay with the transition from republic to empire, when the need for a lingua franca would have been all the more urgent.

While Bright's shorthand project appeared in 1588, two years after the *Treatise on Melancholie,* concerns about the nature of language already had begun to take shape in the earlier work, in fact taking a predominant role. For Bright, melancholy was not easily separated from the specific question, whether English is sufficient in its given state to correctly *describe* melancholy; or rather, can English reasonably *translate* a familiar classical term into a properly English context? When he first introduces this question in the epistle dedicatory to his brother, it has a decidedly off-hand feel about it, almost as though the mere existence of his treatise was proof enough of an affirmative answer. As he asserts,

> I write it in our mother tong that the benefit (how small soever it be) might be more common, & as the practise of all aunciént philosophers hath ben to write in their owne languáge their precepts, whether concerning nature, or touching maners of life, to the end their countrey men might reape the benefite with more ease, and seeke rather for sound judgement of vnderstanding, then for vaine ostentation of strange toys: which is also after a sort followed in translations: so I tooke it meetest to impart these some poyntes of Philosophie, & phisick in English to the end our people, as other natiōs do, might acquaint them selues with some part of this kinde, rather then with friuolous discourses, neither profitable to vse, nor delectable to the vertuous and well disposed minde.[20]

To the extent that English is preferable to Latin, it is primarily a question of speed. Like the book that would follow, the *Treatise on Melancholie* aspired as much to improve the efficiency of communication as to introduce any new discovery.

Of course, such an assertion hardly was ideologically neutral. While English public culture had indeed begun to shift from a Latin-based idiom to a vernacular one—signaled most emphatically by the *Book of Common Prayer* and the several translations of the Bible—by no means was the shift unanimously accepted; nor was English understood to be obviously preferable to Latin in all contexts. Many English linguists dating back as far as

Robert Wakefield—one of the first language historians to advocate the study of Hebrew—clearly understood that languages were not reducible to one another, but in fact that different languages could betray radically different mental dispositions.[21] To speak a foreign language was to think thoughts that literally could not occur in one's native tongue (and in fact it was precisely this realization that led writers like Wakefield to encourage the study of as many languages as possible).[22] By extension, to write in English was to create a chasm, however seemingly desirable, between English writers and continental ones. For his part, though Bright initially does not seem eager to plunge into a direct discussion about the problems concerning multiple languages, as his treatise proceeds these problems become increasingly difficult to avoid. For in the course of promising to cure melancholy, it is necessary to demonstrate that one could truly comprehend it; and to do so, it is necessary further to show that one was capable of putting it in terms that correspond to the way the human body functions.

As early as the first chapter, Bright confronts the problem that melancholy itself is an ambiguous term, referring to entirely different things in different cases: "Before I enter to define the nature of melancholie, & what it is, for the cleare understanding of that wherein my purpose is to instruct you, it shall be necessarie to lay forth diuerse names of taking the name of melancholie, and whereto the name being one, is applied deuerslie."[23] More significant, many readers fail to make the distinction between melancholy fancies and the pangs of conscience that can ultimately lead to despair. In a prefatory letter written to a mysterious character known only as "M," Bright suggests the success of his project depends largely on his ability to make just that distinction:

> The complaints of diverse others also in like case oppressed, droue me, that both they & you knowing the grouds of these passions: what parte nature hath in the tragedie, and what conscience of sinne driveth unto: what difference betwixt them, how one nourisheth another, how ech riseth, and the seuerall meanes, both of preuenting and cure of ech.[24]

Some connection clearly does exist between physical ailments and afflictions of the soul, and Bright devotes considerable time to showing how melancholy can lead directly to despair if not properly diagnosed. But as one might expect, before the work is done he ends up taking great pains to mark them as separate conditions altogether. The opening sentence to chapter thirty-three puts it succinctly (if ever a sentence in Bright's often peripatetic treatise could be called succinct): "By that hath bene before declared it may easily appear the affliction of soule through conscience of sinne is quite another thing then melancholy."[25] As far as Bright is concerned, melancholy is not despair.[26] In fact, as the shorthand book would eventually illustrate, they do not even overlap as categories—to despair is to be concerned with questions of "Hope," whereas to be melancholy is to be concerned with questions of "Blood."[27] Failure to recognize the distinction is failure to properly understand and treat either one. Melancholy thus becomes something of a test case. In the course of taking it as an autonomous subject, Bright ends up putting forth the further demand that English medicine respond to a demand for greater linguistic precision.

This demand turns out to be far more problematic than Bright himself may have anticipated, and in the course of defining melancholy his argument ends up lodged between two positions. In distinguishing melancholy from despair in the *Treatise of Melancholie*, and in categorizing language systematically in *Characterie*, Bright aspires to an ideally referential language; for Bright, the existence of multiple languages is a problem that requires the solution of linguistic reform, if not the all out pursuit of a universal commercial code, wherein symbols could *correspond* with the things they represent. While he believes this ideal is indeed achievable, he nevertheless continues to maintain a physiological model which assumes that one's complexion is ethnologically inflected. He notes in the eleventh chapter of the *Treatise*:

> Howe region, and aire make demonstration of the same, the comparison of the gentle, and constant aire of Asia, with the sharpe & unstable of Europe, doth declare vnto us: wherby the Asians are milde, and gentle, vnfitte for warre, and giuen to subiection: the Europians, naturally, rough, hardie, stearne, right martiall impes, and hardier to be subdued, and raunged vnder obedience: and of the same region, such people as inhabite places barren, open and dry, and subiect to mutabilitie of weather, are more fierce, bolder, sharp, and obstinate in opinion, then people of contrarie habitation.[28]

What makes this lengthy passage so surprising is not only its overtly racialist presuppositions—such references to racial typing were legion, and the conclusions of various authors often contradicted one another—but its silence with regard to the linguistic issues it hints at. Namely, if different habits spring from different habitats, what prevents one from assuming that these respective nations would require qualitatively different languages to inhabit them adequately? To that extent, if a properly English approach to medicine is necessary, it is not only for the overtly nationalistic reasons that he expresses in his earliest writings about medicine. On a more basic level, it is because non-English remedies would not in themselves be of much use.

SPENSER AND THE GALLIMAUFRY AND HODGEPODGE

In the early stages of his career, Spenser's ambitions with regard to linguistic reform are marked by two distinct characteristics. As he indicates in his famous letter to Gabriel Harvey, "Why a Gods name may not we, as else the Greeks, have the kingdome of our own language?"[29] Indeed, depending on how one reads the genitive, Spenser's question may confer upon language the privileged role of a shaping force. Rather than merely ask why the kingdom neglects to adapt the native language presently available to it, Spenser's question suggests that the very notion of a kingdom already presupposes the existence of this language. Meanwhile, to the extent that poetry may both engender and embody political institutions, Spenser's question may already be accompanied by a particular interest in ek-static poetry, modeled after the classical figure of Orpheus.[30]

As a legendary figure Orpheus was renowned for several feats, including: transforming stones into city-walls and beasts into human beings, thereby demarcating the very boundaries between civilized and savage domains; and causing the rivers to stop flowing, a gesture that was subsequently interpreted as the power to halt time and temporality itself. Both Sidney and Puttenhman refer to Orpheus as an example of a poet whose talents include this specifically political dimension (and both suggest that true poetry might once again do the same). By putting political ambitions in the form of a question though, Spenser may already have been wondering just what English poetry could accomplish.

In fact, Spenser's own verse from the period already raises this concern. While the letter itself dates from 1580, in the 1579 *Shepherdes Calender*, under the guise of "The New Poet," he examines his verse in relation to Orpheus.'[31] While the *Calender* as a whole engages with a number of classical and early English authors, specific poems within the work, notably "October," explore Spenser's relation to Orpheus more explicitly. Patricia Vicari has gone so far as to suggest that the *Calender* was primarily an homage to the classical poetic figure, writing, "Spenser's philosophy, as I hope will now be apparent, was deeply imbued with the mythology and theology of the Orphic hymns, and his imagination was also touched by the figure of Orpheus himself, the musician, the lover of Eurydice, and, above all, the poet."[32] To some extent this is plausible, though as a whole Spenser's debt to Orpheus in the *Calender* manifests itself in an irresolute fashion. Consequently, readers are invited to suspect whether the work accomplishes what EK describes as "The power to *make* men immortal for they good dedes" (emphasis added).

In some ways the intermittent references to Orpheus come as a surprise. Orpheus possessed a gift of quasi-divine language—poetic recollections of his career granted him the power of "enthusiasmos," a gift of inspiration that gave him the power to speak a more authentic language. When superimposed against a Christian backdrop, Orpheus' gift bore some resemblance to the miraculous Gift of Tongues, as found in Acts of the Apostles. All this seems to run counter to the *Calender*'s stated concern with reforming the English language. If Spenser ostensibly wished to reform the vernacular, it was because he believed English poetry should assume the power to fashion the nation according to its own domestic needs. In the general epistle to the reader, EK makes known that among the New Poet's objectives, one of the most important is to bring about a widespread reform of the English language by means of his pseudo-rustic word choice and quasi-archaic diction. Regarding the present state of poetry, he writes:

> So now they haue made our English tongue, a gallimaufry or hodgepodge of al other speces. Other some not so wel seen in the English tonge as perhaps in other languages, if they happen to here an olde word albeit very naturall and significant, cry out streigh way, that we speak no English, but gibberish, or rather such as in ole time Euanders mother spake. (Epistle, 95–101)

Insofar as the *Shepheardes Calender* is a project about language with distinctly vernacular implications, the "October" episode invites us to wonder whether even the most carefully crafted English is not a bit wanting in its power.

In that regard, it is important not to lose sight of the fact that during the years preceding the *Shepherdes Calendar* (and in fact continuing well after its publication), Spenser occupied himself with translating visionary poems by various continental authors whose poems made claim to being prophetic statements. Such authors included John van der Noot, Petrarch, and perhaps most notably, Joachim du Bellay, whose own literary ambitions were to rival Orpheus.'[33] These translations offer a clue toward understanding the relation between vernacular and prophetic discourses in the New Poet's officially inaugural work. As Paula Blank has argued, du Bellay's extensive poetic theory combined a fiercely patriotic defense of the French vernacular with a wish no less ambitious than to repair the *confusio linguarum* brought about by the fall of the Tower of Babel. Blank states:

According to Du Bellay, national language reform is dependent on the arts of language. Tracing the contemporary confusion of tongues to the Tower of Babel, he suggests that the diversity of languages is "born in the world of the desire and will of mortals," that "since men are of diverse wills, therefore do they speak and write diversely." The capacity to improve the language consequently lies in the "sole artifice and industry of men."[34]

Spenser may have modeled his own defense of vernacular languages after du Bellay's. More importantly, he shares an active interest in the effects of the Tower of Babel upon the contemporary function of language.

Over the course of his career, this interest takes two forms. In many of his early poems and translations, Spenser explores the notion of prophetic, or visionary poetry, as a potential avenue for transcending the confusion of languages that the Biblical episode foregrounds. In his later years, however, his poetry makes references to Babel as the grounding narrative for understanding all languages as inevitably fallen. As will become clear further below, it is in the course of his references to Babel that Spenser makes recourse to melancholy in his most explicit and sustained fashion. But an implicit sense of melancholy over the fallen state of languages in fact already appears as early as *The Shepherdes Calendar*.

It is in this regard that *The Shepheardes Calender* bears further consideration, as it represents one of Spenser's earliest significant efforts to address the prophetic and political dimensions of the kind of poetry he wanted to write. In doing so Spenser alternates between announcing a poem that aspires to quasi-divine power, and occasionally but forcefully admitting its fundamental limitations on the basis of its fallen condition. To the extent that the *Calender* has a narrative trajectory, it traces the transformation of Colin Clout from a shepherd's boy who breaks his pipes to a man who proves himself fit to mourn Dido, Queen of Shepherds, and who achieves "gentle" status in the process. It is through his elegies, moreover, that he can assume the status of national poet and "To teach the ruder shepheard how to feed his sheepe,/ And from the falsers fraud his folded flocke to keepe" (Epilogue, 5–6). Although Spenser adopted the name Colin Clout as his own fictional persona, readers already would have associated it with a traditional mode of English satire. They would have recalled its use by John Skelton, poet laureate under the service of King Henry VIII. More generally, readers would have associated the plowman and shepherd not only with radical reformist poets, but with a distinctly prophetic style insofar as the humble occupations made them more suitable to receive divine inspiration.[35] Because Spenser represents Colin's career in development, the poem in turn reflects the young writer's own concerns over his literary aspirations.

Meanwhile, to the extent that the poem has a narrator—in fact, there is a nameless figure who makes occasional appearances—he invests nearly all its efforts toward demonstrating that the transformation does occur successfully. Thus the "January" episode introduces Colin as "A Shepheards boye (no better doe him call)," and a boy who breaks his pipes rather than using them to create new verse; by "December" however, his status has undergone a dramatic transformation to "The gentle shepheard satte beside a spring." In addition to Colin's upgrade in status, his location in the final episode adds further to this impression. Earlier, in "June," roughly the poem's midpoint, when Colin complains about his poetic ambitions he refers to the literary talents of Chaucer, "God of Shepheardes" in similar language:

> But if on me some little drops would flowe,
> Of that the spring was in his learned hedde,
> I soone would learne these woods, to wayle my woe,
> And teache the trees, their trickling teares to shedde. (June, 93–97)

To that extent, by the end of the poem the reader is in a position to associate the poem's physical setting with Colin's newly attained poetic genius.

While these moments suggest that the *Calender* does indeed trace Colin's transformation from an ordinary individual to the guardian of the sacred fount of poetry though, it leaves open several questions which, in turn, complicate our understanding just what that transformation consists of. Although one may associate the spring of "December" with literary genius, in the end it is *only* an association, and no more than that. Moreover, it is unclear whether Colin's position "beside" the spring denotes contact with it or yet one more sign of his alienation. Most important, despite "December's" ending, in which Colin's farewells suggest a tone of finality, it is unclear just what is supposed to follow from it. Will Colin's career return to square one (or January), thus imitating the cyclical nature of a calendar; will he continue to evolve as a poet, perhaps even coming closer to the role he has envisioned for himself? What will be the long-term effects of the poem? In light of the poet's Envoi, in what sense has the poem come to an end? Rather than simply trace Colin's development from shepherd to pastor, then, the *Calender* demonstrates how, even in the process of our watching it occur, the entire matter remains unsettled.

To some extent, such readerly skepticism is warranted by the "October" eclogue, the very episode in which Spenser's Orphic ambitions appear in their most explicit fashion, only to converge with an equally explicit awareness of the curse of Babel. As a poem, "October" gives an account of the sacred *furor poetica* and, in one and the same gesture, marks the sign of its own erasure. Indeed, as an indication of Spenser's overall designs for his career, "October" seems at once the most promising and the most disappointing. From the outset, commentary by EK suggests that the poem itself sets out:

> the perfecte paterne of a Poete, whishe finding no maintenaunce of his state and studies, complayneth of the contempte of Poetrie, and the causes thereof: Specially hauing bene in all ages, and euen amongst the most barbarous alwayes of singular accounpt & honor, & being indeede so worthy and commendable an arte: or rather no arte, but a diuine gift and heauenly instinct not to bee gotten by labour and learning, but adorned with both: and poured into the witte by a certaine [enthusiasmos], and celestiall inspiration. (October, Argument)

According to EK, this definition bears a relation to a book by Spenser himself, "Called the English Poete." In fact, this book not only has never surfaced in public, it has never been read by anyone but the semi-anonymous and quasi-fictional figure EK himself; because this character proves less than reliable as the poem's critical interpreter, it is not clear whether his review of the book's contents is reliable, nor whether the eclogue itself is an uncritical application of its precepts.

Given the two characters who actually appear in the dialogue, namely Cuddie and Piers, the episode seems to draw attention to the various failures of poetic authority. Piers has already been compromised by his role in "February," where he had presented himself as a wise man whose experience turns out to be no help to the impetuous youth who needs it most. Cuddie, meanwhile, is presented as "The perfect pattern of a poet," in the introduction, but as a questionable representative of Spenser's own designs:

> I doubte whether by Cuddie be specified the authour selfe, or some other. For in the eyght Aeglogue the same person was brought in, singing a Cantion of Colins making, as he sayth. (October, Note to line 1)

As a character who can sing but evidently cannot make anew, Cuddie finally marks the essential difference between poetry that actually can reshape the world, in the manner of Orpheus, and the type of verse that merely resembles it.

Thus when the two characters actually begin their dialogue, they seem rather to draw attention to the absence of divine enthusiasm than to demonstrate the way to bring it about. Indeed, only once does Cuddie have anything direct to say about enthusuasm at all, and only then at the critical moment in the dialogue—namely, the point where he begins to explain, once and for all, why he will never measure up to Colin Clout, much less the literary predecessors that Colin tries to emulate. As Cuddie laments:

> O if my temples were distaind with wine,
> And girt in girlonds of wild Yuie twine,
> How I could reare the Muse on stately stage,
> And teach her tread aloft in buskin fine,
> With queint Bellona in her equipage, (110–14)

EK takes this verse to be nothing less than the ravishment of a poetical fury itself. On the other hand, EK's commentary is misleading, not least because his very next statement is an expression of extreme disappointment:

> But ah my corage cooles ere it be warme. (115)

Even if the above lines are indeed the expression of poetical fury, and not what Patrick Cheney describes as "A final injection of cynicism,"[36] it is a brief and inconsequential fury at best.

As an alternative to EK's suggestions then, a reader might take the episode as a straightforward complaint that Cuddie lacks the means to achieve the poetical temper he so desperately laments. To that end, it is by no means clear that Spenser would have expected his readers to sympathize uncritically with Cuddie's situation. For what Cuddie expressly desires at this point in the eclogue is not divine ravishment itself, but rather the fruits of Bacchus:[37]

> Who euer casts to compasse weightye prise,
> And thinks to throwe out thondring words of threate:
> Let powre in lauish cups and thriftie bitts of meate,
> For Bacchus fruite is frend to Phoebus wise.
> And when with Wine the braine begins to sweate,
> The nombers flowe as fast as spring doth ryse.
> Thou kenst not Percie howe the ryme should rage.
> O if my temples were distaind with wine,
> And girt in girlonds of wild Yuie twine,
> How I could reare the Muse on stately stage,
> And teach her tread aloft in buskin fine,
> With queint Bellona in her equipage. (103–14)

This is a surprising statement, even if one were to give it the most generous reading possible and assume that by "wine" Cuddie actually meant to speak symbolically of divine fury, rather than the drink one could find at any tavern. In either case, he ends up associating enthusiasm with intoxication too closely for a reader to be certain just how to separate them. If enthusiasm is indeed a divine gift, is it truly as easy to attain as it would be to lift a glass? Cuddie does not seem willing to make this clear.

By the end of the episodes, Cuddie does make perfectly clear that if the resurrection of the prophetic poet does remain a possibility, he himself is in no shape to bring it about. While he had been capable of imagining poetry to be the honor of kings, the sign of Orphic power itself, during the final verses he shifts course and opts for a life of solitude and quiet:

> For thy, content us in thys humble shade:
> Where no such troublous tydes han us assayde,
> Here we our slender pipes may safely charm. (116–8)

With his rejection of the courts and palaces that Piers had referred to in the famous stanza ("O pierless poesie, where then is thy place," (79)) Cuddie opts for a career that has all the earmarks of vice. The call for his pipes refers, of course, to the shepherd's pipes that any pastoral poet would be expected to have, but it also calls to mind earlier, more bitter remarks about poets who live primarily for public praise:

> Sike prayse is smoke, that sheddeth in the skye,
> Sike words bene wynd, and wasten soone in vayne. (35–36)

It is as if Cuddie's readiness to blow on his pipes in the fields where nobody could hear him were in itself the continuation of a process that begins in the court anyway, namely filling the world with smoke and wind. In court or away, Fama is Fama. Likewise, the allure of safe charms calls to mind the "warres and deadly dreade" that once caused the heavens themselves to quake—in that context, Cuddie's final words come across as base cowardice. Rather than fight against the contemptuous reputation that poetry endures then, Cuddie upholds the conditions he complains about midway through the poem:

> But after vertue gan for age to stoupe,
> And mighty manhode brought on bedde of ease:
> The vaunting Poets found nought worth a pease,
> To put in preace among the learned troupe. (67–70)

While he may be capable of observing the conditions that led to the ruin of virtue, his very identity is determined by their effects. He is incapable of rising above the luxurious idleness that he identifies as the cause of the downfall of the poet's career; once it sets in, it would appear, it is difficult for him to fully overcome.

Given the discrepancies between the fanfare with which EK introduces the theme of poetic enthusiasm and the actual dialogue between the two shepherds, a safer approach to the poem might be to dismiss his report of the *English Poete* as just that—namely, report, rumor (Fama)—and to read "October" as the instance of an entirely different kind of poetry, one which neither endorses the presumed enthusiastic frenzy nor the laziness that Cuddie finally expresses. Instead, "October" presents itself as a commentary on the Orpheus legend, a statement on the historical distance between Orpheus' civilizing eloquence and Spenser's own lot. Contrary to what has been the predominant critical opinion about his heroic role in early modern poetics, "October" invokes Orpheus precisely because, as a figure, he so vividly demonstrates the experience of loss and retreat from the civilization he formerly had founded. At one time, poetry had been a force that could subdue both the fiercest animals and the most vicious rulers; indeed, the very existence of an order of virtue implied the trace of a poetic imposition. Over time, however, that power to fashion civilized society so readily has all but disappeared. Such, after all, is the fate of Orpheus, whose loss of Eurydice led him to abandon one poetic lifestyle and take up the solitary lament—until, at last, falling prey to the Maenads (a religious sect that worshipped none other than Bacchus). Taken together, these references suggest Spenser's own self-conscious participation in a literary topos fairly distinct from that implied by the poetics of enthusiasm. If Orpheus is indeed the model whom Spenser imitates, it is not uncritical imitation.[38] Rather than participate in enthusiastic poetry per se, "October" laments it. If he is the ideal, he is the ideal figure of irreparable loss, the figure to whom Spenser can appeal ultimately only in order to measure their radically incommensurable distance.

SPENSER AND THE TOWER OF BABEL (I)

While the *Shepheardes Calender* draws attention to the poem's inability to transcend the trappings of ordinary language, Spenser's later poetry makes direct references to the Tower of Babel in order to underscore the radically fallen nature of contemporary languages as a whole. According to Spenser, the repercussions of this biblical event can be felt on both physiological and political levels. In order to appreciate more fully both the importance of Babel for Spenser's poetry and its political implications, we might turn momentarily to a dedicatory sonnet prefixed to *The Commonwealth and Government of Venice,* translated into English by Lewis Lewkenor in 1599. As a dedicatory poem, it certainly counts as minor verse, albeit verse that has attracted recent critical attention to due its implications concerning Spenser's political affiliations.[39] Because the poem is dedicated to a book about Venetian government—a government which had gained international reputation for successfully sustaining a republican constitution[40]—recent readers have inferred that, at the very least, Spenser saw something appealing about its structure. What is striking about the poem, however, is its persistent invocation of Babel as a political model. In the opening octet, he writes:

> The antique Babel, Empresse of the East,
> Vpreard her buildinges to the threatned skie:
> And Second Babell, tyrant of the West,
> Her ayry Towers vpraised much more high.
> But, with the weight of their own surquedry,
> They both are fallen, that all the earth did feare,
> And buried now in their own ashes ly;
> Yet shewing by their heapes, how great they were.

The reference is all the more captivating in its context as a poem attached to a *translation* which inherently draws attention to the differences among modern vernacular languages. Finally as the final likes suggest, though without specifically saying so, Venice too will enjoy similar fruits, as well as similar disasters, in its own time:

> But in their place doth now a third appeare,
> Fayre Venice, flower of the last worlds delight;
> And next to them in beauty draweth neare,
> But farre exceedes in policie of right.
> Yet not so fayre her buildinges to behold
> As Lewkenors stile that hath her beautie told.

For the first time in the poem, Spenser does not use the name Babel to characterize the poem's subject; but ambiguous lines, such as line twelve, already raise awareness of the problematic nature of Venice's government. As the line suggests, so excellent are its policies, in the end it is their exceeding excellence that will constitute their very transgressiveness.

Although the poem does not explicitly warn Venice of the futility of its political ambitions, which would have been inappropriate for its rhetorical occasion, Spenser does elaborate upon a similar idea in Book II of the *Faerie Queene*. There, Spenser makes reference to the Tower of Babel in order to join together two ostensibly distinct components, namely: the revolt of Maleager's troops, which threatens to pull the castle to the ground; and the various delusions of the melancholy Phantastes. As the following section argues, there is a connection between Phantastes' false images and Maleager's continuous onslaughts. This connection is due to the fact that the castle itself is constituted in terms of what might be called "the Babel effect": if languages are inherently corrupt, the consequences, on a political level, consist of the inevitable failure for healthy institutions to sustain themselves. Like the *Calender* before, this failure has a temporal dimension which also will be discussed below. If the *Calender* had had explored the problem of poetic development within a purely formal arrangement of time (only to suggest that that formal arrangement obscured the decay of language that had occurred between the ancients and moderns), the Castle of Alma episode reexamines what it means to be situated in time. The use of the calendar as a literary model had provided a sense of continuity that combines linear sequences with circular patterns of recurrence. By contrast the Alma episode, with its emphasis on mutiny on revolt, characterizes temporality a force that ultimately *disrupts* the narrative's ability to attain its stated objectives.

SPENSER AND THE TOWER OF BABEL (II): CASTLE OF ALMA

In the middle of the cantos that take place within the Castle of Alma, the heroes of Book II, Guyon and Arthur, read from separate historical chronicles, with the implication that their own histories and destinies are distinct from each other. In perhaps an analogous way, what is distinctive about the Castle of Alma episode is that, over the course of three cantos, the poem demands entirely different sets of reading strategies. Of the cantos that make up the episode, only the last seems particularly plot heavy. Cantos ix and x seem more intent on description and contemplative matters than on narrating sequences of events. In the episode's central passage, canto x, Arthur and Guyon do nothing more than read their respective national chronicles in the chamber of Eumnestes, or good memory. To the extent there is any activity at all, it is activity that has long passed and been preserved—if not fossilized—in the parchments that Eumnestes ceaselessly turns about. By contrast, the action, which occurs in canto xi with Maleger's assault and defeat, poses the greatest danger to the castle. While Arthur does finally ward off the threat, it has not been lost on readers that the only way Spenser finds a way to defeat Maleger is to invoke a salvific power that lies beyond the reaches of temperance itself. Given the way the three cantos fit together, then, it would appear that the things that *happen* to the castle (for instance the encounters, assaults, rebellions) are the very stuff that represent the greatest threat to it. Alma's castle may be safe enough on its own, but it is only insofar as it remains, precisely, on its own, removed from the dangers of events.

In fact, everything about canto ix suggests that the mere possibility that a sequence of events could take place "in time," somehow is itself the problem. Even though, as Sean Kane points out, Temperance is itself a temporal virtue—a temperate person acts according to a measured pace—and even though the book's evil characters seek to annihilate time (Acrasia, Phaedria, even Mammon share this desire), the castle complicates this schema by introducing time and change as the very elements that put its foundations under greatest jeopardy.[41] In fact this is suggested as early as canto ix. There, agents of change interfere with the canto's implicit objective, which is to demonstrate the Platonic image of castle as body entirely through description.

As a whole, the canto inevitably takes on an iconic dimension. As early as the first stanza, the narrator compares the conditions of physical health to a well run commonwealth:

> Of all Gods workes, which doe this world adorne,
> There is no one more faire and excellent,
> Then is mans body both for powre and forme,
> Whiles it is kept in sober gouernment;
> But none then it, more fowle and indecent,
> Distempered through misrule and passions bace:
> It growes a Monster and incontinent
> Doth loose his dignitie and natiue grace,
> Behold, who list, both one and other in this place.[42]

Spenser's incorporation of political terminology in his description of physical health is not altogether surprising in itself—Bright had done the same when he referred the body as a "Vniforme gouernment."[43] The difference between the two writers is that Spenser's language is decidedly more ambiguous. Whereas Bright seems to have the idea of individual comportment in mind, it is by no means clear whether Spenser's fourth line refers to a need to maintain some sense of personal discipline or instead to belong to a well run commonwealth with just laws and customs in place. By extension, it is unclear just what causes monstrosity, as Spenser leaves us to doubt whose misrule and passions base should be held accountable: does misrule refer to personal misconduct, or does it refer to abuse of power and general incivility? Either answer is plausible, given the phrasing of the verse; but neither is obviously preferable.[44]

One way to understand the stanza would be to suppose that this sense of ambiguity between physical and political health is deliberate; Spenser links them as two components of the same grand architecture. As Michel Foucault describes the system (albeit in a slightly different context), "The world is covered with signs that must be deciphered, and those signs, which reveal resemblances and affinities, are themselves no more than forms of similitude."[45] Both the physical body and the commonwealth regulate themselves according to the same principle, or undergo the process of assimilation, which constituted one of the fundamental principles of health. Given the way the bulk of the canto proceeds with its repeated identification of bodily organs as social figures—as though one were a microcosm of the other–such a reading of the opening stanza makes sense. With that in mind, the crucial word in the opening stanza—the word that appears no fewer than seven times—would be the word "and," which not only conjoins two separate elements, but eradicates the sense of differentiation between one body and the other.

What eventually accounts for the episode's uneasy shifts from descriptions of static images to the narration of the castle's greatest threats is the appearance of the melancholy Phantastes, the figure who represents the imaginative faculties of the mind. If this catches the poem's readers off their guard, it is because this figure—who only appears for two stanzas, and not until very late in the episode—does not initially come across as Spenser's main point of focus. In fact, the narrator is dismissive, referring to him as:

> A man of yeares yet fresh, as mote appeare,
> Of swarth complexion, and of crabbed hew,
> That him full of melancholy did shew;
> Bent hollow beetly browes, sharpe staring eyes,
> That mad or foolish seemd: one by his view
> Mote deeme him borne with ill disposed skyes,
> When oblique Saturn sate in the house of agonyes. (II, ix, 52)

In other words, the melancholy that Phantastes embodies is, at best, wrought with ambivalence (as conditional terms like "seemd" or "mote" indicate), and at worst outright repugnance over a character who behaves much like a false prophet. Given the prior description of his chamber, however, it is the latter judgment that appears more likely. His room lies in disarray—indeed, it is "dispainted all within," as the narrator comments, suggesting a kind of antithesis to the plastic arts. And his own adornments, most likely projections of his own fanciful imagination (but not necessarily so) are described in previous stanza with little sympathy:

> All these were idle thoughts and fantasies.
> Deuices, dreames, opinions vnsound,
> Shewes, visions, sooth-sayes and prophesies;
> And all that fained is, as leasings, tales, and lies. (II, ix, 51)

With visions and prophecies—two genres which Spenser the lyricist knew about as intimately as any poet could—juxtaposed among a list of falsehoods and "all that fained is," the narrator seems to reject any sense of prophetic language's claims to truth. Instead, prophecy amounts to a lie, if not an actual symptom of sickness and madness. Phantastes represents a part of the mind which, although natural, is not particularly beneficial. Little wonder, then, that Alma should escort Guyon and Arthur away from his chamber as quickly as she can. In other words, when Phantastes is introduced, he is a minor character—indeed, he is significant only insofar as he reinforces the general framework of the canto, the notion that every aspect of the physical body has its corresponding analogue in the public domain.

But Phantastes does serve a narrative purpose, namely to disrupt the narrative sequence as it is initially laid out. It is only gradually, after readers have read and re-read several stanzas—even, perhaps, reading the stanzas in opposition to the sequential manner that the reading process tends to expect from us—when the melancholy Phantastes takes on an unexpected significance that readers could not have anticipated initially. When readers read through these stanzas they are invited to recall an earlier scene within the canto, which had depicted the castle under assault by a swarm of villains. A cluster of images within the chamber of Phantastes distinctly recalls images from the scene describing their attack. Thus Phantastes' physical appearance is described by the narrator as:

> A man of yeares yet fresh, as mote appeare,
> Of swarth complexion, and of crabbed hew,
> That him full of melancholy did shew;
> Bent hollow beetly browes, sharpe staring eyes,
> That mad or foolish seemd; (II, ix, 52)

This recalls (albeit with modifications) the faces of the "vile caytive wretches, rugged, rude, deformed" which the narrator describes in stanza 13:

Sterne was their looke, like wild amazed steares,
Staring with hollow eyes, and stiff vpstanding heares. (II, ix, 13, lines 8–9)

Similarly, with the appearance in canto xi of the ostensible leader of the rebellion, Maleger, his physical appearance invites further comparison to Phantastes. As the narrator describes him:

As pale and wan as ashes was his looke,
His bodie leane and meagre as a rake,
And skin all withered like a dryed rooke,
Thereto as cold and drery as a Snake,
That seem'd to tremble euermore and quake (II, xi, 22)

Likewise, the chamber itself, which the narrator observes:

Filled was with flyes,
Which buzzed all about, and made such sound,
That they encombred all mens eares and eyes,
Like many swarmes of Bees assembled round, (II, ix, 53, 1–4)

recalls an earlier simile, which describes the swarm of invaders:

As when a swarme of Gnats at euentide
Out of the fennes of Allan do arise,
Their murmuring small trompets sounden wide,
Whiles in the aire their clustring army flies,
That as a cloud doth seeme to dim the skies;
Ne man nor beast may rest, or take repast.
For their sharpe wounds, and noyous iniuries,
Till the fierce Northerne wind with blustring blast
Doth blow them quite away, and in the ocean cast. (II, ix, 16)

Finally, the "idle thoughts and fantasies" that represent the product of Phantastes' restless wit reminds us of the characterization of the villeins as "idle shades" in stanza 15. These repetitions of images suggest that by the end of the canto the reader is expected to make at least an associative connection between the two moments. The revolt against the castle resembles the images of madness within. While the castle preserves itself through stasis, including the static representation of the past by means of historical chronicle and memory, the fantastic visions produced by the disruptive figure of melancholy will continue to usurp Eumnestes' authority until the grace that Arthur represents finally intervenes.

Perhaps most suggestively, the narrator hints early on that Maleger's troops might be grounded in a certain instability of speech even before Guyon and Arthur enter the castle. As they stand at the outer wall requesting entrance from within, the chief sentinel warns them to beware the thousand raving enemies that have been holding the castle siege. As the narrator remarks:

> Thus as he spoke, loe with outragious cry
> A thousand villeins round about them swarmd. (II, ix, 13)

These lines are deliberately ambiguous. The words "Thus as" may just as easily indicate causality as they do coincidence; the villeins' arrival may be the fulfillment of the sentinel's personal fears—and hence the fulfillment of a persecution fantasy. It may also be the effect of a somewhat over felicitous speech act, almost as though the very maintenance and defense of a well run commonwealth were the very cause of the elements that threatened its destruction. Likewise, the narrator gives no indication as to who the low and outrageous cry belongs to. The cry could just as easily be the sentinel's as it can be his foes'. Such indeterminacy in turn suggests a deeper affinity between the invaders and defenders than the participants themselves might be able to recognize; in a sense, they very much share a sense of intimacy which makes it difficult to tell where one side ends and the other begins. And because the narrator characterizes the villeins as idle shades, as semblances rather than substances, it becomes tempting to read them as projections of the sentinel's own terrified thoughts as much as real opposing forces who confront the castle from the outside. Again, either reading is plausible; neither is certain.

As suggestive as this is, nevertheless the entire network of associations outlined cannot help but feel like a typically Spenserian web that the episode expects readers to run into. What gives the lie, as it turns out, is that critics themselves are not clear just what Maleger is supposed to represent. While the dominant interpretation does hold him to be a melancholy figure, other perfectly reasonable interpretations hold up just as well. James Nohrnberg, for instance, sees Maleger as the representation of original sin—and as often is the case with Nohrnberg's book, it is nearly impossible to disagree with him. More recently, Jonathan Gil Harris and David Read have interpreted Maleger alternatively as a syphilitic, and as a New World warrior (equally intriguing insofar as they would take Maleger to be a figure of foreignness).[46] As these alternative interpretations accumulate, the connection between

Maleger and Phantastes gradually becomes harder to sustain. The factor that holds them together, it turns out, is a contingent, rather than necessary reading process. Or rather, it is a trick of language that causes readers to associate Phantastes with the rebels merely by the fact that similar words and images appear in both locations. Readers who note the extensive similarities are falsely led to believe these clusters of words were describing, if not the same things, then the same sorts of things. It might be tempting to identify Phantastes as a kind of homunculus who somehow is linked causally to the forces that invade the castle, even if it amounts to associative causality. In the end, though, there is nothing in the language to guarantee that the link is anything more than a projection of the reader's own fantastic images.

Thus while the melancholy Phantastes may be associated with the rebellions that occur in cantos ix and xi, it is due to an illusory effect that language produces—the effect, close to what Angus Fletcher describes as "magical causality," seems rather to camouflage than to explain how Maleger's troops originate in the first place.[47] Such being the case, the relation between melancholy and rebellion might better be accounted for if we turn instead to the passage's ongoing commentary about the disruptive capacity of language, particularly as it pertains to the very constitution of Alma's castle. For as the narrator makes clear early enough, the castle—both as a castle and as a body—is constituted not only by language, but by fallen languages whose capacity to name things accurately have been destroyed by the Tower of Babel. Indeed, a reader's very ability to recognize the castle both as castle and body in one and the same gesture somehow seems grounded in the corrupted nature of language in the wake of that Biblical event. To the extent that the Castle of Alma demonstrates anything at all, it demonstrates language's capacity to mal-function.

From the outset, the narrator's description of the castle is overshadowed by the Biblical episode, a feature which suggests that the canto is just as concerned with the widespread failures of language—and in turn, failures of a project which holds that language can faithfully and completely describe the world as micro- and macrocosm—as it is with demonstrating an affinity between the individual and political commonwealths. In a sense the story of Babel supplies the very building blocks of both the castle and the episode. As Guyon and Arthur are led through the entrance, the narrator makes a direct comparison between its walls and the walls of the Biblical tower:

> First she them led vp to the Castle wall,
> That was so high, as foe might not it clime,
> And all so faire, and sensible withall,

> Not build of bricke, ne yet of stone and lime,
> But of thing like to that Aegyptian slime,
> Whereof king Nine whilome built Babell towre;
> But O great pitty, that no lenger time
> So goodly workemanship should not endure:
> Soone it must turn to earth; no earthly thing is sure. (II, ix, 21)

In its size, in its strength, in its very materiality, it recalls both the ambition and the profound failure of the Hittites, who had used the same material to build their own edifice. Just as important, it seems to court the same disaster. And while the stanza that follows may present something of a corrective by suggesting that the Castle's frame adheres to the geometrical figures assigned to it by divine will, even there the narrator has difficulties shaking off the story of Babel. In the final lines of the stanza, the narrator describes the correspondence between the sacred and profane realms,

> Proportioned equally be seven and nine;
> Nine was the circle set in heauens place,
> All which compacted made a goodly diapase. (II, ix, 22)

One can hear echoes of the previous stanza, which had invoked the name of King Nine (or Ninus, itself a misnomer for Nimrod), the king whose own tower once aspired to set in heaven's place as well. In other words, the description of the house's exterior repeatedly draws attention to its very design as the source of its own inability to maintain an effective correspondence between words and things. Given these conditions, the house starts to appear less a fulfillment of the ideal given in the first stanza, and more a fulfillment of its (inevitable) perversion. Indeed, the very description of the outer membrane of the castle ought to serve as a warning not to trust the passages that follow, particularly when they pertain to reading written texts—are we really supposed to admire Eumnestes with his worm-eaten parchments, parchments that begin significantly with chronicles of Ninus' own wars themselves?

In a compelling reading of the Castle of Alma episode, Michael Schoenfeldt shows that the image of Temperance that Spenser offers consists of a constant vigilance and regulation of the body's sensual needs. What constitutes "A temperate, well-regulated body is not a classical immured structure but a dynamic and porous edifice continually producing 'superfluous excrements' from the very matter which nourishes it, excrements which must be purged."[48] If the castle is constantly under siege, it is merely because the very nature of the virtue requires constant attention: "Psychological, ethical, and physiological health is an edifice perpetually being constructed, and in need of continual maintenance. The self that Spenser endorses is a profoundly fabricated being, one that discovers individuation in regulating a repertoire of desires possessed in some degree by all. It is, moreover, a structure built in part on the ruins of those forces that threaten it."[49] And yet, as Schoenfeldt also notes, the curious feature of the passage is Spenser's deliberately ambivalent location of the castle's most threatening dangers. If Maleger is the physical embodiment of excessive melancholy, this is because "The figures over whom these rigors are allowed to exert control is not a colonized indigenous population but a series of forces already materially contained within the self."[50] As in the case of jealous anxiety, the biggest dangers may come more from the jealous party's private fantasies than from any real external danger.[51] Rather than merely project all dangers to the health of the physical or political body onto external, foreign agents (such as the Irish, whose description in the *View of the Present State of Ireland* is embarrassingly similar to the swarms of fighters that surround the castle), Spenser warns at least astute readers like Schoenfeldt that the most terrible threats to our well being may be the outgrowth of our own fantasies.

To modify Schoenfeldt's argument slightly, the threat to the castle's well being, or constitution, may be language itself—language, which connects the external world with our inmost thoughts, even to the point of obscuring where one ends and the other begins, but which also causes us to forget that such a connection is tenuous all along. With this adjustment, the sort of ambivalence Schoenfeldt refers to could apply to the castle episode in several additional ways. For instance, is the castle a representation of a public government, or the uncanny (because alienated) interior of Guyon and Arthur's own bodies?[52] Who or what exactly addresses the heroes as they approach the castle in the first place—what sort of speech is it? Finally, does the similarity between Phantastes and Maleger register as such for Arthur, or does this mark a discrepancy between what the reader and characters know?[53] In other words, given the possibility that such a discrepancy exists, is the episode meant to be read ironically? If so, who is the one being ironized, Arthur or the reader who thinks that Maleger must be a melancholic, even a kinsman to Phantastes? The point to all this is not simply to show that ambiguity abounds, but to point out that the ambiguity recurs at moments of division between interior and exterior, public and private locations. In other words, it recurs at moments that have a direct affinity with speech itself, insofar as speech marks that ambiguous border between the private body and public commonwealth.

The more the castle draws attention to itself as a castle constituted, if not in language itself, then in the corrupting agent, the more the threats to its stability seem grounded in language. By reminding us early on not only that the castle resembled the Tower of Babel, and by warning us explicitly of its eventual return to dust—at which point, the line reminds us, "no earthly thing is sure," the real trouble begins—Spenser invites us to search for the cause of its vulnerability. As various possibilities present themselves, they turn out to be illusory, the effect of what Walter Benjamin had referred to, in his own studies on post-Edenic language, as "overnaming."[54] While Spenser seems to define melancholy as the source of bodily intemperance, and analogously, poetic prophecies as the source of political instability, what he shows instead is that these figures are the effect of the fallen condition of language, almost as though there would be no melancholy if language had retained its original sacred status. But in the process he also raises far more critical concerns for, the depiction of Phantastes introduces demands of reading and problems of interpretation that disrupt the principles of a unified commonwealth in direct alignment with the cosmos that mark the major premise of the entire canto. In other words, the figure of the poet functions as the site where the *dis*integration of a long-standing mythology about the relation among individual commonwealth and cosmos finally takes place. To read Phantastes this way is to recognize the limitations and contradictions of that mythology and to begin to search for alternative ways to arrange it.

CONCLUSION

While Bright and Spenser were contemporaries and may have borrowed ideas from similar sources, it is difficult, and perhaps unproductive to believe that melancholy works the same way in their respective texts. For Bright, melancholy belongs to a distinctly nationalist project, wherein diseases and cures are placed within the ethnographic contours defined by the present and ongoing international rivalries. Melancholy further underscores a concern over the English vernacular and its ability to accurately characterize the body and soul as objects in order to treat them according to their specific needs. For Bright, melancholy can be known precisely to the extent it can be spoken about; and it can be spoken about precisely because English can be manipulated to a stable system with clear categories and classes of objects. No poet seems further from these convictions in the case of Spenser, whose own references to melancholy do not necessarily yield a coherent picture. Indeed, if there is such a thing as melancholy, it is the sign of an obscure awareness of the incurably corrupt nature of language. More troubling, insofar as all commonwealths already are products of a language—that is, constituted by the linguistic acts that allow us to see commonwealths as objects—all risk fates comparable to Ninus'. Melancholy ultimately may not *name* anything for Spenser; instead, it serves as a place holder for what might be described as the human ability to comprehend our fundamental inability to comprehend, and the political consequences that follow from this paradoxical arrangement.

Chapter Two

"Reason is Fled to Beasts": Malcontents and Animals in the "Humour" Plays of Jonson and Shakespeare

INTRODUCTION

As the previous chapter argued, during the years when writers began to discuss it as a separate subject in medicine and poetry respectively, at least two versions of melancholy emerged. For a writer like Timothy Bright, writing about the disease had specifically nationalist implications; his *Treatise* had been part of a larger effort to bolster an English medical and spiritual program, which itself depended on both an ethnological and linguistic definition of nationality. For Edmund Spenser, melancholy instead was a symptom of an even more pervasive problem with vernacular languages, namely their inherently fallen condition as the effect of divine punishment at the Tower of Babel. Thus, while Bright's *Treatise* belonged to a larger project that explicitly sought to promote England as both a spiritual and commercial vanguard, Spenser's (admittedly more sporadic and intermittent) use of melancholy wound up unraveling the very concept of nationhood by exposing commonwealths as institutions doomed to failure by the very elements that shaped their existence. If political institutions were the product of human intellect, and human intellect was itself conditioned by languages that were inherently corrupt, it could only follow that there was no political institution that was not in some way involved in this fundamental misprision. Significantly, while Bright and Spenser may well have drawn from similar sources and while their descriptions of melancholy may indeed have overlapped in remarkable ways (both took the surprising step to distinguish melancholy from despair, for instance), the effect of their different approaches to language was to assign melancholy very distinct political undertones.

Meanwhile, on the stages of the public playhouses, a third and perhaps more *popular* version of melancholy emerged: the disaffected malcontent. On the surface the melancholy malcontent is an easier subject for study, for after all, the malcontent is almost exclusively surface. If there is a single example of a relatively consistent Elizabethan stock figure who could correspond to the Warburg school's claim that iconographical representations of melancholy emerged in response to demands to make the condition more recognizable, the melancholy malcontent comes closest. Malcontents appeared in countless tragedies and comedies over a period that corresponded roughly with the public playhouses themselves.[1] The character type quickly became something of a stock figure who embodied a fairly discrete set of characteristics, and who inspired either fear or ridicule, depending on the occasion. If Edmund of *King Lear* offers any clue, melancholy itself was often considered a performance that could be assumed or dropped at the actor's will.[2] Thus whether contemporary literary critics dismiss malcontents as little more than fashionable flirtation with continental philosophies[3] or uphold them as a symbol of the real socio-economic troubles that beset the artisan classes (particularly when its members became better educated and fancied themselves as worthy members of the intellectual elite), they are virtually agreed in recognizing the malcontent as a *type* whose behavior is determined by discrete conventions rather than idiosyncrasies.[4]

Many critics already have provided an extensive survey of the primary characteristics by which malcontents could be identified. They included the following: an exaggerated sense of importance, or more specifically a conscious belief that present society did not provide sufficient avenues for realizing one's potential for success; a propensity for travel, especially for travel to centers of Roman Catholicism, if not Rome itself (thus invoking various deeper concerns about England's own national religion)[5]; and an unusual concern with fashion and dress, so much so that for a critic like Lawrence Babb melancholy during the Elizabethan period was faddish—if not foppish—in its very nature.[6] Above all, the melancholy malcontent was distinguished by deep ambivalence about assuming a disposition that could be mimicked so easily by rivals and status seekers; hence a proclivity among malcontents to distinguish their own "authentic" melancholy from the more "faddish" versions that did nothing but confuse the public on such lofty matters. Taken together, these characteristics add up to a difficult social position. Critics as diverse as Bridget Gellert Lyons and Jonathan Dollimore have noted that the malcontent was the quintessential outsider who paradoxically depended on the presence of others in order to make his condition apparent. Indeed, if social space could be mapped topologically, the malcontent would inhabit a position where interiority and exteriority could not be distinguished from one another. To that extent the stage figure reveals as much about the conditions for forming social relationships that people belong to collectively as it establishes the (all too fractious and unstable) individualistic subjectivity that such famous figures as Hamlet seem to announce in their more ostensibly modern moments.

Thus while they frequently insisted upon their uniqueness and—if one may put it this way—psychological interiority, on a deeper level stage malcontents brought into focus many problems concerning the nature of this public setting in the first place. In particular they drew attention to the conditions of dwelling within a distinctly urban environment, and the role of individuals within a locale whose own dimensions were seemingly in a state of permanent fluctuation. London itself was expanding rapidly, both in population and territory, nearly doubling in size during the second half of the sixteenth century alone. As Jonathan Haynes points out in his study of Jonsonian comedy, for instance:

> The acceleration of fashion in late Tudor and Stuart society is thus functionally related to its social dynamics, as well as to the rapid increase in the quantities of cloth, furniture, and so on available as the material preconditions. The population of London nearly quadrupled between 1500 and 1600, and nearly doubled again by 1660. The increase was the result of immigration, and the immigrants moved into new social relations.[7]

Meanwhile, as L. C. Knights recalls, sixteenth century England witnessed the development of an entirely new phenomenon: unemployment and poverty brought about by man-made conditions, as opposed to the more traditional cause, one's "immediate dependence upon the seasons."[8] From both geographical and social standpoints, then, Elizabethan London could be characterized as a place physical and social disorientation, with overcrowded neighborhoods and displaced populations becoming something of a standard. Meanwhile, as the permanent playhouses themselves suggest—each of which being designed on the assumption that new plays could draw audiences of at least several hundred on a regular basis—Elizabethan London witnessed the emergence of a phenomenon that could rightly be called mass culture. In short, melancholy malcontents were essentially city characters. They became popular among audiences characterized by their large-scale anonymity and virtual alienation toward one another. And to the extent that they appealed to theatergoers their appeal seemed to rely on precisely the condition of dwelling in a place of collective indifference. If malcontents took such pains to distinguish themselves as outsiders within a particular social domain, it was because at heart was a deeper concern that the absence of such gestures would reduce society to an anonymous flock in a city whose composition could change almost as rapidly as the settings in Ben Jonson's more frenetic city comedies.

As the above review suggests, the malcontent's popularity grew in response to concerns about what it means to be a *character*, in all senses of the term. On one level it was to distinguish oneself as an individual, particularly when more gratifying means were unavailable. On another, it was to allow oneself to be classified as a type, and a *written* type at that; at the very least, it offered the security of "knowing oneself" at a time when figures as imposing as King Lear himself could ask the deeply troubling question, "Who is it that can tell me who I am?" (Fittingly, malcontents emerged at approximately the same point in time when new essays on characters began to appear with increasing frequency. These essays were essentially satirical guidebooks for various obnoxious types that one might encounter in public, though the genre did include portraits of "right" individuals as well. As if by coincidence, they were themselves the revival of a literary tradition made popular by Theophrastus.) But in the course of raising questions about the conditions that enable the individual to be recognized qua individual, or even about what enables an individual to participate within a larger social aggregate—which, after all, defines the individual as such—it turns out that malcontents wound up raising an entirely different sort of problem: what does it mean to be a human at all?

To be sure, Jonathan Dollimore made significant headway in this direction when he argued convincingly that theatrical malcontents participated in a larger critique of Renaissance humanist principles, staging what he called (in apparent homage to Copernicus) the Jacobean "decentering of man." In Dollimore's assessment, malcontents helped demonstrate the fictionality of individualism, perhaps best symbolized by Pico's famous *Oration on the Dignity of Man*, and they did so by exposing such claims to individuality as the product of unsustainable social relations:

> Obviously, with the decline of Christian essentialism there did not instantly emerge the humanist ideology of individual man. On the contrary, in the England of the early seventeenth century that decline led to a decentring of man and a corresponding emphasis on the extent to which his subjectivity was to be socially identified.[9]

But while Dollimore's study focuses on the ideological production of competing definitions of humanity as a response to an evolving socio-political climate—for all his distaste for teleological models of history, he writes unflinchingly about regressive and emergent socio-economic relations—his argument remains curiously grounded in anthropocentric definitions of humanity. It is only more recently, through studies such as those by Erica Fudge and Gail Kern Paster,[10] that literary and historical critics have begun to directly address the ways in which both transformations in the urban environment and new speculations about the material composition of physical bodies in turn gave rise to doubts about the differences between humans and other animals—or more specifically, as Fudge argues, about the intellectual categories that allow such distinctions to be made in the first place.

As this chapter argues, a number of theatrical malcontents had a curious tendency to associate themselves, sometimes to the point of identifying with animals. While not necessarily sympathetic toward animals—indeed, the characters who are discussed in the following sections come across as unbearably cruel for many audience members and critics alike—they nevertheless were able to draw attention to the more bestial aspects of everyday human conduct.[11] Nor were stage malcontents necessarily the first figures to make this identification; in fact by doing so they returned to a problem that had already become apparent in more exacting attempts to identify the human as such. If the playhouses lent themselves to this problem, it was because the ability to engage in theatrical performance was itself an obvious way to make the distinction.[12] As this chapter also argues, the theatrical malcontent's identification with animals could be put to very different ends, in accordance with the specific playwright in question.

This will become clear in the final sections, which examine two comedies of humors, Ben Jonson's *Every Man Out of His Humour* and William Shakespeare's *As You Like It*.[13] In many ways these two plays may be considered as a pair. If there was ever a moment when the rivalry between Jonson and Shakespeare erupted into a full-scale public row, the original staging of these two plays comes the closest. While certainly not nearly as cantankerous as the famous "War of the Theaters" that took place a few years later, these two plays traded enough inside jokes and barbs to suggest that Jonson and Shakespeare had each other in mind when they wrote their respective scripts. While the majority of their barbs revolve around the issue of social ambitiousness—their squabble seems to have been occasioned in part by Shakespeare's recent purchase of a mustard yellow coat-of-arms[14]—on a deeper level they are at odds over the issue of identifying the features that define humanity as such. In the course of doing so, both playwrights fill their respective stages with animals, both real and imaginary. In turn, the central melancholy malcontents in the two texts are distinguished in part by the way they interact with the animals that share the stage with them. The differences in conduct that Macilente and Jaques display in turn raise distinct positions concerning the political relations among human beings themselves.

Before turning to those plays, however, it will be useful to reconsider two well-known treatises, somewhat contemporaneous with the plays in question, and whose own attempts to demonstrate the problematic status of humanity were in part shaped by what turns out to be the very difficult task of differentiating humans from animals in the first place. What follows here is not a survey of the historical development of the concept of humanity, but rather an attempt to bring into focus one of the central problems that occurs in positing the human as a unique creature, or a different type of animal. It is a problem that turns out to be particularly relevant for the melancholy malcontents in Jonson and Shakespeare's plays. At the moment when one makes this assertion on the basis of a comparison between humans and other animals the distinction runs the risk of breaking down in the very process of its articulation. And nowhere is this problem more clearly articulated than in the famous humanist text that most emphatically restored the human as the measure of all things, namely Pico's *Oration on the Dignity of Man*.

CHAMELEONS AND TALKING BEASTS: THE PROBLEMATIC STATUS OF THE HUMAN

On the whole, humanism was far more importantly a literary endeavor than a mere attempt to define the status of the human (which, in many ways, was embedded in its understanding of literary scholarship). The purpose of study was to attain familiarity with the *literae,* and in fact the term *humanitas* referred to a certain level of intellectual accomplishment rather than an *a priori* biological condition.[15] To that end, humanism may ironically seem an inconvenient place to begin an examination of the ways in which humans were distinguished from animals among early modern writers of any type. Nevertheless, in a peculiar twist of expectations—and one that has never failed to capture the attention of its readers—the boundaries that mark the distinction between human and animal begin to break down even at the very moment that a writer such as Pico advocates the "human" as a figure of primary significance and subsequently redirects philosophical study to more properly human affairs.[16] (These included, though certainly were not limited to, the arts of rhetoric, history, and political science, all premised on the notion that public life is as much the artistic creation of human activities as it is a reflection of the proper arrangement of the *cosmos* itself.) And in fact, what is most surprising about Pico's text is that this dissolution is not accidental, but rather a necessary step toward securing the very notion that man occupies a place in the universe after all.

Fittingly, he demonstrates the problematic status of humanity in a fable that he uses in order to explain how humanity came to enjoy its dignity as a species. Pico's fable proceeds by stripping humanity of all particular qualities, with the single exception of the faculty for mimesis. Thus, upon finishing his creation of the universe, the Divine maker allegedly proclaims to Adam:

> We have given you, Oh Adam, no visage proper to yourself, nor any endowment properly your own, in order that whatever place, whatever form, whatever gifts you may, with premeditation, select, these same you may have and possess through your own judgment and decision. The nature of all other creatures is defined and restricted within laws which We have laid down; you, by contrast, impeded by no such restrictions, may, by your own free will, to whose custody We have assigned you, trace for yourself the lineaments of your own nature. I have placed you at the very center of the world, so that from that vantage point you may with greater ease glance round about you on all that the world contains. We have made you a creature neither of heaven nor of earth, neither mortal nor immortal, in order that you may, as the free and proud shaper of your own being, fashion yourself in the form you may prefer.[17]

As much as the tenor of this story exhorts mankind to forego the bestial and aspire to the divine, paradoxically it defines the essence of man as a creature without any qualities of its own. In other words, humanity is defined negatively, not for what it possesses as a species, but precisely because there is nothing that belongs to it properly—the very phrase "properly human" is thus a contradiction. And further still, if mankind can claim any genuine aspirations to nobility, it is precisely insofar as the species is effectively devoid of any nature.[18] Significantly, and in a gesture not entirely devoid of irony, not two paragraphs later Pico does identify a creature that humans do in fact remind him of, when he exults, "Who will not wonder at this chameleon?"[19]

This question makes at most only a slight adjustment to Pico's argument, and in fact it goes a long way toward clarifying matters. For Pico, the human is not merely an empty vessel never to be filled; rather, the human is a fundamentally mimetic creature. It is not that mankind lacks reason for instance, but only that it shares the faculty with other creatures (notably, angels) and therefore cannot identify reason as a predicate of humanity. Nor is this to suggest that Pico's fable inadvertently denies the dignity that he assigns his subject matter—indeed, he remains profoundly optimistic that, at the very least, everyone has the ability to aspire to the higher faculties. Instead he denies that mankind owes its dignity to anything that would *differentiate* it from other forms of life. For Pico then, human dignity obtains only inasmuch as humans are capable of recognizing this non-difference as the very thing that differentiates the species in the end.

Perhaps it is only a shift in nuance that separates the belief that humanity is capable of resembling whatever creature it wants to the far more scathing claim that, at bottom, human beings are nothing better than glorified animals. To that end, Michel de Montaigne's caricaturist portraits of humans as beasts may read, at first glance, like a complete rejection of Pico's idealistic project a little more than a hundred years afterward; in many other ways, Montaigne simply reveals the other side of the coin. But in doing so, Montaigne exposes one crucial shortcoming obscured in Pico's glorification all along. Like Pico, Montaigne minimizes the difference between humans and animals, most emphatically in his "Apology for Raymond Sebond," an essay which enjoyed particularly wide readership among early modern audiences.[20] For Montaigne, though, the significance of this non-difference runs in almost direct opposition to Pico, for he uses it to systematically dismantle not only the basis for human knowledge, but likewise its benefits for those who happen to possess it to any degree. In the course of laying out his position, Montaigne completely dismisses the notion that humanity, as a species, is in any way more sophisticated than its animal counterparts. Thus, at least a quarter of the argument consists of anecdotes which seek to eradicate the illusory sense of difference that isolates one species as unique among the rest: "So I say, to return to my subject, that there is no apparent reason to judge that beasts do by natural and obligatory instinct the same things that we do by our choice and cleverness. We must infer from like result like faculties."[21] To that end, this section of his essay maintains, if animals are capable of performing similar tasks as humans, by virtue of our own powers of inference we must conclude that they possess at least an equal, if not occasionally superior, capacity for reason, thought and reflection.

To be sure, at many points throughout the essay, Montaigne appears to anthropomorphize all animal species, almost as though he were incapable of understanding animals beyond the trappings of his experience as a human being. In fact, it is precisely that fundamental shortcoming of human understanding that Montaigne wants his readers to recognize. If there is anything that sustains the perception of difference in the first place, it is essentially an illusion; conversely, though, if there is anything that forces one to recognize a fundamental similarity between human and animal, that too stems from an equally powerful illusion, which renders it impossible for a human to comprehend anything outside its limited human perspective. At the risk of putting it tautologically, to be human is to be incapable of perceiving the world in anything but human terms.

In large part, for Montaigne the illusion of difference involves a trick of language. As he maintains from the outset, it is not that humans possess language while other animals do not. To the contrary, other animals can communicate with one another perfectly well; it is humans who cannot make sense of what other creatures express. Making note of this radical gap, he writes, "This defect that hinders communication between them and us, why is it not just as much ours as theirs? It is a matter of guesswork whose fault it is that we do not understand one another; for we do not understand them any more than they do us."[22] Montaigne offers that such misunderstanding is due in part to a more basic misconception of language itself—while traditional accounts of it restrict communication to vocal expression, a more complete picture would seem to include all bodily gestures, whether voluntary or spontaneous. But on a deeper level, Montaigne's emphasis on the fundamental failure to communicate among creatures across different species underscores the radical limitations to understanding as a faculty. It is not merely that we are condemned to meaning, or that we live in a prison-house of language. More accurately, we are condemned to a meaning that is exclusively our own; and paradoxically, it is this very condition that renders it difficult, if not impossible, to know just what it is we share with other creatures who, in Montaigne's estimation, may be equally condemned.

As the review of these texts suggests, the attempt to differentiate humans from animals on the basis of conduct and physical composition alone results in a curious problem, if not a full-fledged paradox. On one level, even as the grounds for distinction become slippery and quickly disappear, that process itself becomes a new ground for reaffirming it as a distinction after all. Giorgio Agamben describes it nicely in his commentary on Linnaeus, the inventor of modern taxonomy and the one who defined the human as the only animal capable of recognizing it is no different from any other animal; to that end, humanity is defined not by its faculty of recognition but more precisely that by its recognition of the fact that there is really nothing to recognize.[23] Self-consciousness becomes, at once, all-important and perilous insofar as it renders one more consciously beast-like. If this in itself is not dizzying enough, it is compounded by the realization that such non-distinctions are themselves based on a solipsistic error that is itself uniquely human. The ability to say that humans are essentially animals itself is possible only if one is human to begin with; thus one must already be fundamentally different in order to assert that there is no difference to speak of. Or, perhaps to put Linnaeus another way, the human may be the only animal who fails to recognize that there is a difference between humans and animals—but who mistakes that failure as a triumph of consciousness.

At first glance, the problems that Pico and Montaigne touch upon seem remote from the humor comedies and Shakespeare, especially to the extent that their plays revolve around simultaneously establishing and blurring the distinction between the theatrical and "authentic" aspects of human behavior. Jonson's *Every Man Out of His Humour* and Shakespeare's *As You Like It* engage in something of a dialogue over this matter, and they carry it out in part by staging rival versions of the melancholy malcontent. In Jonson's play, the vituperative Asper—who is often taken to be Jonson's mouthpiece, and who doubles as Macilente, following the play's Prologue—is pitted against the foppish Puntarvolo who wears his own "humor" like so many fashionable accessories.[24] Meanwhile, Jaques—who is hardly Shakespeare's mouthpiece, but who is no less theatrical in his mannerisms—is pitted against Touchstone, a seemingly wise fool, whose wisdom and foolishness alike are the product of his refusal to commit to anything whatsoever. Both malcontents seem primarily concerned with demonstrating what makes their own melancholy genuine, and both make tremendously long speeches to that purpose. Asper, in an appeal to classical and traditional learning, gives a lesson on both the proper and improper uses of the term "humor," ranging from grammatical parsing to cultural criticism (for instance, he criticizes those who base their melancholy entirely on clothing and accessories). In contrast, the melancholy Jaques defines himself through a series of negations, which ultimately show that to be authentically melancholy is to be tautologically melancholy as well—or rather, to truly stand out as an individual is to risk becoming an idiot in the strictest sense of the term.

In more ways than one, though, animals are instrumental for both characters. As they attempt to show what separates their own behavior from mere theatricalism, they make extensive use not only of animal imagery, but of actual animals, which turn out to be major components of each play's production. (Jonson's play cannot be staged without a live dog, while Shakespeare's suggests at least the carcass of a hind.) And in a fundamental sense, the differences between the two characters become most apparent in light of the way they relate to the animals who share the theatrical space with them. While Jonson and Shakespeare both use animals in their depictions of Asper and Jaques respectively, it is to very different purposes. As the following section argues, Jonson's play *Every Man Out of His Humour* seems to harbor a genuine dislike for animals precisely insofar as they destabilize the concept of *humanitas* that Jonson would otherwise uphold. While his ostensibly central characters mistreat the animals in the play in order to reassert an essentially privileged conceptualization of humanity, as it turns out this concept remains tenuous at best. Meanwhile, in the case of Jaques, the stakes are substantially different. As Jaques observes the behavior of animals, it is in effort to undo a sense of radical difference among the species. For Jaques, this has specific implications with regard to politics. If it may be stated here provisionally, it is to call into question what it means to define the human specifically as a political animal.

NEVER SO WITTY A JEST BROKEN

Animal imagery appears in *Every Man Out of His Humour* as early as the Induction scenes, when the irascible Asper gives a long (and somewhat pedantic) lecture on the proper and improper use of the term "humor." When it comes to describing a particularly loathsome type of faddish behavior, commonly associated with aspiring gentlemen, he turns straight away to bird imagery:

> But that a rook, by wearing a pyed feather,
> The cable hat-band, or the three-piled ruff,
> A yard of shoe-tye, or the Switzer's knot
> On his French garters, should affect a humour!
> O, it is more than most ridiculous. (Induction, 110–14)

While Asper's remarks draw attention to the histrionic dimensions that inevitably attach themselves to fashionably "humorous" individuals, it is important that the description refers specifically to characters who adopt animal costumes as part of their act. In doing so, Asper sets his sights on a paradoxical phenomenon: it is those very individuals who so blatantly adopt a public persona, and who present themselves as performances, who in the end wind up blurring the distinction between humans and animals. For anyone who does adopt his personality to contemporary fashions to the point where he does so slavishly, as fashionable characters in Jonson's plays inevitably end up doing, does in fact renounce the feature that separates humans from nearly every other animals species, the ability to distinguish ourselves from one another. Curiously, though, as much as Asper's lines suggest an attack on histrionic conduct, other aspects of the play suggest that Jonson's real hostility was directed against animals themselves. To that end, it is necessary to turn to the one figure in the play who does not have a name, and who does not appear in the prefatory "List of characters" that Jonson drew up in order to give the precise nature of everyone who appears in the drama (but who does appear in the "Dramatis Personae"). Significantly, the figure in question is the only one whose business on stage cannot quite be thought of as a performance; when audiences watch this figure, however, any conventional opposition between artificial performance and spontaneous, natural behavior, immediately begins to unravel. This figure is, naturally, the dog.

In many ways, it is the dog who is central toward understanding Jonson's entire play. From a purely material standpoint, it is present on stage for the better part of two acts, where it is the subject for one of the main dramatic plots. The vain-glorious knight Puntarvolo, who fancies himself a knight from a medieval romance, concocts a scheme wherein he will take his wife on a journey to meet the Grand Turk of Constantinople. Accompanying them is the dog (as well as a cat who is mentioned in the "List of Names" but does not necessarily appear on stage).[25] From the moment Puntarvolo is introduced into the action, considerable attention is devoted to his Quixote-like fixation on his imaginary flights of fancy. In particular, characters crack jokes about Puntarvolo's seeming inability to distinguish his dog from a proper human being. Hence, when the scurrilous Buffone describes him it is the dog who occupies pride of place: "Why he loves dogs, and hawks, and his wife well" (2.1.114). When Fastidious chimes in, "They say he has dialogues and discourses between his horse, himself, and his dog; and that he will court his own lady as she were a stranger never encountered before" (2.1.120–21), Puntarvolo positively appears to have reversed the conventional relations between humans and animals. And when Puntarvolo finally does appear onstage, engaging in witty conversation with a gentlewoman, he comments on his own complexion, only to be rebuked by the clown:

> Punt. Mine is melancholy–
> Buff. So is the dog's, just.
> Punt.—and doth argue constancy, chiefly in love. (2.2.39–41)

Indeed, although Puntarvolo may be incapable of recognizing it, his melancholy consists chiefly in his excessive regard for animals, and for his dog in particular.

If Puntarvolo is blind to this fact from the outset, the audience nevertheless has the point driven home by the play's conclusion. During the course of Acts Three and Four, Puntarvolo puts the dog on fairly prominent display, to the point where the play itself seems to become one extended commentary about it. Indeed, the dog becomes something of an accessory, proving, at one and the same instance, its owner's worth (if for no other reason than that it suggests luxury), as well as his *strangeness*.[26] As the play draws to a close, however, Puntarvolo loses not only the dog, but the sense of self-worth he evidently had attached to it. As he prepares to keep company with a small group of the City's social elite, he hands to dog over to a groom, whom he asks to watch over it. The groom eventually abandons it, but not before raising doubts about its actual market value:

> Honesty, sweet, and short? Marry, it shall, sir, doubt you not; for even at this instant if one would give me twenty pounds, I would not deliver him; there's for the sweet: but now, if any man come offer me but two-pence, he shall have him' there's for the short now. 'Slid, what a mad humorous gentleman is this to leave his dog with me! I could run away with him now, an he were worth anything. (5.1.38–43)

It is a disturbing remark in a play filled with all sorts of disturbing elements, for it states explicitly what had been implied before regarding the dog's status as material object. Not two minutes before Puntarvolo had passed the dog off onto the groom, he had turned down an offer to leave it at the porter's lodge, claiming, "His worth is too well known amongst them, to be forth-coming" (5.1.10). While the dog is a living creature with perhaps the most commanding stage presence of all—as Anne Barton points out, it effectively steals the show—in Puntarvolo's eyes it is a material object that can be bought and sold like any other. But while his remarks attest to its alleged monetary value, it is the groom who points out that the market where the dog would fetch a price of any sort turns out to be a figment of the owner's imagination; it is, strictly speaking, worthless.

As unsettling as the groom's remark may be, though, it is not until it is taken away by Macilente (the allegedly authentic malcontent, whom Asper personates) that the performance takes on a genuinely nasty turn. In his effort to draw Puntarvolo "out of his humor," Macilente poisons the dog off-stage and leaves its body in St. Paul's churchyard. While Puntarvolo spends several scenes crying over his loss, Macilente simply gloats:

> Poison'd 'tis thought: marry, how, or by whom, that's left for some cunning woman here o' the Bank-side to resolve. For my part, I know nothing more than that we are like to have an exceeding melancholy supper of it. (5.5.17–20)

Indeed, it is at the point when Puntarvolo is most visibly melancholy that the true punishment begins. Eager to join in the savage mockery, the scurrilous Carlo Buffone offers Puntarvolo two suggestions: either stuff the corpse and place it on display at the next Bartholomew fair, or sell it to the local Jewish craftsman, who will fashion a peruke out of its fur. In both cases, Carlo's remarks merely remind audiences of the prop-like status that the dog had held for its owner in the first place. But while Puntarvolo is obviously shamed to the point of becoming, in Macilente's words, "The melancholy mess," and Macilente further advances his campaign against excessively theatrical behavior, the entire passage cannot help but leave a bad taste in audience's mouths. Anne Barton puts it well:

> However mean and spiteful in itself, Macilente's action here is nonetheless, in terms of the moral scheme of the comedy, a good thing. It causes Puntarvolo to abandon his ridiculous venture, loses him money, and not only gives him pain but brings his accustomed world of singularity and suspect play-acting toppling about his ears. But it is impossible even in reading *Every Man Out of His Humour*—let alone experiencing it on stage—to applaud. Why should Puntarvolo not keep his eccentricity, and his dog? They harm nobody, after all, and they have been theatrically inventive and amusing. Animals are powerful (and potentially disruptive) presences on stage because they are not role-players. Charmingly or anarchically themselves, they force an audience to relate to them as individuals.[27]

Indeed, nowhere does the properly artificial strike such a discordant note; if the play is filled with technically sound bits that strike modern ears as somewhat pedantic, the death of the dog comes uncomfortably close to tragedy.

All this is based on a series of theatrical illusions, though, and to that end it is necessary to bear in mind just what happens to the dog at the end of the play. Surprisingly, it becomes completely absorbed by theatrical apparatuses. Buffone's remarks suggest that the best consolation would involve restoring the dog to the very theatrical marketplace he has just been driven out from. If Buffone had despised Puntarvolo for transforming an animal into something of a prop, his mocking proposals make it clear that this process of transformation may very well continue. More important, while the dog is the only creature in the play to die, the death itself occurs offstage—in other words, it suffers a fate normally reserved for conventionally tragic heroes. This device suggests that the dog's treatment genuinely does violate the expected conventions of comedy that Macilente is so desperate to uphold. It also underscores the genuinely theatrical nature of the dog's life all along. While the various clowns seem dedicated to reducing the dog back to its non-human status that they believe it ought to maintain, the structure of the play itself resists their overtures by insisting that it remains caught within theatrical conventions even past the very end.

In other words, Jonson insists on continuing to draw attention to the dog's stubbornly theatrical nature even after his characters exhaust themselves with reminding each other that, after all, an animal is not a human being. For a point of contrast, one might recall the mechanical Starveling from Shakespeare's *Midsummer Night's Dream*. During the performance of "Pyramus and Thisbe," when Starveling introduces himself as the man in the moon, he finds himself tripped up by the heckling Athenians, only to assert, in exasperation, "All that I have to say it to tell you that the lantern is the moon, I the man I'th'-moon, this thorn bush my thorn bush, and this dog my dog." While Starveling's remark attempts to draw a distinction between objects that can be brought into the mechanisms of theatricality and those that cannot, Jonson's play seems determined to point out (what ought to be obvious anyway) that such a belief is hopelessly naïve. If anything, the dog is incapable of anything but theatricality, and in many ways this seems to be precisely the reason why it cannot survive within the context of the drama. If Jonson requires that the dog suffer the worst fate of all, its punishment seems to owe to the fact that it can participate in a theatrical performance without knowing it.

Two additional aspects of the play help illustrate just what is at stake in Jonson's representation. From the very outset, Jonson's *dramatis personae* includes an unmistakably novel device: a prose description for each of the characters who appear in the script. Jonson seems to borrow and adapt this technique from Theophrastus, whose book on "Characters" would become the basis for a number of seventeenth century authors intent on describing the social character of modern London. For Jonson, it is necessary to be able to describe these individuals as they perform a role in his play, and from the basis of what they say it is clear that his primary objective is to show how they correspond to certain types. The individuals who appear in the play are not unique beings who are unlike any others, but they are capable of description insofar as they can be caught up in a general cast of types. They must be capable of being abstracted into general terms to the extent that they can be articulated at all. Needless to say, while the phrase "Dog and Cat" does actually appear in the "Dramatis Personae," both are left out altogether from the description of characters, thereby assuring that while they have an unquestionably captivating stage presence, they will remain anonymous. On its own, none of this is especially revealing, but it becomes all the more noticeable when the dog's absence is contrasted with that of the minor character, Mitis, of whom Jonson writes: "A person of no action, and therefore we afford him no character." While this description seems to treat Mitis with disdain, there is a radical difference between his status and that of the dog; to that end, the crucial term is "person." The word immediately calls to mind "personate," which Jonson would have understood acting to consist of, according to Andrew Gurr.[28] And while the animal in the play may be fundamentally theatrical, on its own it is not capable, as the other characters are, of *personation*.[29] In making this distinction, then, Jonson, seems to insist on a crucial difference between a person and an animal, though in the end it is perhaps best expressed in the form of a tautology: a person is an animal that is capable of acting like a person.

Meanwhile, although the dog is the only creature in the play who dies, it is not the only character who has an encounter with death. Midway through the play, the wicked Sordido realizes that his plans to reap untold fortunes have fallen apart. He had purchased an almanac in order to prognosticate the heavy rainfall days, and then gouge his customers with exorbitant grain prices. When the rain (predictably) does not fall, Sordido must come face to face with the limitations of the printed words with respect to the actual conditions of lived existence. Thus he enters with a rope and hangs himself on stage. (One must imagine either that this scene was not one of those originally staged but added during the subsequent revisions, or else Jonson had it in for one of his actors.) Eventually he is rescued by a group of rustics, but not before he has performed this act and the audience has been subjected to what appears to be a suicide attempt. It is a deliberately disturbing scene, and when even Mitis interjects from the gallery, "What, will he hang himself?" (3.2.9) the audience is forced to notice just how disturbing. For his part, Cordatus advises that Sordido's death fits within a general scheme of theological ethics: "Faith, ay. It seems his prognostication has not kept touch with him, and that makes him despair" (3.2.10–11). In a profound sense, however, Cordatus seems to miss the point of Mitis' question. For in attempting to hang himself, the individual who impersonates the role of Sordido temporarily disrupts the theatrical illusion and reminds the audience of the apparent limitations to what can and cannot be staged. In other words, Sordido's attempt at suicide disturbs the audience by reminding us that certain gestures may escape the boundaries of performance after all.

In this regard, Sordido's suicide attempt also begins to suggest a certain *potentiality*, a faculty reserved for persons defined as characters in the first place. If all animals can be thought of as theatrical by definition, it is the person who is capable of not being theatrical. As Jonson thus suggests, one is capable of making a distinction between humanity and animality at the very moment it occurs to us that there is at least the notion of escaping this otherwise inescapable world-as-stage. Whether this turns out to be possible or not, what matters is the ability to imagine it, which entails recognizing that one is caught up in it in the first place. What seems shocking to Jonson, inasmuch as he expresses it through the mouths of his characters, is that any person would wish to forego this potential for differentiation, become increasingly animal-like, and—if Puntarvolo is any indication—descend into a particularly loathsome sort of melancholy to boot. In the end, the distinction seems to rest on the flimsiest of criteria, but it is worth pointing out, if for no other reason than to demonstrate the precarious nature of humanity in the first place: to be a human is to be caught up in the belief that one may act differently from other animals after all.

FAT AND GREASY CITIZENS

For Jonson's contemporaries, to say nothing of subsequent generations of audiences, *Every Man Out of His Humour* is notoriously difficult either to perform or watch. Its run was relatively brief with respect to *Every Man In*, and it did not enjoy a revival. Modern day critics have suggested any number of reasons, among them that the play is simply too aggressive to enjoy. Anne Barton draws attention to the dog as an example of the death of the innocent. Meanwhile, though Puntarvolo's melancholy may seem like a bad performance during the play's early scenes, by Act Five it seems positively engrained. By the time Buffone and Macilente ridicule him for it, they are too late, and their punishment too excessive. Fool that he may have been, Puntarvolo seems right to be shocked at what happens to a mere dog at his expense. By contrast Shakespeare's forest comedy proved immensely successful, and as it happens, it contains a character who in many ways is reminiscent of Puntarvolo himself: the melancholy Jaques. Granted, in many ways, no malcontent could have been more unlike Puntarvolo than Jaques. While Puntarvolo uses his melancholy to advance in society, Jaques uses his to avoid it, even to the point that he retires into seclusion when all the other characters in the forest resolve their respective conflicts. To that end, if Puntarvolo is ostracized for overstepping his social position, it is because his misconduct represents a threat to a well functioning social order, wherein everybody can be recognized because everybody occupies a more or less recognizable position. By contrast, there is apparently no room in a well functioning society for someone like Jaques. When he abandons it for the anchorites at the end, he implies that he would be unable to find any place within a court that had been restored to its conventional owner. Finally, if Puntarvolo's greatest character flaw consists of his inability to come to grips with his public persona, even to recognize that as a human being he must conduct himself in a specifically performative manner, Jaques is all too aware of the theatrical qualities of his companions. For the entire community in the forest consists of one version of playacting after another, from the Duke's fanciful games of Robin Hood, to Rosalind's disguise as Ganymede, to Orlando's absurd lovesickness (which requires still more playacting in order to "cure" him of it). But for all these differences, Jaques and Puntarvolo do share one characteristic: a tendency to keep company with animals.

Indeed, as Jaques seems to suggest, humanity might best be regarded as the collision between animality and mimesis. His most famous lines, to be sure, seems to reduce all human behavior to a grand theatrical pageant: "All the world's a stage, and all the men and women merely players" (2.7.139–66). It is perhaps the most well known speech of the play, and the easiest speech to cite out of context (perhaps because the speech itself seems to come out of left field, having little to do with the stage business that has occurred just before it.) In it, of course, Jaques resurrects the notion of the *theatrum mundi,* suggesting that to be human is already to imitate the sort of behavior that had recently become a daily profession along the south bank of the Thames. But that is not the whole story, for Jaques also sees humanity as a disguised version of animal behavior.

Indeed, the very first time Jaques is made mention of, it is in the context of a discussion of animal rights: specifically, the banished Duke Senior and his companions (who the audience meets for the first time) express reservations about whether to embark on one of their favorite pastimes, namely hunting venison. Their conversation has all the marks of a traditional pastoral debate: noblemen are disguised as rustics, dwelling in a space that may or may not be Edenic in its ambience. Meanwhile, as they ponder the question of whether to hunt they frame their concern such that it redirects them to the political subject of natural rights and their usurpation. In true pastoral fashion, this debate reduces the complex to the naïve. Thus, on the one hand their conversation touches on the very foundations of authority, nearly broaching the question whether anything other than violence—a-legitimate, if not illegitimate in its essence—can provide the basis for a system of rights and responsibilities. On the other hand, the Duke's concern for the venison (that he and his companions continue to hunt despite their concerns) is so stilted that audiences rightly doubt just where the Duke's heart truly lies. In an astonishing sleight of hand, the Duke acknowledges a problem that challenges the very basis to all authority—

including his own, one would have to imagine—only to leave it behind, almost as though merely to recognize it were enough to neutralize its potentially damaging conclusions.

It is in this context that the "melancholy Jaques" is introduced into the play—as one of the Duke's noblemen points out:

> Indeed, my lord,
> The melancholy Jaques grieves at that,
> And, in that kind, swears you do more usurp
> Than doth your brother that hath banish'd you. (2.1.25–28)

At first glance Jaques appears to question the anthropocentric basis for political associations since, strictly speaking, only a creature with rights is capable of having its rights usurped. To that extent the political distinction between human and animal turns out to be, for Jaques, a matter of artifice. While humanity may be predicated on certain qualities, those qualities on their own are not sufficient to guarantee unique privileges that other creatures—such as deer, for instance—do not themselves enjoy. As his soliloquy proceeds, however, it becomes increasingly apparent that in removing a clear distinction between human and animal his concerns consist less of extending the concepts of political rights to animals than with impugning animals on the very same grounds that determine his apparent contempt for the Duke's own party. If humans and animals are alike, they are alike in their collective indifference both to their public responsibilities and the private suffering of its members.[30]

Nothing captures Jaques' complaint more clearly than the moment when an anonymous flock passes by the wounded deer who is the subject for Jaques' ruminations. As the lord reports:

> 'Poor deer,' quoth he, 'thou makest a testament
> As worldlings do, giving thy sum of more
> To that which had too much:' then, being there alone,
> Left and abandon'd of his velvet friends,
> ''Tis right:' quoth he; 'thus misery doth part
> The flux of company:' anon a careless herd,
> Full of the pasture, jumps along by him
> And never stays to greet him; 'Ay' quoth Jaques,
> 'Sweep on, you fat and greasy citizens;
> 'Tis just the fashion: wherefore do you look
> Upon that poor and broken bankrupt there?' (2.1.47–57)

The comparison between deer and citizens is deliberately ironic, especially insofar as the privileges of citizenship are determined by public attributes such as duty and collective sacrifice. As Jaques observes, however, the conditions of citizenship have been effectively reversed: if there is a community among the forest animals, it is a community founded on collective indifference and anonymity.

To be sure, this soliloquy has been exhaustively analyzed by critics, and more often than not the verdict holds Jaques more than a little unfavorably. At best he has been seen from the perspective of Duke Senior himself, "full of matter," and hence enjoyable, but full of a particularly inconsequential matter all the same.[31] It is enough for the Duke later to remind him that Jaques had once himself been a libertine in order to suggest that his melancholy and hedonism are two sides of the same coin (a preference of self-interest at the expense of the common good). At worst, Jaques' imposition of political terms onto deer betrays him as a solipsist who is so caught up by his fantastical believes that he takes them for reality itself.[32] In other words, Jaques' equation of human and deer turns out to be anthropocentric illusion after all, and curiously his language ends up "killing" the deer through the very gesture that allows him to identify with it as a suffering deer in the first place. If there is any truth to the claim that Duke Senior himself may be a usurper—along with the implication that all ostensibly legitimate power is in fact based on a faction which effaces the violent gestures that had brought it about to begin with—that truth is somehow lost in the absurdity by which Jaques makes it known.

As out of step as Jaques may come across in this scene, however, an even deeper absurdity emerges, and while it unfolds throughout the course of the play, elements of it already are present during this scene. To begin with, as much as Jaques presents himself as an outsider, even to the point that he seems to inhabit a physical space entirely separate from the Duke's party, the attitudes that most explicitly designate him as an outsider bear a striking resemblance to the characters from which he seeks the most distance. It is difficult not to notice just how much he and Duke Senior are alike. (Even the Duke, thick as he is, brings it to Jaques' attention.) For what is most striking about Jaques' defense of the deer is that it is presented as though it were a direct response to the Duke's own original ruminations:

> Come, shall we go and kill us venison?
> And yet it irks me the poor dappled fools,
> Being native burghers of this desert city,
> Should in their own confines with forked heads

Have their round haunches gored. (2.1.21–24)

Jaques either is clairvoyant or he has heard the Duke's complaint many times before. In that regard, Jaques' ventriloquism underscores not only his own narcissism but the Duke's as well. The only real difference is that the Duke is enthralled by it at the very moment he thinks himself free. From his first moments onstage the Duke strives to convince himself (if not his companions) that the discomforts of rustic forest life are nevertheless an improvement on a court oversaturated with flatterers (presumably such flatterers as helped blind the Duke to his own vulnerability in the first place). In doing so, though, he goes the extra step of comparing it to prelapsarian paradise, when he declares:

> Here feel we not the penalty of Adam,
> The seasons' difference, as the icy fang
> And churlish chiding of the winter's wind,
> Which, when it bites and blows upon my body,
> Even till I shrink with cold, I smile and say
> 'This is no flattery: these are counsellors
> That feelingly persuade me what I am.' (2.1.5–11)

This is not just hyperbole. In one critical aspect the reference to Adam is what bites the hardest, for among the various changes in worldly conditions that collectively amounted to the "penalty of Adam" had been the loss of communication with other animal species. If Jaques demonstrates the gulf between human and animal by imposing a fiction of humanity on the animal world, Duke Senior exposes the gulf by pretending as though it no longer exists.

But in the long run, there is more to Jaques' complaints than simply to draw attention to the narcissism that seems to be the prevailing force throughout the play. His real interest seems to lie with what the (anonymous) lord of the scene calls the "careless herd," and what he himself refers to as "fat and greasy citizens." For Jaques, animal behavior as much as human is marked by a fundamental indifference to suffering. If on the one side there is the wounded deer who stands in solitude, on the other side there is the anonymous flock—one can hardly call it a community—so united in its collective anonymity that it ultimately is incapable of recognizing any single member as an individual, let alone responding to its plaints. To that end, Jaques' use of the term "citizens" carries a potentially harsh connotation, for what unites the deer is the mere fact of their dwelling together; meanwhile, any sense of citizenship as a political privilege that is bought with sacrifice and collective responsibility has been drained, assuming that there ever was room for it in the first place.

For Jaques, what makes humans and animals most alike seems to consist of this collective indifference within which the primary sense of individuality available amounts to little more than helpless isolation. To that extent, the question whether or not Jaques engages in solipsism is overshadowed by his suggestions that the political bonds that hold people together—even when they are most demonstrative—are based on an even deeper neglect, unwillingness, or perhaps inability to respond to the needs of any individual member when circumstances may call for it. The significance to this pessimistic conclusion becomes more clear when we turn from Jaques, the malcontent of the play, to Orlando, who is perhaps only a shade or two away from Jaques himself. Like Jaques, he defines himself from the very first sentence by his sadness—and indeed, in Orlando's case, sadness much more explicitly rooted in thwarted ambition. He is the only character other than Jaques to identify Arden forest as a melancholy site. Within the forest, he bears a striking resemblance not only to Duke Senior (if the Duke pretends to find tongues in trees, Orlando takes the conceit one step further); but when he is in the presence of Jaques, he cannot help but come across as something of a mirror image. Indeed, if there is a single difference between Jaques and Orlando, it lies in the latter's persistent desire not to regard himself as an animal—with the consequence that his own sense of individuality starts to harbor characteristics of aggressive self-interest, despite the fact that he repeatedly finds himself in pleasing social arrangements.

In fact, when the play begins with Orlando recollecting his circumstances to the servant Adam he positions himself somewhere between denying his animality in the name of familiar nobility and advocating a lifestyle that resembles the very anonymity that Jaques eventually comes to decry. Thus when Orlando complains about his older brother's refusal to let him enjoy the fortunes allegedly bequeathed to him by the late Rowland de Boys, he compares himself to livestock:

> My brother Jaques he keeps at school, and report speaks goldenly of his profit: for my part, he keeps me rustically at home, or, to speak more properly, stays me here at home unkept; for call you that keeping for a gentleman of my birth, that differs not from the stalling of an ox? His horses are bred better; for, besides that they are fair with their feeding, they are taught their manage, and to that end riders dearly hired: but I, his brother, gain nothing under him but growth; for the which his animals on his dunghills are as much bound to him as I. (1.1.5–15)

It is this, more than anything else that Orlando has in his sights when he asserts, not that he is human and thus entitled to certain rights, but that he is another version of his father. As he notes twice, his father's spirit has been growing inside him, and the implication is not only that he possesses the same strength of character, but—in a gesture that simultaneously defies and reaffirms the system of primogeniture that has forced him on the outs in the first place—he shares a claim to privilege. Given this claim, however, it is perhaps a little surprising when, failing to gain his brother's assent, he demands the right to become something of a venture capitalist:

> therefore allow me such exercises as may become a gentleman, or give me the poor allottery my father left me by testament; with that I will go buy my fortunes. (1.1.71–74)

Rather than perpetuate a traditional social order based on patrilineal authority, then, Orlando from the outset seeks to transform it, either by borrowing some of its language and applying it to radically different purposes, or by renouncing it altogether in a gesture that, when taken to its extreme, implies the dissolution of traditional family structures altogether.

As the play unfolds, Orlando engages in a two-fold movement, which disavows the animalistic dimensions of his own status while simultaneously promoting a lifestyle based on aggressive individualism. (It is hardly a surprise that he should first distinguish himself as a wrestler, or that his brother should be the one who most fervently desires that Orlando injure himself; it is perhaps more unsettling that, when Orlando and Oliver first encounter each other on stage, they address each other as "sir," as though they were already on the cusp of becoming strangers to one another.) All this comes to the foreground in a crucial scene, when Orlando first encounters Duke Senior's party in the forest. The scene itself enacts a startling movement from savageness to civility. When Orlando first intrudes upon the Duke's meal, he is full of threats and commands. Indeed, in a subtle parody of the prelapsarian narrative, Orlando becomes the absolute usurper when he warns, in his own name, "He dies that touches any of this fruit / Till I and my affairs are answered" (2.7.99–100). In a matter of seconds, several transformations occur. Orlando's aggression gives way to the most demonstrative civility imaginable. Anonymity gives way to familiarity, as the Duke comes to recognize the young man as the offspring of his late father (who had himself been a close associate of the Duke's). Most surprising, though, the language of suffering and relief is recast as a type of animal situation, and in an apparent reversal of terms Orlando compares himself to an animal as part of the rite of passage to the civilized banquet that has been spread out before the Duke. Thus he requests leave to find his servant Adam:

> Then but forbear your food a little while,
> Whiles, like a doe, I go to find my fawn
> And give it food. (2.7.127–29)

It is a striking simile, not only because it reminds us how little Orlando had wanted to be regarded as an animal earlier, but because he puts the simile to such an entirely different purpose than Jaques had done earlier. Ironically, by comparing his situation to an animal's Orlando winds up underscoring the very gulf that his metaphor seeks to elide. The Duke and his party can join Orlando in the belief that their generosity really is what they make it out to be; and in turn they affirm the values of a traditional community that is under effacement even during the very moments when they celebrate its power.

For all the claims to civility that the Duke makes here, it is a deliberately old fashioned civility—the general report has been that he and his men have been playing make believe, alternately as Robin Hood and his merry men, as members of the Ovidian Golden World, and as exiles returning to the lost Garden itself. And indeed the very sense of longing for a better era hints that their comportment toward Orlando is largely imaginary. Significantly, it is at this point in the play when Jaques makes his famous observations concerning the radically theatrical nature of human behavior, and if his speech seems excessive, his insistence on the fact that men and women are merely players draws attention to the theatrical aspects of the Dukes' demonstrations of civility. If the Duke thinks of himself as someone who cares for the suffering of others—and whose care takes the form of recourse to deliberately old-fashioned "values"—Jaques in turn suggests that such overt displays of generosity end up obscuring the more brutish conditions that give rise to such needs in the first place. And indeed, such seems to be the general condition of Arden forest, which is defined not only by its brutality, but by its ability to disguise its brutality in the language of traditional customs. (Such a case may be made for the two shepherds Corin and Silvius, whose own pastoral debate—a highly conventionalized dialogue between youth and age over the subject of unrequited love—turns out to cover up an altogether different dialogue about rising rent prices that threaten to render the older shepherd Corin homeless precisely by transforming his "home" into property that can exchange hands more or less indiscriminately).

For Jaques, it would seem, it is preferable to denounce the overtly theatrical nature of the Duke's civility precisely because that theatricalism permits him to sustain a fantasy of legitimization in the face of far more disruptive social conditions.

To that end, it is telling that, as Jacques' Seven Ages of Man speech reaches its conclusion, Orlando and Adam return for what more or less amounts to Adam's "farewell speech." During the scene's few remaining moments, Orlando takes it upon himself to thank the Duke on Adam's behalf. Thus as the Duke invites Orlando to "Set down your venerable burden / And let him feed," Orlando replies, "I thank you most for him" (2.7.168–169). For his part, Adam's response is not to thank, but to offer an apology for not thanking: "So had you need, I scarce can speak to thank you for myself." It is a surprisingly unsettling remark; for all its apparent graciousness, it abruptly calls to mind the suggestion that the Duke and Orland may well have taken their figures of speech, which had reduced the old man to suffering fawn, perhaps more literally than they should have.

Adam is not made mention of after this scene, when the Duke's party carries him off by the arm to their cave. For the purposes of the story, he is more or less forgotten; nevertheless, it is difficult for audiences not to wonder just what becomes of him. In fact, the play had offered something of a hint during an earlier scene, when Adam agreed to accompany Orlando on his flight to Arden forest. During this passage, it is Adam who makes the truly astonishing gesture of generosity, offering his life savings of five hundred crowns to the youthful Orlando, promising the service of "a younger man" as well (2.38.38–55). In thanking his servant profusely, Orlando observes:

> Thou art not for the fashion of these times,
> Where none will sweat but for promotion,
> And having that, do choke their service up
> Even with the having; it is not so with thee. (2.3.59–62)

Clearly, Orlando is studied in the art of thanking, but evidently he is quite comfortable exhausting Adam's generosity all the same. So much so, that by the time they reach the forest, Adam no longer is capable of walking on his own; it is not long afterward that he is silently passed over.

As exits go, it pales in comparison to Jacques' overly ostentatious departure from the wedding party at the end of the play. Witnessing his extensive farewell speech, it is easy for audiences to recognize Jacques' departure as the sign that there is no longer any room for him in the community that Arden forest represents. But it is also worth bearing in mind that his departure amounts to a refusal to endorse the marriage between a character like Orlando, and the daughter of Duke Senior—or a union between families that uses play-acting to nostalgically recreate a lost Golden World even as they grow oblivious to the only individual in the play whose misfortune seems to have been to embody the principles of that lost world in his daily life.

Jacques departs right as preparations for the wedding between Orlando and Rosalind begins, a ceremony supervised by a mysterious character, named Hymen, who virtually comes out of nowhere. It is an unexpected moment of "supernaturalism" in a play otherwise not very supernatural in its tone, and indeed, Hymen's very presence suggests that a union between these two lovers cannot take place without such a shift in register. In other words, only a god would be powerfully absurd enough to obscure relations between Orlando and Rosalind which, in his departure, Jacques alone is perceptive enough to see. Meanwhile, if they have not done so already, are the members of the party themselves not at risk of becoming fat and greasy?

The differences between Jonson's and Shakespeare's comedies might be expressed in the following manner. Jonson insists on a notion of humanity can claim an authenticity for itself only insofar as it pretends to maintain a radical difference between humans and animals. Thus, to be human is to resemble humanity, but a humanity that is formally empty. By contrast, Jacques seems to reject the overt theatricalism that the other characters in Arden forest live by, and he does so on the grounds that it eradicates the very basis of legitimacy that those same characters take for granted. However, he does so at the cost of being unable to do anything but abandon it. What is curious about both plays is that authenticity itself becomes more problematic than the various types of overt theatricality it is usually expected to counter.

Because both plays considered in this chapter are comedies, the melancholy malcontents are treated as the objects of scorn and ridicule, rather than outright fear. To that end, they stand out in marked contrast to characters whose melancholy was the register of political discontent and who used their condition as instruments for their own acts of usurpation. The number of melancholy malcontents who appeared in revenge tragedies alone suggests at the very least a widespread interest in the relation between these two phenomena, and it is this relation that will be taken up in the following chapter. However, rather than focus on plays that make the connection between melancholy and revenge explicit—plays such as *Hamlet, King Lear, The Revengers Tragedy, The Duchess of Malfi*, to name only the more well known—the following chapter presents a reading of Shakespeare's *Julius Caesar*. While *Julius Caesar* does not include as clear a melancholy malcontent as the plays listed above, it is helpful insofar as it interrogates what will be recognized as a related phenomenon: the relation between individual grief (or grievances) and the responsibilities of the state.

Chapter Three
Civil Dissension and its Malcontents, or States of Melancholy

"Such men are dangerous."

–*Julius Caesar* (1.2.195)[1]

INTRODUCTION

The present chapter focuses on Shakespeare's *Julius Caesar,* a play which presents something of an intriguing problem in the stage history of malcontents in that it does not easily fit recognizable patterns that would have been available for use. The play was first performed in 1599, during a period when the playwright was producing his most famous melancholy characters, including Jaques, Don John, and Hamlet, wherein personal discontent was a manifestation of a larger dissatisfaction over political affairs. By all accounts, the Roman play easily could have followed a similar pattern, and in many ways it is striking that it does not.[2] If any topic would have been suitable for exploiting the malcontent type as the defender of liberty against tyranny—or rather, for granting a sense of legitimacy for political melancholy as a justifiable response to an oppressive political order—the assassination of Caesar was among the more inviting.[3] Brutus seemed particularly well suited for the role. Throughout Europe, the name of Brutus regularly was invoked among factions who either defended their liberties against oppressive governors or used the rhetoric to advance their own ambitious interests.[4] In England, the *Vindiciae Contra Tyrannos*—written under the name of what seems to be Marcus Brutus' namesake, Stephanus Junius Brutus—was still a widely known tract. For those who rebelled against the prevailing political order, the name of Brutus was virtually synonymous with protecting the integrity of virtuous (i.e. republican) ideals. And in a very compelling sense, Brutus served as the exemplary historical figure of rebellion as cure.[5]

Just as important, if any year in the Elizabethan period would have been appropriate for staging the assassination of Caesar, 1599 was among the most likely.[6] James VI had published "The Trew Law of Free Monarchies" the year before, and his assertion that "Kings are called Gods . . . because they sit vpon God his Throne in the earth," would have struck many English subjects as unsettling, if not downright appalling.[7] James' disparaging remarks against liberty in the same pamphlet were precisely the stuff that shaped Brutus' cause; and when Brutus orders his fellow conspirators to march through the streets shouting "Peace, Freedom, Liberty," one of the possible implications may have been for Londoners to do the same in the event that their own sense of liberty should become refigured as the symptom of what James refers to as "broiling spirits and rebellious minds."[8] Enough circumstances were in place not only to stage assassination as a legitimate, albeit highly daring response to tyranny, but also to cast it in the familiar dramatic conventions of melancholy discontent and revenge.

Finally, while his discontent is entirely political in origin, it manifests itself largely in psychological troubles that could easily have been associated with contemplative melancholy. And in fact for many writers—among whom Shakespeare was familiar with at least one—Brutus was understood in precisely those terms.[9] A small but definite literary tradition was emerging, which identified Brutus as melancholy, either by disposition or as a result of Caesar's unprecedented rise to power. More famously, his historical namesake had himself feigned madness as part of his plot to banish the Tarquins and found the republic itself. Within his play, Shakespeare drops hints that his own Brutus has been cut from the fame fabric. Portia's catalogue, in Act Two, of Brutus' anxious behavior were common symptoms of melancholy— even lover's melancholy, or erotomania.[10] Brutus himself complains early on of being troubled by "passions of some difference," and when he is alone he compares his state of mind to a "phantasma, or a hideous dream," terms which call to mind the type of melancholy that Spenser described in Book II of *The Faerie Queene*.[11] Without wishing to suggest that Brutus has hitherto not been properly "diagnosed," it is nevertheless clear that his behavior and his state of mind—at least insofar as he reports it—conform to a pattern that would have made a connection with melancholy appropriate. In the end though, what is most striking about Brutus is precisely how much he differs from his ancestral namesake. For Shakespeare's Brutus, adopting the posture of madness curiously becomes less an option than it seems to invite.[12]

In this fashion, *Julius Caesar* seems rather to hint at melancholy discontent than to foreground it. For while the text makes use of the terminology of melancholy discontent, the play never gives it prominence, and it never makes clear just how melancholy is supposed to figure in the assassination at all. The term appears only once in the entire script, when Messala (a relatively minor character) laments about the strategic mistakes that Cassius and Brutus make in the aftermath of the assassination and ensuing civil war. There are no genuine malcontents in Rome. Caesar hints that he thinks Cassius might be one, and he concludes, "such men are dangerous," but that fact in itself goes as far to show how little help such knowledge provides Caesar when it comes to protecting himself. And while some of his contemporaries did suggest that Brutus was given to the illness, in Shakespeare's play it ultimately does not emerge as an adequate motivation. Finally, while an eerie and highly unnatural atmosphere lurks over the players at critical moments, there are no "melancholy boughs," such as Orlando describes them in *As You Like It*. On the eve of the assassination, the streets of Rome are filled with prodigies. Cassius himself identifies them as the "terrors of this night," a phrase which may perhaps call to mind Thomas Nashe's essay on melancholy apparitions, entitled *The Terrors of the Night*.[13] The profusion of signs, wonders, prophetic dreams, even ghosts might suggest a Rome anthropomorphized, suffering from a kind of melancholy sickness. Portia herself refers to "the humours of the dank morning" (2.1.261–2). To that extent, a humoral disorder seems to be present everywhere without touching any one character directly.

If this is an omission, it is perhaps best accounted for when we examine the terminology that Shakespeare *does* use in effort to characterize the psycho-physiological dimensions that the Caesar assassination embodies. While Shakespeare does not make much use of humoral psychology, he does use a political analogy which had been popular among Roman political theorists, and which had been undergoing something of a revival among sixteenth century political commentaries, namely the notion of the body-politic. In particular, Shakespeare's play seems concerns with establishing the relation between political troubles and disease, with the perhaps more ambitious goal of indicating whether rebellion against an unsuccessful political system represented a fresh outbreak of new symptoms or an actual remedy. By no means would this have been an easy task, and indeed part of what makes the play compelling is that in the course of using the terms from this analogy, Brutus ends up exposing it as a fairly ineffective rhetorical maneuver.

This situation is in some ways close to what Robert Miola and Rebecca Bushnell have observed with regard to the term "tyrant" as it operates in the play.¹⁴ To the extent that the play is about tyrannicide, it is about the way different political factions appropriate the term; there is no abstract concept of a tyrant, only contested definitions. Extending this idea, there is hardly a term that does not escape this ambiguity, including melancholy. When the play adopts language from traditional body-politic ideology then, it is precisely in order to show how poorly such terms express the complaints and objectives among the faction. Put simply, they cannot articulate their plot against Caesar in physiological terms. As Sharon O'Dair has argued, "Brutus misjudges the 'health' of the Republic. Brutus believes that the Republic's 'illness' is the result of one man's action and that only his sacrifice is necessary to 'cure' the state."¹⁵ Taking this one step further, Brutus' mistake may well be to imagine the Republic in the normative terms of health and sickness in the first place.

In the course of this explication, something that might be called melancholy does emerge, but ultimately it is a melancholy unlike the sort comes out of theories of the humors.¹⁶ What distinguishes Shakespeare's Brutus from any number of political malcontents who had appeared in plays before him is that his anguish does not manifest itself as a condition of privilege or as the clear response to a political condition he finds unacceptable. It is not simply a matter of conspiring against Caesar as direct redress for the wrongs Caesar inflicted, as though wrongs and redress could be converted into sums and measured against each other accordingly.¹⁷ If there is melancholy at all, it refers to a condition of radical uncertainty—not an inability to understand one's role within the political arena, but the gradual recognition that such an ability in fact does not exist.

THE CRISIS OF THE BODY-POLITIC

If we turn more broadly to writers who applied the body-politic analogy in one form or another, particularly during those instances where they sought to establish a correspondence between rebellion and disease, we can observe just how unstable the device had become by the late Elizabethan period. During the 1590s and 1600s, the analogy's popularity rose dramatically, and as King James himself came to compare his own duties to a physician's, it became one of the dominant terms in theoretical discussions of disorder and rebellion. Its dissemination, not only in political treatises, but in sermons, psychological and physical guidebooks, and character studies, meant that there was a great deal of interchange between political and corporeal terminology. (Indeed, the analogy's usefulness seems to have depended on its flexibility, its ability to be recombined to fit a writer's immediate needs.)

While such flexibility might have made it useful on one level, though, it also had the counter-effect of rendering it meaningless. As a result, during the period in question, competing versions of the commonwealth-body analogy in turn contributed to ongoing debates about how to understand sedition, faction and rebellion. Indeed, the analogy appealed precisely because it could claim to interpret disorder within a representation of society as a generally more stable entity. Edward Forset's defense of monarchy, *The Body Natural and Politique*, is a clear example of how the device worked. Forset's book essentially boils down to noting and delineating similarities between body and state, as he puts it in the Preface: "And (by the way) it were a paynes well bestowed, to obserue the good correspondence betweene euery the particular parts or faculties in man, and the other distinct parts, power and operations of that bigger bulk."[18] The key word here is "correspondence," as the entire book is virtually a catalogue of the various resemblances between body and state. In the course of charting them out, he makes no bones about the monarch's infallibility. As for the things that cause disorder, he attributes them entirely to the "lower" parts of society:

> Diseases arise as in the body naturall by distemper of humours; so in the politicall, by disorder of manners: and as in the bodie naturall they doe hinder, peruert, and corrupt the orderly actions of nature; so in the politicall they do impeach, infringe, and resist the proceedings and regiment of a iust gouernance.[19]

Even in cases where the king may appear to be at fault, Forset explains them away; concerning errors in policy, then, he assigns blame not to the king but to the king's favorites, who are more or less akin to Spenser's Phantastes:

> The fauorites of a Prince may be resembled to the fantasies of the Soule, wherewith he sporteth and delighteth himselfe; which to doe (so the integritie of iudgement, and Maiestie of State be reteyned) is in neither of both reproueable. Which of vs is there that doth not (especially in matters rather pleasing than important) follow and feed his fantasies, giue scope vnto them, suffer them to preuaile with him, reckoning it a great part of his contentment to haue them satisfied?[20]

In the end, Forset does little to explain either the nature of government or the nature of the body, but that is not his objective. What interests him is to note similes and "resemblances"—the word or device appears on nearly every page—in order to assert royal prerogative, reinforce a doctrine of obedience, and to denounce factions as corruptions of the otherwise stable monarchy.

Forset's was hardly the most original adaptation, his argument being in many ways an extension of what could be found in texts ranging from the *Homily Against Wyfull Disobedience and Rebellion* to Thomas Wright's *Passions of the Mind in Generall*.[21] Indeed, part of what makes him significant is precisely that he is typical in so many ways, his book thus becoming a confirmation that rebellion could be situated in somewhat recognizable terms. But typical as he may have been, Forset's account was hardly neutral, and the basic terms of his position did not go unchallenged. Other writers adapted the body-politic analogy for altogether different ends—assigning culpability for civil unrest to prevailing institutions themselves. Some, beginning from the second half of the sixteenth century, went so far as to advocate political assassination, a form of decapitation, as a justifiable remedy for social ills. John Ponet's suggestion for restoring order to a corrupt commonwealth, for instance, is of a sort that might have inspired Mary Shelley almost as much as it evidently inspired readers in 1642, when they perused a reprint of his *Short Treatise of Politike Power*:

> Commonwealthes and realmes may live, when the head is cut off, and may put on a newe head, that is, make them a newe governour, when they see their old head seke to muche his owne will and not the wealthe of the hole body, for the which he was onle ordained.[22]

By contrast, Francis Bacon's essay on sedition may offer an example, reversing tenor and vehicle, and thereby suggesting entirely different grounds for the interpretation of rebellion: "As for discontentments, they are in the politic body like humours in the natural, which are apt to gather to a preternatural heat and to inflame."[23] Bacon envisions the state as body with the implication that every member of the "politic body" holds a specific position within it as a measure of its viability. But what truly distinguishes Bacon from someone like Forset is his consideration of the entire body-politic's responsibility in cases of sedition: "The first remedy or prevention is to remove by all means possible that material cause of sedition whereof we spake; which is want and poverty in the estate."[24] Bacon's attention to the state's responsibility for removing causes of discontent hints at a certain toleration of sedition (although it would have been limited toleration at most).[25] Even if sedition can be defined as a type of political madness the revolt itself may turn out to be no more than a symptom of political troubles located elsewhere. If seditious discontent cannot fully be justified by that premise, at the very least it can be mitigated.

While contemporary critics have noticed this problem before, they have been divided as to its significance. In an important study of body-politic imagery in the Renaissance, David G. Hale has argued that overuse effectively ruined it as a useful explanatory model: "But while the organic analogy was being used more widely and more artistically than ever before, the challenges to its validity increased in number and importance."[26] As Hale notes, Ponet (along with others, such as Roger Parsons, who followed a similar strategy) pushed things too far: "To argue seriously . . . that decapitation is a feasible remedy for a diseased body-politic is to wreak havoc upon the metaphor," and many of Ponet's contemporaries did spill plenty of ink showing just how he went wrong.[27] More recently, literary critics and historians have argued that the analogy's malleability was precisely what made it so popular, as it enabled writers to stage a critique of power, and as it adopted the language those institutions of power had used to give themselves legitimacy.[28] As Jonathan Gil Harris has suggested, for instance, the critique of power was more subtle, even inadvertently subverting its own commitments to royal authority.[29] Rather than reinforce common beliefs, then, the body-politic analogy challenged and redefined them.

Whether they did nothing more than "wreak havoc upon the metaphor," or whether they exploited the discursive strategies of the dominant class in order to develop a legitimate vocabulary of resistance and rebellion, as others have maintained, writers such as Ponet, Bacon, or Robert Parsons destabilized the significance of the analogy. For in developing an ethics of resistance by adopting the terminology from the very political orders they meant to resist in the first place, they ultimately exposed the fact that such terminology had been entirely arbitrary all along. No natural organic relation between body and state could be claimed independent of the situation in which it was being deployed; its meaning depended entirely on context. As a consequence, active resistance or rebellion against the commonwealth could be either justified or condemned with exactly the same topoi. To that extent, the image of the body-politic was neutralized, and a stage figure who embodied the persona of disaffected plotter could come across with a high amount of moral ambiguity. To the extent that malcontents can be characterized as stock types at all, they might be characterized as embodiments of the question whether sedition could be legitimately defended—a question audiences presumably could have ruminated over indefinitely.

While such radical ambiguity has been noticed before, it overlooks another crucial dimension, namely the role of temporality in descriptions of the body-politic. What has generally escaped critical attention (perhaps because it is so self-evident) is the fact it represents body and state alike as *static* images. As the title to Thomas Floyd's political treatise indicates—*The picture of a perfit common wealth*—commonwealths can be portrayed as though they were not subject to time. To that extent there is something of an Orphic fantasy at the heart of the entire operation: a political theorist must stop time *in order to* represent the commonwealth as a body in the first place. We can observe just how much temporality becomes a problem by turning again to Forset, who refers to only refers to it briefly, almost as though the mere recognition of temporality threatened to undermine his overall project. As Forset writes:

> The mutabilitie of this earthly state stirred by the diuersitie of causes, admitteth no such certeintie or stabilitie in either of the said bodies, as can quite keepe off or exclude alterations. Let vs then as in the naturall, so in the politicall bodie gouerne the question of change with such choice & discretion, as vnlesse either vrgent necessitie constraine, or euident vtilitie do entise our assent, we may still retain our wonted orders and vsages with all permanent firmenesse, not affecting or enduring any nouelties.[30]

For Forset, to recognize change and mutability not only is to admit that commonwealths, like infants, eventually age and die; more dramatically, it is to expose the illusory quality of his project, as it forces him to concede that neither bodies nor commonwealths ever are so stable as their literary representations make them out to be. Significantly, he addresses it just before he ventures into his survey of diseases to the state, as though the mere acknowledgment of mutability were in itself enough to bring to mind the dangers of disorder and rebellion that threaten otherwise stable institutions.

It is in this context that the body-politic imagery in *Julius Caesar* becomes significant. Two processes are at work in the drama, and each factors in what finally gets named as melancholy—though this does not occur until the fifth act, by which point it accounts for very little. On the one hand, Brutus, along with his fellow conspirators, try to rewrite body-politic imagery in order to suit their own interests. As they recognize, the success of their plot depends entirely on their ability to have it make sense to the populace. Thus, while traditional body-politic ideology rejected revolt as a form of disease, their own version had to portray their specific revolt as though it was well grounded in that same tradition. On the other hand, for the conspirators—and it is Brutus who seems particularly attuned to this problem—there is the deep sense that time functions as a disruptive force. It is meaningful insofar as it signals just how little is in their control.

As some critics have observed, none of Shakespeare's plays are as attentive to time as is *Julius Caesar*. References to clocks and calendars abound, specific dates have both dramatic and thematic relevance. Nor is there a play more attentive to the question of how we measure time—the ultimate question of power. As Sigurd Burkhardt has pointed out, the play's deepest conflict—a conflict that would have resonated for Elizabethans undergoing the same conflict for nearly two decades—boils down to the question, not of what the time is, but by whose calendar?[31] This uncertainty over time is further reflected by the fact that most of the play takes place either during a holiday (the Lupercal) or what Linda Woodbridge refers to as Saturnalian festival, a period when the regular order of time is suspended.[32] In fact, the play can be understood largely as a conflict among competing experiences of time, including: the sense that the traditional devices by which people arranged their lives have been disrupted and need to be restored, as Brutus implies when he refers to "The time's abuse," no doubt in anticipation of Hamlet; and the eerie sense that despite such organizing devices, one never truly feels such orientation after all, as exemplified by Cicero's remark, "Indeed it is a strange disposed time." Rather than take a stand against the world at a particular moment in history then, the characters who come closest to malcontent figures in *Julius Caesar* seem radically uncertain whether such a world and when such a moment in history can truly be said to exist.

FROM THE BODY-POLITIC TO THE POLITIC BODY

"Till then, think of the world."

–Julius Caesar (1.2.307)

At first glance, Cassius' farewell remark to Brutus, which concludes their first on-stage encounter, seems to be an appeal to what Brutus himself refers to as "the general good" (1.2.85). A slightly more cynical reading might note that Cassius alludes to Brutus' ambitions to world domination—whether they are his own desires or not at this point in the play is beside the point—thus taking the remark to mean, set your eyes on the world as your reward for ridding Rome of this new self-proclaimed god. But this is not the first time in the scene that Cassius has brought that lofty term, "The world" to Brutus' attention; in fact, he refers to it no fewer than four times in the few minutes they spend alone with each other. When commenting on Caesar's unparalleled rise to power, for instance, he notes:

> Why, man, he doth bestride the narrow world
> Like a colossus, and we petty men
> Walk under his huge legs and peep about
> To find ourselves dishonourable graves. (1.2.134–137)

In other words, by sending Brutus on his way with the instruction to think of the world, Cassius would have him continue the thought process that their brief exchange has just established, namely to conceive of Caesar's rise to power in terms of the way it has transformed the traditional "world picture" into a grotesque.

Clearly, what has been on Cassius' mind is the inexplicable suddenness of Caesar's metamorphosis. What matters is not only the superhuman qualities Caesar has assumed, or even the way Caesar's power has threatened the traditional values of Roman republican politics;[33] just as startling is the sense of spontaneity that accompanies the changes. Twice in the scene, Cassius depicts Caesar's former personality in equally exaggerated, if correspondingly diminutive terminology. During a swimming contest, he recalls, Caesar had conducted himself as a feeble senex (Anchises), and during his bout of sickness, Caesar cried "As a sick girl" (128). While critics have noticed the way Cassius' images have feminized Caesar, what has not been noted is just how quickly they give way to their opposites.[34] In both cases, Cassius' descriptions end mid-line, only to be followed by hyperbolic reversals:

> I, as Aeneas, our great ancestor,
> Did from the flames of Troy upon his shoulder
> The old Anchises bear, so from the waves of Tiber
> Did I the tired Caesar: and this man
> Is now become a god, and Cassius is
> A wretched creature (1.2.112–7)
> 'Alas' it cried, 'give me some drink, Titinius,'
> As a sick girl. Ye gods, it doth amaze me
> A man of such a feeble temper should
> So get the start of the majestic world
> And bear the palm alone.(1.2.127–31)

In both cases, Cassius seems inclined to rhetorical abuse, though it is hardly because he is not in control over what he says. Quite the contrary, he is only too well aware just how easily one simile can stand in for another and how unnerving this process of substitutions can be. For it is not as though there is a real Caesar that somehow lurks behind these rhetorical embellishments—for all intents and purposes, rhetorical embellishment is exactly what he is.

As for Brutus, there is every indication that Caesar's fate will somehow depend on the way he can be represented. When he appears alone on stage, the night before the assassination, he searches busily for an image that would make the assassination appear legitimate:

> And, since the quarrel
> Will bear no color for the thing he is,
> Fashion it thus, that what he is, augmented,
> Would run to these and these extremities;
> And therefore think him as a serpent's egg
> Which hatch'd would as his kind grow mischievous,
> And kill him in the shell. (2.1.28–34)

It is Brutus himself who needs the most convincing, not only that Caesar is a monster in the making, but that such fashioning, as he refers to it, ultimately will do the trick. For on the one hand, Brutus seems to doubt that Caesar would really ever fit this image—the mere fact that it has to be fashioned (or made, coming from the Latin word *facere*), reminds us that it can always be re-fashioned at some later date.

Given both these misgivings and Cassius' earlier litany of complaints though, it is not a little surprising to see just how eager Brutus seems when he tries to fashion the factioners in terms of body-politic imagery, once they arrive in his orchard. Brutus' critics, beginning with Plutarch himself, have noted just how much of a blunder it had been to leave Antony untouched following Caesar's murder. In his translation of Plutarch, North mentions that Brutus commits two "faultes," each with respect to Antony: the first was to not kill him, the second to let him speak at Caesar's funeral.[35] As Shakespeare portrays it here, Brutus is simply tenacious:

> Our course will seem too bloody, Caius Cassius,
> To cut the head off and then hack the limbs–
> Like wrath in death and envy afterwards–
> For Antony is but a limb of Caesar. (2.1.161–164)

Doubtless, some spectators would have heard, within Brutus' remark, language that echoed Ponet and Parsons; and doubtless they would have responded according to their own predilections. If there is a reason why audience members traditionally have projected their own desires onto the play and passed them off as interpretations, as Sigurd Burkhardt comments, it is because by and large the play is about exactly that trick of mind, as well as the disastrous consequences that follow from it.[36] But the mere fact that Brutus uses it at all, and with such conviction, is what seems to be the real issue.

In his "Life of Brutus," the source for Shakespeare's play, Plutarch identifies two faults with Brutus' strategy: he lets Antony live; more foolishly, he lets Antony speak at Caesar's funeral. The first assumes that Antony depended entirely on Caesar's life for his political vitality, while the other overlooks Antony's talents as an orator. If we stick to Shakespeare's version of the event, we might reconsider Brutus' two faults as follows. To begin with, Brutus' mistake is to take his metaphors too literally, to believe that in referring to Antony as a limb, he has hit upon some essential discovery about the present Roman body-politic. As Brutus becomes carried away by his own imagery he becomes particularly impervious to the threat that Antony might become equally imaginative. That Antony does eventually employ a similar device of anthropomorphism, but to radically different purposes, when he promises to ventriloquize Caesar's wounds:

> Over thy wounds now do I prophesy
> (Which like dumb mouths do ope their ruby lips
> To beg the voice and utterance of my tongue) . . . (3.1.259–61)

only underscores just how shortsighted Brutus' depiction turns out to have been.[37]

To that end, Brutus' mistake is to think that there is substance to his figures of speech, rather than to recognize that, to a certain degree, the public persona that goes by the name Caesar never was about substance. On a still deeper level though, Brutus errs the moment he starts to make predictions about how the conspiracy will be received. When he describes the manner in which they ought to conduct themselves, always appealing to the most delicate terms possible, he concludes:

> Let's carve him as a dish fit for the gods,
> Not hew him as a carcass fit for hounds;
> And let our hearts, as subtle masters do,
> Stir up their servants to an act of rage
> And after seem to chide 'em. This shall make
> Our purpose necessary and not envious,

Civil Dissension and its Malcontents, or States of Melancholy   97

> Which so appearing to the common eyes,
> We shall be call'd purgers, not murderers. (2.1.172–9)

Again, Brutus adopts terminology that anyone even partly familiar with political theory would have recognized—in particular, anybody who knew James' *Basilikon Doron,* which makes use of the same trope of the king as purger, would have recognized it right away. What matters here though is the grammatical construct; Brutus represents the conspirators in the future perfect tense, a device that enables him to perceive some future as though from the comfortable perspective of hindsight. It is a strange maneuver: he makes note of the passing of time in order to reinforce the notion that the body-politic image is the static image he wants his followers to believe. And while he speaks of the highly unstable and ambiguous task of portraying the faction as a legitimate cause, he imagines a point in the future almost as though it were a foregone conclusion. In short, at the moment when it least serves the interests of the plotters, Brutus argues that there can be an element of necessity to their actions.

Of course we have seen Brutus struggle with this sort of temporal disorientation at least once before in this scene. While alone and waiting for the conspirators to arrive, he notes to himself:

> Between the acting of a dreadful thing
> And the first motion, all the interim is
> Like a phantasma or a hideous dream:
> The genius and the mortal instruments
> Are then in council, and the state of man,
> Like to a little kingdom, suffers then
> The nature of an insurrection. (2.1.63–69)

The irony of this observation is that it actually does represent one of Brutus' greatest moments of clarity—virtually everything that he does in the moments that follow can be explained by referring back to this peculiarly uncertain simile. (Is it like a phantasm, or is it more like a hideous dream?) Similarly, the convoluted sequence of the first two lines captures a genuinely twisted mental state, for in a very real sense he must act first and then muster up the will, if for no other reason than to explain it to himself. Finally, while he had been making furtive references to inner conflict from his first moment on stage:

> Vexed I am
> Of late with passions of some difference . . .

> Nor construe any further my neglect
> That poor Brutus, with himself at war
> Forgets the shows of love to other men. (1.2.39–47)

It is only when alone that he expresses his grief in terms that suggest his constitution truly is imbalanced. While the body-politic analogy may ultimately prove fatal to the conspiracy, here it strangely does seem to work. At any rate, it works insofar as it both shows Brutus at a moment of lucidity *and* shows that he utterly lacks the language necessary to account for himself in a truly lucid way.

If Brutus can be called mad at this point in the play, his madness consists of two factors. While he senses something is wrong with Rome, his desire to inscribe civil disorder within the unstable ideology of the body-politic prevents him from knowing just how to articulate whatever sense of grief he thinks he has.[38] To that extent, his identification of Caesar as the cause—both because of who he is and what he might someday represent—feels like a hasty conclusion, a convenient place to direct his own murderous desires when a better one is not readily available. In short, Caesar is a scapegoat.[39] Just as important, Brutus seems to recognize his indecisiveness as a crisis of temporality; his decision to act is marked by his sharp awareness of a future not only unwritten, but obscured by fantasies and delusions.

Nothing conveys this crisis of temporality more emphatically than the moment when Shakespeare commits his so-called "most notorious boner," namely the references to the clock, which seem to pile up during the moments that surround the murder.[40] When Brutus interrupts the conversation in the orchard, "Peace count the clock," it reminds us just how poorly mechanical time provides an organizing principle for the conspirators. (And in fact, because it is supposedly such an anachronism, one cannot help but wonder whether they hear the clock differently from those of us who cannot get away from chronometric devices that divide our days and nights into manageable units.) What Brutus needs is a glimpse of the consequences to his own future actions, something that will stop him from projecting his own fantasies onto the conspiracy's future legacy. What he has instead is an arbitrary arrangement of time which, in itself, contains no small element of what is implied by the term, "phantasma or hideous dream," insofar as knowledge of what time it will be in an hour can serve as a substitute for knowledge of what the future will be like.

To that extent though, when Brutus likens his moment of personal crisis to a phantasma or a hideous dream, we might put to one side questions of whether his decisions will be correct or not, or even of whether being correct is the final word. It is absolutely crucial that Brutus structures his state of delirium as a simile:

> All the interim is
> Like a phantasma or a hideous dream (2.1.64–5)

By stressing that his uncertainty merely resembles a hallucination, he refrains from rejecting his every thought as mere error. The problem is not that he is always in the wrong, but, in anticipation of what Pascal would describe in years to come, he simply cannot know when he is and when he is not.[41] What finally distinguishes Brutus from other theatrical malcontents, even the malcontent that Cassius is taken to be, is that Brutus somehow recognizes the extent to which his decisions are dependent on a standard of knowledge that exceeds his powers of comprehension. Because he cannot know whether his commitment to the faction will emerge as the sign of his nobility or of his delusional ambitions, he lacks the ability to invoke the rhetorical devices normally available to the political malcontent. He cannot seek revenge against definite wrongdoing. He cannot properly justify the assassination, except by the most outrageous flights of fancy that verge on paranoia themselves. He cannot even make an actual promise to the people whose complaints he intends to resolve. As he declares in the lines immediately preceding his admission of delirium:

> O Rome, I make thee promise.
> If the redress will follow, thou receivest
> Thy full petition at the hand of Brutus. (2.1.56–58)

Since he cannot know the significance of his actions before he completes them, all he can do is act; only on the condition that his action would produce its desired effect will he allow himself retroactively to reinterpret his actions as a pledge to answer his petitioners' complaints.

What finally characterizes Brutus' discontent, though, is not some sense of privileged knowledge that only a political outsider could have, but the awareness that he is just as much in the dark as everybody else (and therefore not entitled to right what he perceives as injustice). After all, Shakespeare does not show much sympathy for characters who comprehend their circumstances accurately. For instance, when Caska attests to Cicero that lions and screech owls have invaded the city, while a hundred women swear to have seen men walking up and down the streets in flames—visions that would be taken as possible symptoms of madness, or as projections of melancholy fumes upon the senses—Cicero is technically "correct" to caution him against superstitiously converting them into signs of Rome's crisis:

> Indeed it is a strange disposed time;
> But men may construe things after their fashion,
> Clean from the purpose of the things themselves. (1.3.33–35)

The soothsayer is also correct when he warns Caesar to beware the Ides of March; so too is Calphurnia correct when she has the prophetic dream of her husband's murder. In each of these instances, Shakespeare toys with the notion of a prophetic knowledge that seems to hover just far enough out of reach for anyone to use it to their advantage. For the citizens of Rome, knowledge—even the forms of knowledge that resemble the enthusiastic rhapsodies of the prophets—hardly amounts to power. If anything, their knowledge merely intensifies their powerlessness.

In other words, on one very important level Brutus is not unique, since there is nobody in Rome who is capable of performing a political act without that act being grounded in a fundamental confusion with regard to its significance. Brutus may well be the only character on stage to grasp this fact, but merely to grasp it is not enough to overcome it. Brutus' inner conflict might be thus be characterized as being caught in two positions. On the one hand, he is consumed by a desire to use rhetoric in order to determine, and hence to render legitimate, the course of action that he and his fellow conspirators undertake. On the other hand, he is beset by an awareness of a radical *disorientation*. For Shakespeare, the latter seems to carry the weight of intrigue, and in many ways his play explores the dangers, not only of false rhetoric, but of a basic premise that political actions can be boiled down to an affair of language. It would be tempting to speculate on a definition of melancholy that might apply to this condition that Brutus articulates, in lieu of the humoral terminology that does not appear very prominently. One might say that melancholy stems from the fact that Brutus' plot is marked by an ambiguity that is both fundamental and inescapable, an ambiguity which both compels him to fight for his political liberties and assures him that doing so will necessarily have tragic consequences.

However, the actual term "melancholy" does appear once, toward the end of the play, and one would be remiss not to make note of it. The word appears in a speech by Messala, one of the play's minor characters. Significantly, he speaks not of one body, but two:

> O hateful Error, Melancholy's child,
> Why dost thou show to the apt thoughts of men

The things that are not? O Error, soon conceived,
Thou never com'st unto a happy birth
But kill'st the mother that engendred thee. (5.3.66–71)

Melancholy and error are configured as mother and son, engaged in a conflict that is more destructive than nurturing. To be sure, there are about a dozen or so references to mothers, fathers, and children throughout the play; and childbirth itself is a major part of the play's central conflict. (It is enough to recall that Caesar's weakness is first represented by the fact that his wife is not pregnant.) To that end, Messala's remarks respond to the problematic status of childbirth and parenting during the fall of the republic and rise of Caesar's empire. But it is also worth noting that melancholy appears explicitly, at this one and only moment, and precisely a moment when a character stops thinking about the body as a relatively stable entity and starts seeing it in terms of gestation and growth, of reproduction and division, and of differences—the differences in gender being only the most prominent. In that sense, Messala's reference to melancholy may ultimately expose the biggest problem underlying body politic terminology in the first place—in order for it to work, it must regard the body itself as though it had been a corpse all along. In contrast, according to Messala's comment, if there is melancholy, it is very much due to the fact that bodies are alive, and therefore ultimately resistant to the various attempts to represent them through rhetorical strategies, more commonly known as anatomies.

Section II
Melancholy and the Question of Government

Chapter Four
"And Yet I Am My Own Executioner": Rumor, Suicide, and Textual Authority in John Donne's *Devotions*

> "That how desperate soever our case be, how irremdiable soever our state, we our selfes, and not God, are the cause of that desperate irremediableness . . . There is no such matter, there is no such desperate irremediablenes declared to any particular conscience, as is imagind, but you, any, mare returne to me, when you will, and I will receive you."
>
> —John Donne, Sermon preached at Whitehall, 24 February, 1625/6[1]

Donne's readers have grown accustomed to thinking of at least two Donnes—in fairness, the author himself actively contributed to this impression by referring to himself in those terms. Whatever the number of stages, Donne's melancholy had a prominent function in all of them, so much so that some critics have gone so far as to suggest that he anticipated what Freud discovered concerning the death drive—and without having to live through the mass destruction of World War I, as the founder of psychoanalysis had done.[2] Surely, if the lines from his first Holy Sonnet are any indication, which read:

> I run to Death, and Death meets me as fast,
> And all my pleasures are as yesterday

Donne seems to have been less uncomfortable embracing death than even Freud himself (whose favorite line of poetry may well have been Sophocles' "Best never to have been born"). Significantly, Donne nearly always used it to represent alienation—if not outright opposition—either to social, political, or ecclesiastical institutions. During his so-called years of exile at Mitcham, most famously, Donne wrote a defense of suicide, entitled *Biathanatos,* in which he defended the early Christians who martyred themselves by the thousand in the face of the Roman empire. Indeed, reading *Biathanatos,* one gets the impression the very merits of Christianity as a religion originally lay in its status as a cult of mass immolation. Donne does not use the word "melancholy" once in the entire treatise—a stunning omission, given that he makes reference to his own melancholy and despair in letters from the same period. Nevertheless, he does suggest that the modern Christian association of suicide with madness is in fact the result of a conspiracy between Roman statesmen, "subtle heretiques," and the Devil himself, all of whom combine to reinterpret the church's official position on suicide in order to accommodate itself to the massive state bureaucracy that the original martyrs had resisted in the first place.[3] As Donne audaciously suggests, to argue that people commit suicide out of madness is to tacitly accept the conclusions of the early Roman church, even if there remained the possibility that their conclusions may have been the first step in a long history of irrevocable damage to the church as an institution.

During the latter part of his career, as preacher (and spokesman) for the crown, Donne frequently represented rebellion as a sickness, or melancholy—a melancholy which, as some critics have noticed, bears a curious resemblance to the melancholy that he himself was thought to be afflicted with.[4] In a 1621 sermon preached at St. Paul's, for instance, he equates melancholy with religious rebellion. Or rather, melancholy signals self-exclusion from (his version of) the Universal Church:

> For to exclude others from that Kingdome, is a tyrannie, an usurpation; and to exclude thy selfe, is a sinfull, and a rebellious melancholy. But as melancholy in the body is the hardest humour to be purged, so is the melancholy in the soule, the distrust of thy salvation too.[5]

More emphatically, when preaching before King Charles in 1625/6, Donne refers to melancholy as a form of self-exclusion in order to promote a doctrine of universal grace. In this sermon, Donne uses melancholy to characterize a fundamental misinterpretation of God's universal grace:

> Look also if this Bill [ubi est Libellus, where is the Bill of Divorcement] be not dropt upon and blotted; The venim of the *Serpent* is dropt upon it, The Wormwood of thy *Desperation* is dropt upon it, The Gall of the *Melancholly* is dropt upon it, and that voydes the Bill.[6]

Regular comparisons between rebellion and illness may have caught the attention of King James, whose own early textbook on governance, *Basilikon*

Doron, compared the office of kingship to that of the physician.[7] So too did King Charles seem to approve of Donne's sermons, at least insofar as his advocacy of universal salvation corresponded with Charles' own early ideas of ecclesiastical policy.[8]

In terms of Donne's own career though, it is a noticeable contrast to the fashionably melancholy outsider of the early years, or even the outright suicidal depression he mentions in his letters during the so-called period of exile at the Mitcham estate. For the younger "Jack" figure, melancholy literally was a pose, as we know from his famous Lothian portrait as a melancholy lover. If Jonson had spewed his venom at people who associated the humors with costumes, Donne's portrait offered visible proof why anyone would aspire to such affectations at all. There, he is hardly pale, hardly swarthy. In fact, his lips are a deep red. He is clad in a black outfit, but he wears it well indeed, with an enormous hat, along with white lace and an ermine cuff for contrast. Even his right eye has a certain glow of light about it. Everybody should be lucky to be so melancholy. During the course of his career, melancholy consistently remains both the physical manifestation and metaphorical expression of rebellion against established institutional norms; if anything changes, then, it is his attitude about rebellion itself. One might suspect that as he aligned himself with the Jacobean church, Donne's references to sickness and melancholy as rebellion always had one eye on his past as a type of self-reproach—but all the same, self-reproach for something he could not have done much about had he wanted to.

Given his use of the analogy between disease and rebellion in his sermons, it hardly is surprising that he would not only invoke it but develop it more extensively in his *Devotions upon Emergent Occasions,* the autobiography of his own illness of 1623. There, he links both under the more general category of disorder: "Everything that disorders a faculty, and the function of that, is a sickness."[9] Evidently, Donne expected to demonstrate that the same forces that contribute to illness also are at work in political situations. As he asks in the same section, invoking a phrase that recurs throughout the text, "Is it not so in states too?" (59) In asking this question, he reveals that–at least in part—Donne's illness had political implications by nature. How much so, is of course a matter of doubt. To the extent that the *Devotions* can be read politically at all, though, it might be read as a study of the ways in which states and bodies alike are agents of their own ruin.

Of course there is something profoundly indecorous about making political analogies in a treatise whose primary concerns are to trace a physical illness, and to use that illness as a vehicle for examining one's spiritual condition. In fairness, though, there is something indecorous about the genre as a whole. Like the very illness the text itself refers to, the publication of a book like the *Devotions* never really could have occurred at an opportune moment. At the most basic level, the lesson behind a book about illness is that it replicates the illness it depicts. Specifically, it has the attributes of an interruption, but an interruption that nevertheless commands its readers' attention away from other affairs. There is always something more pressing, or at least something that had felt more pressing until, without warning, we are called upon to contemplate our own mortality. Even if readers are particularly well versed in an *ars moriendi* tradition,[10] doesn't that very tradition itself already betray a not so hidden wish to turn dying into something manageable, a technical program like any other, such as shipbuilding, medicine, even book-writing? And finally, as a distraction from our normal affairs, is there not perhaps something just the slightest bit false about a meditation on one's own sickness unto death, at least insofar as nobody is ever in a position to write the truth of their own death (which is, naturally, impervious to personal experience)? To that extent, Donne's own tone of *gravitas* and repeated gestures of sincerity notwithstanding—there is no reason not to take him at his word in the text—the *Devotions* nevertheless takes on an unexpectedly gossipy quality. It represents a process that one never really can become more than merely curious about, let alone master. At the very least, as will become clear shortly, Donne cannot represent his own sickness, nor what his sickness might signify within a larger cultural scheme, without attending to the concepts of rumor and idle curiosity as obstacles that stand in his way.

While there may never be a great moment to publish a book like the *Devotions,* the actual publication date of 1624 appears to be, in retrospect, the mark of especially poor timing. In 1624, Donne's own failing health might well have been the last thing on the mind of Prince Charles, to whom the book is dedicated. Charles himself was on the verge of embarking on a secret trip to Madrid, where he would eventually become involved in one of the more spectacular diplomatic fiascoes of the Jacobean court to date. (Charles would eventually be fortunate to return from Spain with his hat in hand, let alone momentarily one of the two most popular public figures in the entire realm.) Meanwhile, Charles' father, King James, was already showing the effects of age and failing health—as it turns out, the king did pass away a little over a year later, just shy of his own sixtieth birthday. With these things in mind, a book about Donne's illness likely would have been taken as a conceited gesture of self importance.

On the other hand, it may have been an indirect intervention on Charles himself, perhaps even a suggestion on how the heir apparent ought to conduct his own public affairs. And while there is no evidence that

Charles read the text to that effect, modern criticism has suggested Donne may well have harbored such an intention. After all, the treatise does furnish a moderate amount of material that discusses political affairs abstractly. This material, which Robert Cooper once famously described as "an almost endless webbing of political imagery," has taken on the status of a clue, if not a "symptom" of Donne as an unexpected political adviser.[11] Cooper's approach raises as many questions as it answers. Why, for instance, should readers of a spiritual treatise give privilege to political imagery which in fact is not endless but only appears in limited sections of the text, and which occurs in a text that makes use of all sorts of imagery from any number of discursive fields? The political imagery that he refers to is quite specifically limited to the subsections marked for meditation. In contrast, throughout the Expostulations and Prayers, which comprise about two thirds of the treatise, Donne's imagery generally comes from other discourses.[12] Even when he does make use of political imagery, it is so general and metaphorical that a reader might suspect Donne of deliberately *avoiding* even an accidental reference to specific Jacobean policy. In other words, while a reader could perhaps make the case that certain instances do respond to contemporary political concerns, as a whole they do not necessarily conform to any pattern that might constitute an actual set of directions or even an indirect address (to the extent that an indirect address is even possible). The effects of Donne's nonspecific terminology bear out in contemporary critical attempts to identify just what he would have been addressing the prince about in the first place. While Cooper (and others) have assumed that Donne would have been thinking of the Spanish match, and the attendant fears of Catholicism that marriage to the Infanta would have generated, the scandal itself did not fully break until October 1624, well after Donne had been restored to health. Because Donne raises the topic of how kings should make use of their advisors, some readers have assumed that Donne was offering Charles advice about how to manage Parliament more effectively. (If this is correct the advice was poorly received, if in fact it was received at all.) More recent critics have even noticed a tone of political quietism within the text. In an article that challenges not only the immediate context for Donne's remarks but the very principles by which his political terminology ought to be read, Mary Papazian argues that the political imagery heads toward isolation and quietism rather than continued struggle and intervention.[13] In fact, a specific reference point never does emerge, and to the extent that the text does not affirm much of anything, it mirrors James' own policy with regard to the Spanish, a policy which even the King's closest friends had a difficult time comprehending.

Such discrepancies among generally astute readers ultimately say quite a bit about the hermeneutic difficulties that the *Devotions* poses as a text, especially when it comes to properly interpreting illness. If readers are sometimes at a loss to explain the political subtext within a treatise such as Donne's, is this not in part because the very treatise so often stages anxieties about what the author's disease consists of, what causes it and cures it, what prevents it from returning as relapse, and above all what it says about sin and redemption?[14] Just as important, if the *Devotions* is less than clear about what it might be saying to Charles regarding public policy, this itself owes to a deep concern within the text about what constitutes appropriate forms of political address in the first place. In many ways Donne's language parallels the very disease he uses to write about it; it is contagious, it is fundamentally enigmatic, it is capable of unexpected permutations, and it is a complete embarrassment to those who rely too heavily on cause-effect models to account for it. Viewed in this manner, the illness that Donne writes about serves as a vehicle for exploring questions—and additionally for exposing anxieties—regarding agency and authority within a public arena. The *Devotions* foregrounds a deep anxiety over the absence of any devices that might regulate the circulation, and the meaning, of language.

Frequently Donne's anxiety takes the form of criticizing a phenomenon which, while hardly new, nevertheless was beginning to take on new dimensions under James' rule: a widespread obsession with gossip and rumor.[15] As Elena Levy-Navarro has recently noted, "A persistent fear of rumor pervades the *Devotions*."[16] Thus when Donne defends the propriety of Nero's empire for instance, in a passage that incidentally can be understood as a comment about tyrants and a largely supportive endorsement of King James' authority, his attention ends up falling not on the ruler but of those who speak ill of him. As he addresses his God, "Certainly those men prepare a way of speaking negligently or irreverently of thee, that give themselves that liberty in speaking of thy viceregents, kings; for thou who gavest Augustus the empire, gavest it to Nero too" (52). Later, Donne points out the threat that conspiracies pose to a kingdom: "Twenty rebellious drums make not so dangerous a noise as a few whisperers and secret plotters in corners" (64). When he describes the vapors that afflict him—those substanceless substances that, at bottom, characterize what is so dangerous about his illness—Donne again turns to rumor as an analogy:

> That which is fume in us is, in a state rumour; and these vapours in us, which we consider here pestilent and infectious fumes, are, in a state, infectious rumours, detracting and dishonourable calumnies, libels. (79)

"And Yet I am My Own Executioner"

The concern about rumor persists through the very end, when he worries about relapse:

> How easily thou passedst over many other sins in them, and how vehemently thou insistsedst in those into which they so often relapsed; those were their murmurings against thee, in thine instruments and ministers, and their turnings upon other gods, and embracing the idolatries of their neighbors. O my God, how slippery a way, to how irrecoverable a bottom, is murmuring; and how near thyself he comes, that murmurs at him who comes from thee! (154)

Indeed, rumor takes on such extreme dimensions that not even God is entirely impervious to it. In a passage which inadvertently invites us to compare God to Iago, of all villains, Donne writes, "But where there is but a suspicion, a rumour, of such a relapse to idolatry, thine anger is awakened, and thine indignation stirred" (156). These few instances help to exemplify what is ongoing throughout the *Devotions* from start to last, with regard to the nature of public discourse. Like illness itself, rumor poses a fundamental threat to the preconceived order of commonwealths. As a disruptive force that catches rulers off guard, yet nevertheless demands attention *and* escapes the responsibilities one could demand of, say, a royal counselor, rumor literally sickens the state.

To some extent, Donne shares this concern about rumor with a number of professional writers who had been taking notice of the fact that cheap print made public discourse both more accessible and more precarious. As historians have pointed out, late sixteenth century England witnessed the emergence of anonymous and semi-anonymous forms of print, including broadsides, verse libels, and (those precursors to modern dailies) news separates. Such devices caught on like a fever, and by the time James took the throne, London had a distinctly newsy culture.[17] The newly coined phrase "news-mongers," described people who craved updates on public scandal. In the wake of such prominent scandals as the murder of Thomas Overbury, the imprisonment of MPs in 1621, Lord Vaux's refusal to surrender his arms in Northamptonshire, and Buckingham's virtual betrayal of England for thirty pieces of silver, there emerged an audience of anonymous readers who presumed to make it their business to know the affairs of court. Meanwhile, in the wake of the crisis over the Spanish match, Londoners produced what Thomas Cogswell describes as an "unprecedented flood of pamphlets."[18] In a fairly perverse sense, then, by the time Donne wrote the *Devotions,* the personal very much had become the political.

By all accounts the relatively sudden appearance and circulation of news separates produced a number of substantial shifts in the nature of political discourse. Most immediately, it greatly expanded the range of people who had the authority—or at least believed they had the authority—to intervene indirectly within affairs of state. Individuals, or small groups of individuals, could thereby find themselves participating in discussions— albeit unofficial and unwieldy ones—about topics that hitherto had not been of their concern. As Dagmar Freist describes it, by the 1640s, "Men and women of this period displayed an active interest in matters that were outside their immediate local context, and they had some basic 'knowledge' of national politics."[19] To the extent that official Stuart ideology believed in the principles of rule by *arcanum imperii* and top-down proclamation, such widespread interest in state affairs inevitably struck the crown as, at best, unthinkable. At worst, it was a variant of what King James had described in *Basilikon Doron* as, "The naturall sicknesse that I haue perceiued this estate subject to in my time . . . a fectlesse arrogant conceit of their own greatness and power."[20] Just as important, as Freist's remark suggests, people who actively took an interest in the news were largely *mis*-informed to the extent that they were informed at all. Inevitably, what people learned about was not affairs of state so much as a pamphleteer's representation of affairs of state. And in the interest of cultivating as certain cult of personality for themselves, many pamphleteers did not shy away from inventing anecdotes in place of events that might be substantially verified. The news-mongering public's expertise was thus pseudo-expertise, wherein nobody knows anything, as everyone has an opinion about everything.

While the sermons thus promoted a doctrine of inclusion when it came to matters ecclesiastical, in no way did his church views extend to embracing the culture of news pamphlets and separates. In matters political, the incursion of such pamphlets represented a public nuisance at best, and at worst a full-fledged sickness. Donne himself was keenly aware of just how much one's reputation depended on the rhetorical construction of a public persona, and in turn he was aware just how easily that persona could be disrupted. Given the extensive anxiety about rumor throughout this fairly public display of personal affliction, it is not hard to imagine that Donne was suggesting that Charles do likewise. In other words, by claiming that rumor functions as a kind of social disease, Donne effectively admonishes the king, so-called physician of the state, to do something to curtail it. At the very least, the crown should become more cognizant of the damage that anonymous libels and newsbooks could cause by virtue of their marginality. But the concern about rumor in the *Devotions* was more than simply a bid to fashionable sensibility. Rather, the specific appeal of rumor—what the very idea of rumor calls out to Donne, as it were—is its largely untraceable origin. In this regard, the analogy between rumor and illness ends up complicating Donne's representation of illness as rebellion, and most extensively when it comes to questions of agency. What causes such disruptions to occur in the first place? Where do they originate? Why do they appear at the specific moments that they do? What does the persistence of rumors suggest about the fate of commonwealths, even the best of commonwealths, over a long-term scale? How can they be prevented, if indeed they can be prevented at all? If not, to what extent can a physician-king effectively manage them, and to what extent do they ultimately do damage? In short, what do rumor and illness, characterized as *interruptions* of a well-ordered body politic, finally suggest about the nature of good governance?

What is particularly noteworthy about this approach is that it allows him to account for sedition and rebellion while maintaining a distinctly loyal posture. As a rule, when it comes to making any statements as to how commonwealths should be governed, Donne enthusiastically supports Jacobean ideology of monarch as absolute ruler. If the king promotes stability and order, by contrast those who oppose it become usurpers who work toward its dis-composure and eventual collapse. To be sure, he does advise that the king should seek counsel with others:

> It diminishes not the dignity of a monarch that he derive part of his care upon others' God hath not made many suns, but he hath made many bodies that receive and give light. The Romans began with one king; they came to two consuls; they returned in extremities to one dictator: whether in one or many, the sovereignty is the same in all states, and the danger is not the more, and the providence is the more, where there are more physicians; as the state is the happier where businesses are carried by more counsels than can be in one breast, how large soever. (43)

If anything in the entire text stands out as a sharp challenge to the king, it is this statement, with its implications that to turn away from a large government to a rule of one is to become a dictator. In light of James' eventual dissolution of Parliament over the Spanish affair, Donne's remark have might been understood as a reminder that the commonwealth depended on the two houses for its perseverance. However, as a text primarily about disease as usurpation, the *Devotions* directs its attention to those critics and conspirators who represent the much greater threat. There is nothing ambiguous about his response to open detractors:

> What ill air that I could have met in the street, what channel, what shambles, what dunghill, what fault, could have hurt me so much as these home-bred vapours? What fugitive, what almsman of any foreign state, can do so much harm as a detractor, a libeller, a scornful jester at home? (79)

Likewise, even in the potentially legitimate case where a tyrant sits on the throne, Donne adopts a position that is distinctly royalist:

> Is it not so in states too? Sometimes the insolency of those that are great puts the people into commotions; the great disease, and the greatest danger to the head, is the insolency of the great ones; and yet they execute martial law, they come to present executions upon the people, whose commotion was indeed but a symptom, but an accident of the main disease; but this symptom, grown so violent, would allow no time for a consultation. Is it not so in the accidents of the diseases of our mind too? Is it not evidently so in our affections, in our passions? If a choleric man be ready to strike, must I go about to purge his choler, or to break the blow? (57–8)

The tone of this remark resembles that of King James himself, whose own speeches to parliament regularly admonished his audience to remain obedient to the state, even in cases where a tyrant was on the throne.[21] In short, Donne's area of political concern—if indeed he does express a political concern within the treatise—is not so much to offer a programmatic for the king to follow. More plausibly, and as James would likely have understood it, it is to worry about those members of the commonwealth who pose the greatest threat to it, namely those who meet in secret places and plot against it.

Still, if Donne equates the commonwealth with the physical body and prescribed order as the sign of health for both, he seems to shore up over the question of how to preserve that order—to purge the state (as it were) of its more threatening components. Unlike what numerous preachers and writers offered throughout the seventeenth century, Donne does not simply admonish people to remain obedient subjects at all costs. Instead his depiction of political dissidents raises many disturbing problems about the state's constitution. And curiously enough, it is not under the sign of disease, but rather of suicide that these problems become most acute. According to Donne, even a well-ordered commonwealth runs the risk of committing a form of self-murder, insofar as the diseases of the state that he points to are inevitable. While not exactly supportive of them, he nevertheless assigns them a fairly prominent role in the functioning of public affairs.

As a rule, when it comes to suicide, Donne's rhetoric is strained, and never more strained than when determining what role the self plays in self-murder. In his so-called defense of suicide, the paradoxical essay *Biathanatos*, Donne had argued that suicide could in fact represent the will of God. At any rate, it is Divine prerogative to decide not only the time of our deaths but the instrument by which we are taken; whether God sends a fatal illness or directs our own hands to the knife is not for anyone else to decide. To that extent, the very term self-murder is a potential misnomer, as it obscures the role that God may play in the process. Unsurprisingly, Donne would controvert this very argument in *Pseudo-Martyr*, which he wrote and published in the years following, by characterizing human will as the custodian of the soul. What is common to both texts though is a prevailing concern over just what directs an individual to commit *felo de se* in the first place.

While Donne was not necessarily beset with the same curiosity about the ethics of suicidal martyrdom during the later years of his life, nevertheless his sickness in 1625 gave him cause to return to the subject of suicide. In the text of the *Devotions*, Donne uses the term suicide to refer to the body's inevitable process of decline toward death; while Donne does not necessarily express a desire to take his own life, his body seems willing to give itself up all the same, and the result is an internal conflict between the various faculties which, taken together, make up the individual John Donne. Thus he foregrounds it in critical passages—critical not only in terms of stages of the illness (the onset, the crisis and the recovery when he fears relapse), but also in terms of the order of the narrative structure (the first, twelfth, and twenty-third meditation, marking precisely the beginning, middle, and end of the text). In addition, suicide has a central thematic importance: it is explicitly linked with the melancholy and sin that he believes have been responsible for his illness. As he makes clear in the twelfth meditation, the melancholy that besets him and the suicide that he runs the risk of committing are of a piece:

> But what have I done, either to breed or to breathe these vapours? They tell me it is my melancholy; did I infuse, did I drink in melancholy into myself . . . But I do nothing upon myself, and yet am mine own executioner. (78–9)

When Donne subsequently links suicide with the problem of vulnerabilities within the state, the prevailing rhetoric of apologizing for political order (even when that order is represented by a Nero) becomes complicated, if not altogether compromised. Like the body, which in its melancholy disorder becomes its own willing-unwilling executioner, the state becomes, in its very composition, the unintending cause of its own dissolution.

This relation between physical illness and political vulnerability is most fully developed in the twelfth meditation, midway through the text and right before the moment when Donne's own disease enters its critical stage. Here, in this passage, he turns explicitly to the question of what constitutes the biggest threats to both body and state. And it is here that his objectives become significantly more mysterious. Perhaps the most striking feature of the political commentary in this meditation is that he feels the need to include it at all. For in a certain sense, it more or less comes out of nowhere:

> But extend this vapour, rarefy it; from so narrow a room as our natural bodies, to any politic body, to a state. (79)

While the analogy may in fact be plausible enough, strictly speaking he has no compelling reason to offer it. By and large when Donne makes use of political imagery, it is with the purpose of making an argument by analogy; the illness, not the state, is what remains important.[22] In the twelfth section, Donne turns to political imagery without relating it to his own condition. In fact, the meditation ends instead with a comparison between fleas and libellous jesters, and a reader might well suppose from this that he has gotten carried away with his own rhetorical endeavors.

The entire section hinges on the significance of what he refers to as vapors—a cloudy term if ever there was one. What makes vapors such a problem for Donne is that they destabilize his sense of agency in illness:

> But when I have said a vapour, if I were asked again what is a vapour, I could not tell, it is so insensible a thing; so near nothing is that that reduces us to nothing. (79)

After acknowledging that vapors are the type of trifling matter that somehow always finds a way to do the most damage, he offers a series of statements that leave in suspension the role that he himself plays in producing his illness. Initially, he seems certain that their origin is internal, as he writes,

> But when ourselves are the well that breathe out this exhalation, the oven that spits out this fiery smoke . . . who can ever, after this, aggravate his sorrow by this circumstance, that it was his neighbour, his familiar friend, his brother that destroyed him, and destroyed him with

a whispering breath, when we ourselves do it to ourselves by the same means, kill ourselves with our own vapours? (77–8)

But he becomes much more indecisive when he turns to the role of the will. Like the vapors themselves, whose constitution is significant precisely because they are insubstantial substance—"so insensible a thing; so near nothing" (79) as he calls them—the will appears curiously present and absent in the progress of his illness.

A closer examination of Donne's rhetoric should make this point clear, since he poses his commentary on the will in conditional language, and in a commentary against those who engages in licentious practices:

> Or if these occasions of this self-destruction had any contribution from our own wills, any assistance from our own intentions, nay, from our own errors, we might divide the rebuke, and chide ourselves as much as them. Fevers upon wilful distempers of drink and surfeits, consumptions upon intemperances and licentiousness, madness upon misplacing or overbending our natural faculties, proceed from ourselves, and so as that ourselves are in the plot, and we are not only passive, but active too, to our own destruction. (78)

The difference between the suffering brought about by riot and excess, and the suffering that Donne endures as a sick patient consists of his level of assurance. Heavy drinkers and philanderers clearly engage in activities that cost them their health and sanity, and anyone can point to their faults as the cause for their misery. By contrast, although an illness such as Donne's resembles the rioters' it does not exactly reveal a specific fault within him:

> But what have I done, either to breed or to breathe these vapours? They tell me it is my melancholy; did I infuse, did I drink in melancholy into myself? It is my thoughtfulness; was I not made to think? It is my study; doth not my calling call for that? (78)

By refuting his supposed critics with a series of questions, rather than with more emphatic assertions, Donne seems to leave the matter open, suggesting genuine confusion on the question of responsibility. Either his study and thought, along with his melancholy, are genuine errors that he should have avoided, or else he must face the unfortunate verdict that the body kills itself in performing its natural functions.

Perhaps it is not surprising that, in the face of such a problem, Donne should revert to paradox as a solution. It is at this point that he invokes the image of suicide—the act of willfully ending one's own life—in order to further distinguish the peculiarities of his own condition:

> There are too many examples of men that have been their own executioners, and that have made hard shift to be so: some have always had poison about them, in a hollow ring upon their finger, and some in their pen that they used to write with; some have beat out their brains at the wall of their prison, and some have eat the fire out of their chimneys; and one is said to have come nearer our case than so, to have strangled himself though his hands were bound, by crushing his throat between his knees. But I do nothing upon myself, and yet am mine own executioner. (78–9)

Many suicides, like the intemperate individuals he compares them to, can be defined as people who are both active and passive in their own demise in the sense that they both commit and suffer the action. At the last moment though, Donne distinguishes his own condition one step further. He finds himself acting by not acting, doing by not doing. If his will plays a role in his own death, it is not the same type of role that a criminal's might play. Instead, it is much closer to a spectral role, where the will performs without quite being present for the performance. Like the substantial/insubstantial vapors that threaten his well being, this will seems to escape traditional methods for figuring responsibility, guilt, and violation. Such terms are only meaningful when they can be identified with a particular individual. By the same token, it seems to escape such verdicts as accident or fate. For Donne, neither description is accurate. The closest he can come to correctly describing his own complicity in his illness is to locate some liminal region that can only be identified by the temporary suspension of contradiction: "But I do nothing upon myself, and yet am mine own executioner." His own responsibility becomes possible only as impossibility.

In short, the dangers that threaten the state, the persistence of rumor and anonymous libelling that seems to circulate without being traceable to a definite origin, parallel the dangers that turn Donne into his own executioner despite all his efforts to do otherwise. This analogy might hold a certain fascination to Donne for its own sake, but also calls attention to it for deeper reasons. For one of the predominant assumptions he holds throughout the text—if not the single assumption that allows him to write about his illness at all—is that the symptoms he experiences have their root in a divine plan. In the thirteenth prayer, he refers to his disease as a type of code, a Boehme-like signature of God:

> These heats, O Lord, which thou hast brought upon this body, are but thy chafing of the wax, that thou mightest seal me to thee: these spots are but the letters in which thou hast written thine own name and conveyed thyself to me. (87–8)

Similarly, at his moment of sleeplessness, he assures himself that, even though he cannot read it on his own, his condition nevertheless is readable:

> Let not this continual watchfulness of mine, this inability to sleep, which thou hast laid upon me, be any disquiet or comfort to me, but rather an argument, that thou wouldst not have me sleep in thy presence. What it may indicate or signify concerning the state of my body, let them consider to whom that consideration belongs. (101)

Even the tolling of the bells, which critics have recognized as a sign of Donne's acceptance of Laudianism, if not all-out Arminianism,[23] hold significance for him only insofar as he can hear God's voice through them:

> O my God, my God, what thunder is not a well-tuned cymbal, what hoarseness, what harshness, is not a clear organ, if thou be pleased to set thy voice to it? And what organ is not well played on if thy hand be upon it? Thy voice, thy hand, is in this sound, and in this one sound I hear this whole concert. (110)

While he uses the funeral bells to assert the universal community of the human species, he also regards them as ciphers for the voice of God rather than mere noise. The entire economy of the text depends upon this assurance.

Alongside the wish for his disease to become meaningful, however, is a deep concern over idolatry, superstition and misinterpretation, such as when he criticizes the Jews, in his nineteenth prayer, for placing too much emphasis on the mere signs and types of God. Likewise, his attack of idolatry in the twenty-third expostulation has its basis in the fear that a fetishization of the instruments would do more to occlude God's glory than disclose it. Such outrages might not have seemed so glaring to him were it not for the fact that they affect even the ostensibly more reliable instruments of God's voice. In the case of the church bells, however, this is exactly what happens. As the physicians lead Donne out of his bed for the first time in weeks, the sound of the bells transforms from divine instruments to mere noisemakers. God's voice becomes absent from them:

> Why doest thou not call me, as thou didst him, *with a loud voice,* since my soul is as dead as his body was? I need thy thunder, O my God; thy music will not serve me. (141)

What is striking about this remark is that it occurs at the very onset of his recovery. Even as Donne begins his return to physical health, the bells lose their power to convey the voice of God directly. While they still remain God's music in one sense, in another, they embody at least one of the characteristics that make rumor a threat, namely semi-meaningful sound that fails to convey the intentions of any specific author. In the absence of a guarantee that the church bells convey the voice of God, then, their ringing takes on self-referential characteristics. To the extent that they represent anything at all, they represent the collective fantasy held by those who attribute more than human significance to them in the first place. And as human devices, which may or may not express God's mystery at all, the differences between them and the disembodied voices of the libelers and scornful jesters that Donne finds so odious begin to collapse. Although he maintains a distinctly hostile position toward those who deliberately plot to overthrow the states that harbor them, the precarious nature of the bells as signifying devices ends up reminding his readers that, even as official proclamations of the church, they cannot escape challenges to their own authenticity.

In one sense, Donne's anxiety about rumor is purely conventional. As traditional literary representations of the allegorical figure Fama make clear, what makes rumor so insidious is not that it spreads falsehood or even nonsense, but rather that it doesn't discriminate. One might recall Virgil's description, for instance:

> She is a terrifying
> Enormous monster with as many feathers
> As she has sleepless eyes beneath each feather
> (amazingly), as many sounding tongues
> And mounts, and raises up as many ears . . . By day
> She sits as sentinel on some steep roof
> Or on high towers, frightening vast cities;
> For she holds fast to falsehood and distortion
> As often as to messages of truth.
> Now she was glad. She filled the ears of all

> With many tales. She sang of what was done
> And what was fiction.[24]

In other words, rumor tears away not at truth but at our own ability to make distinctions between truth and falsehood. By extension though, rumor tears away at the ability to distinguish meaningful statements from nonsense, insofar as we can always partially understand it even when the context it refers to does not in fact exist. Most importantly—and it is this that gives Donne so much cause for alarm—rumor undercuts the ability to distinguish proper political allegiances from usurpation and rebellion, a distinction he seemed determined to make throughout his sermons. To that end the *Devotions* suggests a substantial shift from his highly public representation of the well ordered commonwealth as a healthy body, and his equally public denunciation of sin and rebellion as signs of political disease. When he comes to the question of what causes sickness though—and this holds for both the individual and the state—he very quickly discovers that such normative patterns cannot hold up. The very attempt to define what is normal and what is diseased, much like the attempts to determine what is Orthodox and what is Puritan (as would eventually become the personal obsessions of King Charles and Archbishop Laud), already is based on the flawed assumption that such concepts as healthy, legitimate, or orthodox ever exist, except in the mental trappings of those who try to employ them. Perhaps this had been the idea behind the *Devotions* all along, and it hardly seems an accident that it would appear in a text that deliberately blurs the distinction between private meditation and public performance, as well as the distinction between public discourse and interruption. For by publishing a text that draws attention to its own inopportune dimensions—the disease which "overthrows all" (7), and the text which cannot but feel like a public intervention—Donne ends up drawing attention to the interruptive dimensions that constitute even officially sanctioned discourse. Donne's examination of disease thus enabled him to interrogate the grounds of all authority. More important, though, it enabled him to challenge the legitimacy of state authority even during the very moments when he would end up publicly defending it.

Chapter Five
Robert Burton and the "Language" of Melancholy

"The *Anatomy of Melancholy* is almost unreadable."
—Excerpt from the New York Review of Books Review of
The Anatomy of Melancholy.

"And yet it is the ultimate book, a volume that one can not but return to over and over, constantly."
—Excerpt from the same review.

INTRODUCTION

As massive as it is—it began as an eight hundred page folio and grew larger with each subsequent edition—at the core of Robert Burton's *Anatomy of Melancholy* lies the question: is melancholy dead? By the seventeenth century, this ought to have been the case; melancholy discontent had been so thoroughly overused that it had given way to stereotype. And given the way melancholics had been ridiculed on stage and in poetry, it is doubtful anyone would have wanted to be associated with the condition in any capacity.[1] Meanwhile, as Theodore Spencer has observed, the very people who had popularized melancholy as a mark of status in the first place—the generation of courtiers born around 1560, or so—no longer held power at court (if they were even still alive).[2] The one famous melancholic who does stand out prominently—John Donne, Dean of St. Paul's—repeatedly denounced it throughout his sermons as, at best, a character flaw and at worst the mark of sin. All of these factors must have made the publication of a *magnum opus* on the disease seem a little belated. To that end, the huge corpus that did appear

123

in 1621 reads just as its title suggests: as a post mortem examination.[3] Melancholy must be presumed dead in order for an anatomy to get underway. At the very least, the body of knowledge in question would have to hold still long enough for its anatomist-author to describe the essential components. As readers discover within the first few pages however, Burton begins to give an account of melancholy that does anything but hold still.

On many levels, the *Anatomy* addresses the disjunctive relationship between the living worlds of bodies, diseases, even commonwealths, and their symbolic representations (which invariably fail to capture the very liveliness that makes them subjects of interest in the first place). In the introductory epistle, entitled "Democritus Jr. to the Reader," Burton creates a picture of the world that ends up exposing the entire science of geography as little more than a fool's errand. Thus he writes, seemingly in full earnestness:

> And if thou should either conceive [a mountain] or climb to see, thou shalt soon perceive that all the world is mad, that it is melancholy, dotes; that it is (which Epichthonius Cosmopolites expressed not many years since in a map) made like a fool's head (with that motto, *Caput helleboro dignum* [a head requiring hellebore]; a crazed head, *cavea stultorum,* a fool's paradise, or as Apollonius, a common prison of gulls, cheaters, flatterers, etc., and needs to be reformed. Strabo, in the ninth book of his Geography, compares Greece to the picture of a man, which comparison of his Nic. Gerbelius, in his exposition of Sophianus' map, approves . . . If this allusion hold, 'tis sure a mad head.[4]

In quintessentially baroque fashion, the world has gone mad.[5] And while, in the course of his description, Burton proclaims, "it needs to be reformed," it is hard to imagine what such a reformation would consist of.[6] For if the world was indeed mad, who or what could possibly present itself as the cure?[7] In this fashion, Burton performs at least two separate, if not entirely incommensurate tasks (almost as though the book were written by two separate hands). One seeks an innovative way to address the need for political and religious reform. By diagnosing political troubles and religious controversies as symptoms of melancholy, and by addressing the physical and psychological defects of the nation's governors, Burton suggests that someday, after enough analysis, a cure may be possible. The other acknowledges melancholy as infinite in scope, a condition that has taken over the world in its entirety, and that will not stop expanding even at that point. One sees melancholy as the temporary aberration of an otherwise healthy world; the other more or less equates madness with the world itself.[8]

Part of the reason these two trajectories can coexist, unhappily, in the same text has to do with the sort of world-outlook Burton invokes in the first place. While the above description suggests that madness more or less defines his world picture,[9] it is still crucial to remember that his description is based on the literary device of ekphrasis. The passage is written in the conditional tense. It depends on the author positing an imaginary vantage point located somewhere beyond the terrestrial realm that would allow the reader to sit in Scipio-like fashion, simultaneously seeing and dreaming the planet as a whole. In fact, Burton himself recognizes that the very idea of such a vantage point harbors the fantasy of an all-encompassing gaze from without. To that extent, the world he tries to anatomize must itself be fictionalized as a unified and organic entity—so long as one does not get too caught up in its details.[10]

Specifically, Burton represents his world in pictorial terminology, but only to draw attention to the imaginary aspects that such terminology inevitably depends upon. What else could be expected from a writer who very famously proclaims to have "never travelled but in map or card" (Preface, 18)?[11] This obsession with pictures (more broadly, with categorizing systems and their limits) is apparent in some form or another on nearly every page, from the table of contents, which he fashions in the shape of a diagram, to the end (or rather, the point where the text simply stops, seemingly arbitrarily). But again, while Burton uses melancholy to give a picture of the world, he constantly finds himself so badly bombarded by the details of description that his writing ultimately becomes the pursuit of an impossibility. To the extent that Burton cannot discuss his topic conclusively, the book seems to fail; ironically, it is a happy failure for the very fact that it allows him to pursue his subject indefinitely.

The *Anatomy* is structured as a potentially limitless engagement with a problem that is strangely both frivolous *and* all-important, and Burton is not without his reasons. In particular, he is ambivalent about addressing contemporary religious controversies, a subject that would have been more than a little personal for a member of the church, and which undoubtedly would have put more at stake. Thus in the Preface, Burton defines the anxious relationship between these two topics:

> Not that I prefer it before divinity, which I do acknowledge to be the queen of professions, and to which all the rest are as handmaids, but that in divinity I say no such great need. For had I written positively, there be so many books in that kind, so many commentators, treatises, pamphlets, expositions, sermons, that whole teams of oxen cannot draw

them . . . But I have been ever as desirous to suppress my labours in this kind, as others have been to press and publish theirs. To have written in controversy had been to cut off an hydra's head, *lis litem generat,* one [dispute] begets another, so many duplications, triplications, and swarms of questions *in sacro bello hoc quod stili mucrone agitur* [in this sacred war which is waged with the pen], that having once begun, I should never make an end. (Preface, 35)

And indeed had he wanted to write about religious matters during the 1620s, when fears of both Catholics and Puritan uprisings occupied the attention of most divines, he would have had more than enough opportunity. This ambivalence persists throughout the entire book: as he suggests, one of the reasons he writes about melancholy is to avoid writing about religious disputes; such furtiveness notwithstanding, he is at his most innovative (and most concerned with revisions in subsequent editions) in the final subsection, concerning religious melancholy. If there is a single section other than the Prefatory epistle that is read in isolation, it is the section on religious melancholy, and undoubtedly this section caught the interests of readers during the 1650s, when the *Anatomy* went through two reprints. And yet for Burton, it is only a subspecies of a more common (and presumably less controversial) type, namely love-melancholy. If the book is peculiar stylistically, it puts him at a certain advantage concerning more controversial topics; by writing about melancholy, he can simultaneously engage in and refrain from more pressing matters.

These conflicted objectives are reflected in the somewhat disparate nature of his critical reception. Roughly, critics have tended to view the *Anatomy* in one of two ways.[12] The book is, on one level, a political intervention that simultaneously advocates radical social reform and cautiously defends the establishment.[13] Alternately, it functions more or less as a work of literature. These positions have been refined and significantly reshaped in the wake of both new-historicist and reader-response approaches to the text. Thus critics who read the *Anatomy* as social intervention have shifted attention away from its utopian sections and toward the sections concerning religious melancholy.[14] In doing so they read the *Anatomy* as the inaugurator of a wide-scale cultural critique of religious enthusiasm, the results of which included an effective silencing of more radical religious sects during the Protectorate and Restoration alike.[15] During this period, the relation between melancholy and prophetic faculties underwent a sudden and dramatic shift—if adherents to the Ficino circle had popularized the notion that melancholy, under the right circumstances, endowed the individual with poetic and prophetic talents, writers who participated in the invectives against religious enthusiasm became more inclined to treat it as the symptom of a disease that left its victims lost in their private delusions. Burton's name thus stands at the forefront of a genealogy that continues with Henry More and Meric Casaubon, and ends with Swift's invectives against the Puritans (although the connection between Burton and these subsequent writers is by no means as obvious as such critics contend).[16]

By contrast, critics who read the *Anatomy* as literature, largely building on Stanley Fish's influential reading from *Self-Consuming Artifacts*, Burton's prose method deliberately produces the tools for its own undoing.[17] Recognizing the similarities between the *Anatomy* and the encyclopedic method, many have claimed that Burton launched an all-out assault on the Renaissance textual tradition of *compilatio*. The notion that a writer could say something definitive about a topic simply by gathering together what others had previously said apparently proved so odious that he undertook his project ironically to demonstrate its futility.[18] For others, Burton's persona, in a demonstration of the way melancholy destabilizes the integrity of the speaking subject, continuously undercuts its own statements, making one promise only to both fulfill and deny it at once, making a judgment only to both uphold and violate it a few pages later. More than a mere hermeneutics of suspicion, the alert reader leads to a full-scale hermeneutics of bewilderment. Given these conditions, the *Anatomy* takes on political implications entirely unrelated to the goal of marginalizing or pathologizing the more radical segments of the population. Instead, Burton's project demonstrates that the act of writing always finds itself at odds with the phenomena it wants to describe, that no human discourse can ever hope to be a discourse of mastery, and that the ultimate end of writing is more writing.

On their own, neither stylistic approaches to Burton's writing technique nor examinations of the *Anatomy*'s cultural significance in the field of psychiatric oppression seem to do justice to the book as a whole. As it turns out though, these various approaches may not be as incompatible as they have been characterized to this point. For Burton, the notion that discourse on melancholy essentially amounted to an infinite dilation, and the recognition that political and religious institutions stood in dire need of reform—with due emphasis on the cognate word *form*—do in fact converge. The point of convergence becomes clearer when we examine the opening epistle, "Democritus Jr. to the Reader," in conjunction with the final section, "On Religious Melancholy." These two sections have far more resemblance than critics hitherto have recognized. For Burton's characterization of religious melancholy not only repeats the concerns he raises in the introduction, but often re-invokes the same images and phrases. As these parallels suggest, his treatment of religious melancholy at the end of the book—and more importantly, his inability to cure it—has quite a lot to do with the problems he encounters when he tries to describe a utopian commonwealth in the Preface.

Burton refers to this utopian society as "poetical," a word which appears only once in the entire *Anatomy*, but which performs a crucial task for him all the same. At first glance, it seems to resolve the author's deep ambivalence over the possibility of political reform. As Ruth Fox argues, a bit pessimistically,

> The Preface suggests that the reformation is possible only poetically, not really, and this view of the superstitious state of men making uncivilized empires by ignorance out of unlawful laws confirms the essential barbarity of a universe not annexed to its Creator by love, but formed into perverse imitations of the community of God and men.[19]

If melancholy has become too pervasive throughout the real world for anyone to reverse its effects, at the very least he could imagine a space within language itself that could model a society that escaped it. Granted, his project contains a self-contradictory element, for among the things he found to have been corrupted by melancholy, language itself was among the worst to suffer—thus the prospect of using language to escape the effects of melancholy seems highly improbable. Just as important, by invoking the term "poetical," Burton indulges in the Orphic fantasies that we have seen in previous chapters. In devising his so-called "New Atlantis," explicitly as a "poetical" commonwealth, Burton endeavors to portray his ideal society at a standstill, impervious to the onslaughts of time and corruption.[20] In the end though, this utopia is compromised by the question of its own legitimacy. If Burton is troubled by his inability to represent melancholy in sufficiently stable terminology, he is positively confounded by the fact that, in actual societies, objects are constantly on the move. As Burton demonstrates throughout, the traditional languages of political description cannot sufficiently account for this movement. As a corollary, there can be no utopia without usurpation. As a political institution, its authority is founded entirely on force. He readily admits his willingness to tyrannize over its inhabitants, were any to actually dwell within its boundaries. This fact may ultimately explain why he devises a utopian solution in the introduction, but must revert to a conservative position in the final one, namely to defend the Laudian church against its critics despite his tacit recognition that its

Robert Burton and the "Language" of Melancholy 129

authority was in fact wide open to dispute. What seems at first to be a reversal turns out to be a reiteration of the same principle in a new context—in both sections, Burton recognizes that the basis for authority ultimately rests on a false claim. As will become apparent in the sections that follow, if no political system emerges which does not simultaneously raise questions about its own legitimacy, this is because no political system ever escapes a conception of the poetic that is not itself fundamentally compromised regarding the nature of its own authority.

"NO NEWS HERE": ON THE EPISTLE TO THE READER

Before proceeding further, it might be useful to reconsider a question that must, by this point, seem incredibly naïve: what does Burton write the *Anatomy* for? Or rather, what exactly does he want to accomplish? Part of what makes the question at once so easy and so impossible, is that the text itself seems to provide its own answer, and that answer seems to be: not much.[21] We observe this when, under the guise of his persona Democritus Jr., he renders the following account: "I can allege more than one. I write of melancholy, by being busy to avoid melancholy" (Preface, 20). This would be astonishing enough on its own, but the narrator takes it one step further: it stands out in contrast to what he further claims had been the motive for his antecedent and namesake, Democritus, when he himself undertook a study of melancholy. For this original figure, the one whose book had provided the model for the *Anatomy* itself, the reason for writing on melancholy had been, "to the intent he might better cure it in himself, and by his writings and observations teach others how to prevent and avoid it" (Preface, 20). In other words, there had been little doubt that the relation between writing and knowledge, writing and technical ability (in this case, the ability to cure a disease), or writing and instruction is stable enough to make a book about melancholy seem a worthwhile endeavor. His book had actually provided a practical service; if only it hadn't been lost to oblivion, it might still do so. By contrast, while Democritus Jr. does imagine himself picking up where his namesake Democritus had left off—indeed, to re-create the now missing treatise—he substitutes the notion that writing produces knowledge with the notion that writing is a good form of busy-ness. As he expounds upon his own rationale, it becomes clear that idleness alone is the great bogey that he worries about the most:

> There is no greater cause of melancholy than idleness, "no better cure than business," as Rhasis holds: and howbeit *stultis labor est ineptiarum,*

> to be busy in toys is to small purpose, yet hear that divine Seneca, better *aliud agere quam nihil,* better do to no end than nothing. I writ therefore, and busied myself in this playing labour, *otiosaque diligentia ut vitarem torporem feriandi* [to escape the ennui of idleness by a leisurely kind of employment. (Preface, 20–1)[22]

For a moment, we may even suspect that, although writing afforded Burton great pleasure, he may just as well have found an equally pleasing alternative in backgammon, as David Hume would claim to do in response to his own melancholy several decades later.[23]

Under this second model, writing about melancholy does not necessarily mean he will make sense of melancholy, let alone find the cure for it. These reservations in turn inform his description of his own literary style. It is a defensive description, as far as such things go, although he defends himself on the grounds that most writing fails to achieve any practical results anyway. Thus he compares his book with all the bad writing his contemporaries have published:

> 'Tis most true, *tenet insanible multos scribendi cacoethes,* and "there is no end of writing of books," as the wise man found of old, in this scribbling age especially, wherein "the number of books is without number" (as a worthy man saith), "presses be oppressed," and out of an itching humour that every man hath to show himself, desirous of fame and honour (*scribimus indocti doctique* [we all write, learned and ignorant alike]), he will write no matter what, and scrape together it boots not whence. (Preface, 22)

This appears to be, at first, a standard complaint against verbiage; but the purpose of the standard device usually was to establish a context in which a writer could assert that his own contribution would hopefully put an end to the supposed cacophony. For Burton, the image of the "paper-kingdom" is invoked precisely in order to situate his own work squarely within it, as he concedes that his own text adheres to every bad habit it points out:

> How many excellent physicians have written just volumes and elaborate tracts of this subject! No news here; that which I have is stolen from others, *Dicitque mihi mea pagina, fur es* [my page cries out to me, You are a thief]. If that severe doom of Synesius be true, "It is a greater offence to steal dead men's labours then their clothes," what shall become of most writers? I hold up my hand at the bar among others,

and am guilty of felony in this kind, *habes confitentem reum* [the defendant pleads guilty], I am content to be pressed with the rest" (Preface, 22).

Again, this appears to be a classical trope of affected modesty—at any rate, it would be were it not so flamboyantly self-deprecating.[24] In fact, so much does he flaunt his lack of originality, so much does he compare his own techniques to the worst faults of others, that a reader might wonder if he does not perhaps envy them a little.[25] He effectively complains, "If everybody else gets to write such lousy books merely to sustain an entirely parasitical print industry and even make a profit at it, why should I be expected to write something useful, let alone a book that would put an end to the chatter that occurs everywhere from the booksellers' booths at St. Paul's to the public lavatory?"[26] If writing is itself marked by excessiveness, insofar as the various combinations, re-combinations, and redeployments can lead to novel statements, none of which say anything genuinely new, Burton is hardly troubled by it. Quite the contrary, it seems to be the condition that makes his project readable in the first place.[27] Again, the effects are two-sided. He complains about the excess in verbiage, knowing that the sheer volume of writing becomes a hindrance to good communication. He quotes other writers extensively, knowing full well that to do so is to wrench the written statement out of its original context and potentially distort its original meaning.[28] If he invokes a stylistic rule, such as "much certainty in fewer words," it seems only to let his readers know that he flouts it deliberately. Indeed, any reader can be forgiven for suspecting that the purpose of the *Anatomy* is to produce madness rather than cure it.

Ultimately, Burton makes this point himself when he declares that melancholy and language amount to much the same thing. Thus in Book I, he identifies the symptoms of melancholy with the written word itself:

> Who can sufficiently speak of these symptoms, or prescribe rules to comprehend them? as Echo to the painter in Ausonius, Vane, quid affectus, etc., Foolish fellow, what wilt? if you must needs paint me, paint me a voice, *et similem si vis pingere, pinge sonum;* if you will describe melancholy, describe a phantastical conceit, a corrupt imagination, vain thoughts and different, which who can do? The four-and-twenty letters make no more variety of words in divers languages than melancholy conceits produce diversity of symptoms in several persons. They are irregular, obscure, various, so infinite, Proteus himself is not so diverse; you may as well make the moon a new coat as a true character

of a melancholy man; as soon find the motion of a bird in the air as the heart of man, a melancholy man. (I.3.2.1, 408)

On one level, the above passage reads as though it could have been culled from a chapter on hyperbole in perhaps any textbook concerning rhetorical tropes and figures. Because it is written language itself that serves as the image of hyperbolic excess, however—and in a text where writing has already demonstrated a clear tendency to overtake the author's life altogether—something more seems to be at work. Namely, to write about melancholy is not to convey an idea about melancholy (an idea that could somehow be separated from the act of writing); rather, writing produces it. There may be as many symptoms as there are words and phrases in any language, along with the implication that every combination of letters somehow discloses another symptom of melancholy, even if it is not certain how. As long as the possibility of writing remains, so too does melancholy unfold in its symptoms and manifestations; and as long as writing falls short of saying everything, of completing itself, so too does melancholy elude full description. In that sense, and as the *Anatomy* demonstrates through its continual rewritings (which still occur even after the author's demise, fittingly enough) to write on melancholy is to be unable to exhaust the subject. To that end we must wonder in just what sense the *Anatomy* hopes to anatomize.[29]

This is not simply a crisis in language; it raises serious misgivings concerning the effectiveness of political commentary. As is well known, what is most striking about Burton is his description of melancholy as a social disease, rather than an individual one. Melancholy does not affect the body alone, but rather the entire world:

> Examine the rest in like sort, and you shall find that kingdoms and provinces are melancholy, cities and families, all creatures, vegetal, sensible, and rational, that all sorts, sects, ages, conditions, are out of tune, as in Cebes' Table, *omnes errorem bibunt,* before they come into the world, they are intoxicated by error's cup, from the highest to the lowest have need of physic, and those particular actions in Seneca, where father and son prove one another mad, may be general; Porcius Latro shall plead against us all. For indeed who is not a fool, melancholy, mad? *Qui nil molitur inepte,* who is not brain-sick? Folly, melancholy, madness, are but one disease, delirium is a common name to all. (Preface, 39)

Whereas previous medical books had focused on the physiognomy of the patient, Burton simply extends the physiognomy to describe everything else as well. Social conditions are thus the equivalent to symptoms of an illness. Moreover, by recasting melancholy as a public problem—a complete contrast from the melancholic who craves solitude and retreat—he lets on that to write about melancholy is to engage in a critique of these institutions. Put briefly, society needs to be cured.

Burton's extensive catalogue of social maladies thus has its counterpart in what Robert Appelbaum refers to as utopian experimentalism, inasmuch as he suggests that a full remedy does indeed exist.[30] To the extent that Burton can be considered a political reformer, as he sometimes hints that he wishes to be understood, his survey of socio-political affairs reads much like a predecessor to the sort of ideological criticism that regards the conditions of the world as the effects of fundamental forces. Ill kingdoms are the effects of the failures of the people who rule it:

> Kingdoms, provinces, and politic bodies are likewise sensible and subject to this disease, as Boterus in his Politics had proved at large . . . But whereas you shall see many discontents, common grievances, complaints, poverty, barbarism, beggary, plagues, wars, rebellions, seditions, mutinies, contentions, idleness, riot, epicurism, the land lie untilled, waste, full of bogs, fens, deserts, etc., cities decayed, base and poor towns, villages depopulated, the people squalid, ugly, uncivil; that kingdom, that country, must needs be discontent, melancholy, hath a sick body, and had need to be reformed. (Preface, 79–80)

For Burton the would-be reformer, political troubles are treated according to a model of normal and pathological, which, in itself, seems grounded in a series of deep-seated presuppositions about the nature of healthy bodies. Specifically, he holds on to the premise that stable political entities do exist; moreover, they exist as a rule, not as the exception, since they can account for both healthy and diseased commonwealths alike:[31]

> Where they be generally riotous and contentious, where there be many discords, many laws, many lawsuits, many lawyers, and many physicians, it is a manifest sign of a distempered, melancholy state, as Plato long since maintained: for where such kind of men swarm, they will make more work for themselves, and that body politic diseased, which was otherwise sound. (Preface, 83)

It is in the name of this image of the melancholy "state"—which suggests, at once, a stable political entity and a clear moment in time—that Burton criticizes everything from idleness at court to the Jack Cade uprising. In that sense, political reform corresponds to the medicines that cure people in a corporeal sense; if a public physician could rightly cure the nation on this level, certainly other reforms would be sure to follow.

So long as Burton writes of political problems in the most general terms, he is at his most confident; the strategy ultimately fails him when he turns to address the current problems of his own nation. For while writing in abstractions Burton can maintain the illusion of a relatively stable state; by switching to domestic troubles, he cannot avoid noticing that such stability is an illusion of writing. Thus in the Preface he embarks on a survey of England's public troubles. It runs only twelve paragraphs, during the course of which his outlook very quickly changes from relative optimism to complete discouragement. (It is so dramatic that it takes a moment to remember he is still writing about the same England.) The change in tone is reflected primarily in the figurative language he uses to represent England's overall condition. When he initially calls upon the island to serve as "a sufficient witness, that in a short time, by that prudent policy of the Romans, [it] was brought from barbarism" (Preface, 86), he compares the foundation and corruption of kingdoms with good horticulture. Thus he describes pre-Roman England "They were once as uncivil as they in Virginia, yet by planting of colonies and good laws, they became, from barbarous outlaws to be full of rich and populous cities, as now they are, and most flourishing kingdoms" (Preface, 86). And from the outset, it would seem, Burton shares the general opinion of the nation, namely that "we have besides many particular blessings, which our neighbors want" (Preface, 87). Even when he admits that problems afflict the nation, he still makes recourse to floral imagery: "Yet amongst many roses some thistles grow, some bad weeds and enormities, which much disturb the peace of this body politic, eclipse the honour and glory of it, fit to be rooted out, and with all speed to be reformed" (Preface, 87–8). As such imagery suggests, Burton sees flourishing governments as organic institutions, in which all parts are conjoined in a continuous relation with one another and no part can survive on its own. Just as important, his imagery is teleological; to the extent that he allows for historical development, he implies that good governments move continuously toward the fulfillment of their respective destiny. Like flowers, some commonwealths may live past their prime, but such after all is the nature of both. Some weeds may have crept in, but weeds can always be removed. While a bit of cleaning may be necessary, in most respects it is still a garden, with a proper destination.

It is not until he faces the difficult task of producing an actual policy that he abandons these floral images. In fact, he abandons the notion of natural organic processes altogether, substituting for it a pessimistic fantasy of the supernatural hero:

> We have good laws, I deny not, to rectify such enormities, and so in all other countries, but it seems not always to good purpose. We had need of some general visitor in our age, that should reform what is amiss; a just army of Rosy-cross men, for they will amend all matters (they say), religion, policy, manners, with arts, sciences, etc.; another Attila, Tamerlane, Hercules." (Preface, 96)

Curiously, none of Burton's exemplary figures are English; there is no Arthur, no St. George. Instead, the heroic figure, if he comes at all, must come from somewhere else—a suspicion reinforced by the ambiguous term "general visitor." Whether he hopes for an actual invasion from another country (unlikely) or a visitation of a strictly theoretical sort (more probable), it is clear that the source of reform will not come from anything inherent to the commonwealth itself. If true reform ever occurs, it will occur as a sudden rupture. Someone, or something, will have to usurp the normal course of events and interrupt the current sequence of time. Otherwise, the process of decay will likely continue unabated.

What separates these two passages, and indeed what seems to cause the shift from an optimistic view of reform as gardening to reform as waiting for messianic salvation, is a brief digression on commerce. More important, it is a particular aspect of commerce that destabilizes the market value of commodities, namely international trade.[32] Burton is fully aware that England lacks an industry of its own. He refers to the failed cloth-dressing and dying ventures as signs of the nation's economic troubles. Similarly, he is acutely aware of the disadvantages that the French mercantilist system had begun to impose upon England's economic health, as he makes clear:

> We send our best commodities beyond the seas, which they make good use of to their necessities, set themselves a-work about, and severally improve, sending the same to us back at dear rates, or else make toys and baubles of the tails of them, which they sell to us again, at as great a reckoning as the whole. (Preface, 91–2)

In his esteem, even a public works project that served no other purpose than to give people something to occupy themselves would be an improvement. He recalls the example of ancient Egypt, which had an advantage over present conditions despite the overall uselessness of its civic projects:

> And rather than they should be idle, as those Egyptian Pharaohs, Moeris, and Sesostris did, to task their subjects to build unnecessary pyramids, obelisks, labyrinths, channels, lakes, gigantic works all, to divert them from rebellion, riot, drunkenness, *quo scilicet alantur et ne vagando laborare desuescant* [that they might support themselves and not become vagrants and idlers]. (Preface, 93)

The point here is not to decide whether his assessments of England's economic conditions were accurate, or even whether they were enough to warrant the tone of resignation he adopts throughout the passage.[33] More important is that the very idea of commerce interferes with the teleological model he had hitherto employed for his political discourse. As David Hawkes has recently reminded us, if a government can be said to have a moment of constitution, a period of growth and decline, and a standard of health, the commercial activity that sustains it seems to operate autonomously, and without the same kind of trajectory.[34] Among other things, commerce is ongoing, and it does not necessarily develop along predictable lines. Likewise, if the nation proves itself impervious to reform, it is because political institutions attempt to govern activities that operate according to entirely separate principles. Burton may recognize that the inability to account for this disjunctive relation between political and economic activity may be, as a failure, the "common consent of all geographers, historians, politicians" (Preface, 87). Nevertheless his early commitment to a teleological portrait of commonwealths leaves him curiously incapable of addressing the problems of trade insofar as they correspond to a model of perpetual circulation of goods. Merely to acknowledge it is to concede that "only a god—or at least a very strong hero—can save us now."

Still, while Burton recognized that the task of defining coherent political structures—whether that coherence be iconic or teleological—are compromised by the continual emergence of particularities that expose such coherence as idle fantasy, he does not give up on his dreams of political reform. On the contrary, he is at his most utopian at precisely the moment where his faith in reform meets its greatest challenge. What he identifies as utopian might thus be understood as the attempt to resolve the contradictions that have, to this point, undermined his earlier attempts to define political organizations in terms of health and pathology. Significantly, it is here that he invokes the "poetical," a term which allows him to retain his passion for reform:

> Because, therefore, it is a thing so difficult, impossible, and far beyond Hercules' labours to be performed; let them be rude, stupid, ignorant,

> incult, *lapis super lapidem sedeat* [let stone sit on stone] . . . I will yet, to satisfy and please myself, make an utopia of mine own, a New Atlantis, a poetical commonwealth of mine own, in which I will freely domineer, build cities, make laws, statutes, as I list myself. (Preface, 97)

While critics have interpreted Burton's excursus on the utopian commonwealth as a further attempt at practical reform, in fact his understanding of the ideal hinges on the status he assigns to poetic language and, by implication, the concept of *poiesis* that it refers to.

For Burton, to devise an effective commonwealth is to invoke one's creative energies, or to fashion public affairs into a suitable arrangement. The word "poetical" is not in the least to be taken lightly; nor does he want simply to invent merely imaginary solutions to social crises. All the same, when he appeals to it, he quickly runs into familiar problems. If poetry emerges as a possible solution, it has to do with more than the mere notion of artistic license that he cites from the Horation *Ars Poetica*, "*Pictoribus atque poetis etc.*" Poetry offers the allure of a coherent pictorial arrangement; in the end, its counterpart is the image of the world as Pasquil's madcap he has already shown his readers.[35] From the location of its cities (which he would arrange geometrically), to the assignment of industrial activities, to the regulation of family conduct, or the economic sphere in the proper sense of the term, everything is well disposed. To that extent his utopian project is unabashedly totalitarian in outlook, leaving the suggestion that only the complete organization of every last aspect of human conduct under a single corporate unity could possibly cure the commonwealth of its melancholy.

Meanwhile, the utopian commonwealth also is remarkably well proportioned, as its harmony is at least in part a matter of arrangement. Much like More's utopia before him, the landscape is arranged along regular intervals, and only briefly does Burton let on that such a landscape would in fact be a mathematical impossibility:

> It shall be divided into twelve or thirteen provinces, and those by hills, rivers, roadways, or some more eminent limits exactly bounded. Each province shall have a metropolis, which shall be so placed as a centre almost in a circumference, and the rest at equal distances. (Preface, 98)

In short, the utopian commonwealth is the counterpart, perhaps the mirror image of the melancholy world insofar as that world can be arranged according to a rule of madness. His insistence that madness is all encompassing ultimately leaves him without a position from which he can make a clean break. His own imaginative faculties lead him more or less to the very place from which he originally started out.

Such being the case, the most telling feature about his utopia is that it concludes with a reference to Hercules that bears a striking resemblance to the resignation that gave rise to his need for a utopian solution in the first place. After descending from cities to families to types of individuals, and after shifting from an account of his own objectives as the imagined ruler of his kingdom to the kind of relentless pile-up of examples and anecdotes for which he is renowned, Burton finally concludes:

> To insist in all particulars were an Herculean task . . . it would ask an expert Vesalius to anatomize every member. Shall I say Jupiter himself, Apollo, Mars, etc. doted? and monster-conquering Hercules, that subdues the world and helped others, could not relieve himself in this, but mad he was at last. (Preface, 116–7)

The conditions that made a utopian section so desirable, if not necessary, in the first place, paradoxically become the same conditions that render it impossible. The attempt at proper disposition becomes a vicious circle in the poetic register as much as it does in any other, insofar as the principle of arrangement gives rise to more particularities than any general concept seems capable of handling. If poetic discourse does anything, then, it holds the contradiction together in a way that allows Burton to maintain both positions at once. While the turn to a poetical commonwealth ultimately returns to the same madness that had predicated it, nevertheless it offers the promise of organization and the component ability to continue writing of the world in terms of form, thereby giving him at least the possibility of coming to understand it.

"I HAVE NO PATERNE TO FOLOW": ON RELIGIOUS MELANCHOLY

In many ways, the *Anatomy* is asymmetrical. While it begins with an introduction, it seems to break off without much of a conclusion, ending instead on a subsection that details an allegedly minor variation of the disease, namely religious melancholy. As Burton claims, it is not a subject writers have addressed in the past; hence the tentative nature of the argument, for at last the author is exploring uncharted territory. In fact, the author overstates his case in several ways. He is hardly the first person to discover a connection between religion and melancholy, or to note that religious melancholy shares many common features with love melancholy. (It is difficult to imagine how Petrarch's *Rime* would have made the transition from Laura to the Virgin if these two versions of melancholy were not, in some way, obvious.) Throughout the section, his general purpose is to point out the despair and fanaticism of Catholics and Puritans respectively, and explicitly in defense of the reformed English church. And while he claims not to have a model or pattern to follow, in fact the section repeats many of the maneuvers he had used in "Democritus Jr. to the Reader." In both sections, the author recognizes widespread public illness while conceding, after making some gestures toward reform, that one has to make peace with tyranny.

The difference between the two sections lies primarily in the way he comes to grips with this fact. While, in the Preface, Burton had made recourse to the "poetical" in order to hold together (if not resolve) otherwise antithetical viewpoints—melancholy as the symptom of a commonwealth in disorder, and thus suitable for reform, versus melancholy as the perpetual dilation of its own symptoms—he offers no such hope in the final pages. Indeed, as Ruth Fox points out, whatever resolutions he offers in the final section are deeply unsatisfying. Commenting on the prevalence of superstition, one of the commonest causes of madness named in the section, Fox writes:

> The cure for superstition is no cure at all. With this topic, the *Anatomy* has reached its lowest ebb. The image of the universe is a fearfully tangled one: Love and hate, legalism and tyranny, mad men and mad empires, religion and superstition, gods and men are heaped together in monstrous disorder that "can never be remedied." Burton's effort to cure is lame and he knows it.[36]

Thus, while many themes and images found in the preface to recur in the final section, giving Burton's discussion of religious melancholy the feel of a recapitulation, of sorts, it is repetition with a difference.

A short list of examples shows just how this works. In the Preface, Democritus Jr. coyly suggests building his New Atlantis at the hitherto undiscovered *Terra Australis Incognita*. Moreover, he recommends it precisely because it was a charmed place, a place full of hope. In the final section it reappears as yet one more territory among a long list of nations that have yet to see the true light of religion set in (III.4.1.1, 322). Where Democritus Jr. had called his fictional utopia a New Atlantis, in anticipation of Bacon's famous treatise and seemingly with the same enthusiastic eye toward scientific progress as the Bacon's, in the final section, when he turns to the problem of religious enthusiasm, scientific progress gives way to the most brutal form of physic. For the first and only time in the entire text, the author recommends hospitalization at Bedlam (III.4.2.1, 379). And while Democritus Jr. had actually regarded tyranny optimistically—at any rate, as optimistically as anyone can—in the final section it is something the Anglican divine must accept only when he admits that England's theological problems are incurable. Indeed, it is in this final section where the author starts to lose control over his own literary persona, as he watches it give way to its conventional opposite: "*Fleat Heraclitus an rideat Democritus?* in attempting to speak of these symptoms, shall I laugh with Democritus, or weep with Heraclitus?" (III.4.1.3, 346). Is there any clearer a sign that religious melancholy disrupts whatever sense of authorial control he may have had when he began his composition?

As had been the case in earlier parts of the *Anatomy*, the survey of religious melancholy is shaped by two demands. On the one hand, Burton is compelled to write of it precisely because it gives way to a vast expanse marked by radical instability. Throughout the section, Burton characterizes religious disorder as a body of water. Thus he promises:

> Give me but a little leave, and I will set before your eyes in brief a stupend, vast, infinite ocean of incredible madness and folly: a sea full of shelves and rocks, sands, gulfs, euripes and contrary tides, full of fearful monsters, uncouth shapes, roaring waves, tempests, and siren calms, halycionian seas, unspeakable misery, such comedies and tragedies, such absurd and ridiculous, feral and lamentable fits, that I know not whether they are more to be pitied or derided, or may be believed, but that we daily see the same still practiced in our days, fresh examples, *nova novitia*, fresh objects of misery and madness in this kind that are still represented unto us, abroad, at home, in the midst of us, in our bosoms.[37] (III.4.1.1, 313)

The choice of imagery is no accident. It bears the trace of Heraclitus (to say nothing of Orpheus)—after all, it was the weeping philosopher who had pointed out that we cannot step twice into the same body of water. By turning to water imagery in order to characterize chaos in this final section, not only does Burton draw attention to the temporal nature of religious practices, he continues to shift his allegiance from the laughing philosopher toward the weeping one.

Nevertheless, the demands of writing require a different approach, one that at least makes an effort to gain some measure of systematic comprehension. Thus, while he would appear to want it otherwise, he resigns himself to a certain organization:

> The parties affected are innumerable almost, and scattered over the face of the earth, far and near, and so have been in all precedent ages, from the beginning of the world to these times, of all sorts and conditions. For method's sake I will reduce them to a twofold division, according to those two extremes of excess and defect, impiety and superstition, idolatry and atheism. (III.4.1.1, 318–9)

Burton admits he is being reductive; it is difficult to imagine an alternative approach. Instead he finds himself in a contradictory position. To represent religious melancholy in its genuine shape would be to represent chaos so chaotically, that he would not be able to speak of it at all. Conversely, to make sense of the picture is to distort it to such a degree that he can only fail to do justice to it.

At first, Burton uses the terms superstition and idolatry to distinguish false religious practices from what he calls "this true love and worship of God" (III.4.1.1, 318).[38] What he finds objectionable about false religion is its mimetic character:

> Which is religion's ape, religion's bastard, religion's shadow, false glass. For where God hath a temple, the devil will have a chapel; where God hath sacrifices, the devil will have his oblation: where God hath ceremonies, the devil will plant superstition. (III.4.1.1, 321)

What is most immediately striking about this litany is how little it explains. Or if, after all, it does, what it explains is not that true religious practices are incredibly easy to mimic, but that they are so easy to mimic precisely because they are about ceremonious imitations to begin with. There is little about the true religious ceremonies Burton alludes to that is not potentially subject to the condition that Fox explains as follows: "Through superstition's ignorance and the fear that accompanies it, man creates gods out of men and recreates God in his own image."[39]

As a result, when Burton actually does set out to give a portrait of true religion he qualifies it extensively every step of the way. While he sets up his survey of religious practices in innocent enough terms, then,

> For as Zanchius well distinguished, and all the world knows, religion is twofold, true or false (III.4.1.1, 320)

he invokes the distinction only to pass it over with little commentary. Indeed, in the few lines that he does devote to true religion, he appears more interested in its effects than in what it actually consists of:

> Where the true God is truly worshipped, is the way to heaven, the mother of virtues, love, fear, devotion, obedience, knowledge, etc. It rears the dejected soul of man, and amidst so many cares, miseries, persecutions, which this world affords, it is a sole ease, an unspeakable comfort, a sweet reposal (III.4.1.1, 320)

And when he attempts to locate people who do follow acceptable practices, he resorts to methods of calculation that seem predestined to include the fewest possible number:

> At this present, *quota pars!* how small a part is truly religious! How little in respect! Divide the world into six parts, and one, or not so much is Christians . . . That which remains is the Western Church with us in Europe, but so eclipsed with several schisms, heresies and superstitions, that one knows not where to find it. (III.4.1.1, 322–3)

Whether he meant to be taken at his word, or whether he wanted desperately to steer clear of a politically sensitive subject is difficult to say.[40] Meanwhile, concerning what exactly such true religion consists of, meanwhile, he is conspicuously silent.

Moreover, what little he does have to say in favor of true religious worship is highly qualified. Burton accepts Calvinists (and perhaps their Lutheran counterparts) insofar as they avoid the greater infractions of more radical protestants, say, Brownists, Anabaptists or Catholics. That said, he recognizes that even Calvinists and Lutherans contribute as much to civil unrest as they do to Church reform:

> The remnant are Calvinists, Lutherans, in Germany equally mixed; any yet the emperor himself, dukes of Lorraine, Bavaria, and the princes electors, are most part professed papists. And though some part of France and Ireland, Great Britain, half the cantons in Switzerland, and the Low Countries be Calvinists, more defecate than the rest, yet at odds amongst themselves, not free from superstition. (III.4.1.1, 324)

John Stachniewski attributes to Burton the occasional insight that his fellow Anglican divines may harbor the same tendencies to error as their enemies, and undoubtedly this passage documents that sort of skepticism.[41] It is worth emphasizing, however, that Burton's assessment of Calvinism is motivated by a sense of superstition as an all-powerful force that manifests itself even in cases where people seem most committed to warding it off. The most one can hope for is a temporary defense against its perpetual pressures, an act he compares to staving off a flood: "As a dam of water stopped in one place breaks out into another, so doth superstition" (III.4.1.1, 324). What counts as true religious practice turns out to be an ongoing effort to impose order on a torrent of behavior whose very nature, it seems, is antithetical to the principles of organization.

The task does not become any easier when, later in the section, he attempts to provide a history of the true church, with due attention to the Reformation. While he ostensibly desires to trace a real development, Burton ends up denouncing contemporary religious conduct as a radically mimetic affair. Thus he begins with a praise of Martin Luther which is sincere enough, but which quickly runs into problems. The figures of rivalry and emulation that give shape to the passage suggests that what actually occurred during the early 1500s had been a seductive imitation of true reform, but an imitation nonetheless. Thus it was beset with all the dangers that make seductive imitations so hateful for some in the first place:

> In the meantime, the true Church, as wine and water mixed, lay hid and obscure to speak of, till Luther's time, who began upon a sudden to defecate, and as another sun to drive away those foggy mists of superstition, to restore it to that purity of the primitive Church. (III.4.1.3, 369)

Regardless of whatever respect and admiration Burton may have had for Luther, he still remains attuned to the element of mimetic rivalry that had gone into his reformist efforts. As "another sun," he may indeed stave off what is, yet once again, characterized by its protean essence, namely "wine and water mixed," and the "foggy mists of superstition"; but this does not preclude the fact that as another sun he establishes his ethics on competitive grounds. In fact, by characterizing Luther as another sun, Burton goes so far as to suggest that what Luther wanted to emulate was precisely another *image* of God's glory (even if that image was the source of light), rather than the glory itself. Even at his best moments he wound up succumbing to an act of idolatry.

More than an unfortunate accident, this moment of emulation is precisely what made Luther's reforms so dangerous in the end. For in the act of imitation, so close to the thing it imitates that we have trouble telling one from the other, there emerges a peculiar side effect. A zealous and horrifying dynamic of iconoclasm develops out of Luther's most sincere (and undoubtedly well-meant) efforts to restore the Church to its proper mission. It is iconoclasm that remains blind to its own adherence to the power of imagery even as it discovers and destroys similar false images quite literally everywhere it looks. Thus, while Burton admires Luther, he finishes his description with a complaint:

> But see the devil, that will never suffer the Church to be quiet or at rest: no garden so well tilled but some noxious weeds grow up in it, no wheat but it hath some tares: we have a mad giddy company of precisians, schismatics, and some heretics, even in our own bosoms in another extreme (*Dum vitant stulti vita in contraria currunt* [fools in avoiding one fault rush into the opposite]); that out of too much zeal in opposition to Antichrist, human traditions, those Romish rites and superstitions, will quite demolish all, they will admit of no ceremonies at all, no fasting days, no cross in baptism, kneeling at communion, no church music, etc., no bishops' courts, no church government, rail at all our church discipline, will not hold their tongues, and for all the peace of thee, O Sion! (III.4.1.3, 369–70)

To the extent that his reticence is motivated by the suspicion that even true religious practices always are accompanied by their devilish double, he seems unwilling to perpetuate the dynamic of reform that leads to the very internecine conflicts that reform had tried to defecate away.[42]

Instead he appears to offer his allegiance to prevailing ecclesiastical institutions, a gesture of political conservatism, if not "chameleonism,"[43] in the name of protecting civil order. Given that such pressures concerning representation reemerge in the final section as prominently as they had appeared in the Preface, we might have expected a similar turn to utopian discourse for the resolution. And all the more so when, in the course of giving his prognosis, he once again finds himself invoking the name of Hercules—this time, among other gods—for assistance:

> To purge the world of idolatry and superstition will require some monster-taming Hercules, a divine Aesculapius, or Christ Himself to come in His own person, to reign a thousand years on earth before the end, as the millenaries will have Him. They are generally so refractory, self-conceited, obstinate, so firmly addicted to that religion in which they have been bred and brought up, that no persuasion, no terror, no persecution can divert them. (III.4.1.5, 375)

But as his awkward conjunction of mythological heroes with the ostensibly more authentic messianic figure suggests—almost as though, for a brief moment, Burton himself regards them all as interchangeable—this time around, there is something more dire at stake. Hence, rather than develop a fictional society that could successfully accommodate conflicting demands, as he had done when considering political reform in the preface, Burton instead opts for an uneasy acceptance of prevailing ecclesiastical doctrine.

In a passage that has generated moderate interest among modern readers,[44] Burton announces his qualified allegiance to the Church of England. Burton makes his position known while writing on the problem of despair, brought on by too much contemplation over predestination. In many ways, merely to touch upon the subject was to invite criticism from some section. More rigid versions of Calvinism had indeed been associated with an extreme form of despair, and preaching on the question of predestination was officially looked on unfavorably (even if many preachers ignored the official sanctions against delivering sermons on the subject).[45] Meanwhile, Arminianism was unavailable as an alternative, since Parliament had prohibited it on grounds of treason.[46] In the course of his analysis, he makes a sudden, unsettling retraction. Indeed, it is a retraction that seems to raise more question than it answers (although, to be sure, that is what retractions do as a rule), since in the process he quotes a passage from Erasmus' preface to his *Colloquies:*

> I might have said more of this subject; but forasmuch as it is a forbidden question, and in the Preface or Declaration to the Articles of the Church, printed 1633, to avoid factions and altercations, we that are university divines especially, are prohibited "all curious search, to print or preach, or draw the article aside by our own sense and comments, upon pain of ecclesiastical censure," I will surcease, and conclude with Erasmus of such controversies: *Pugnet qui volet, ego censeo leges majorum reverenter suscipiendas, et religiose observandes, velut a Deo profecas; nec esse tutum, nec esse pium, de otestate publica sinistram concipere aut sereer suspicionem. Et siquid est tyrannidis, quod tamen non cogat ad impietatem, satius est ferre, quam seditiose reluctari* [Let him dispute who will, I hold that the laws of our ancestors are to be treated with reverence and scrupulously observed, as originating from God; and that it is neither safe nor pious to harbour and spread suspicions of the public authority. It is better to endure tyranny, so long as it does not drive us to impiety, than seditiously to resist.] (III.4.2.6, 424)

What is so astonishing about the reference to Erasmus is the fact that he includes it at all. One would think that the question's mere status as a forbidden one would have been reason enough to refrain from further commentary;

on the surface, it seems to add nothing to his account except a satirical bite. By linking the clergy's decision to tyrannical regimes, he seems deliberate about including them among the innumerable private fanatics whose personal commentaries and prophecies he denounces throughout the section as tyrannical impositions upon proper conventions.[47]

In fact, while critics may be right that the decree in question, *Articles Agreed upon by the Archbishops and Bishops of Both Provinces and the whole Cleargie*, may have been just what Burton needed to avoid a topic he felt uncomfortable discussing anyway—namely, the doctrine of double predestination advocated by Calvinist preachers[48]—nevertheless he seems to go out of his way to link the decree, along with its tyrannical undertones, to Laudian policy. The prohibition against making one's "Owne sense or Comment to bee the meaning of the Article," and instead submitting to "the plaine and full meaning thereof,"[49] had actually preceded Laud's appointment to Archbishop by a good five years. The original date of publication had been 1628, a detail which Burton apparently overlooked when he referred its date as 1633. To be sure, the Preface to the Articles was reprinted several times—well into the Restoration and eighteenth century, when it was reprinted on over two dozen known occasions—and Burton may have had in mind a reprint from 1632, or perhaps even one from 1633 that has not survived. Still, given that he felt the Declaration to be intended for members of his own profession, as he makes clear when he notes "we that are university divines especially, are prohibited" (III.4.2.6, 424), it seems improbable that Burton wouldn't have been familiar already with an earlier version. A more likely explanation is that the Declaration had escaped Burton's attention—it would not have occurred to him to comment on it—until 1633, the year that Laud took the position as Archbishop of Canterbury. By inserting the reference into his fifth edition (which probably went to print at Edinburgh in 1635), Burton points out, in an understated tone, what Laud's critics had been complaining about much more noisily—namely, that the Church of England was a tyrannical institution whose claims to legitimate authority were therefore unfounded.

This does not mean Burton would have felt comfortable with an assault on Laud's policies and doctrines, or even that he was making an obliquely subversive remark. As mannered as it may be, his retraction expresses a determined unwillingness to respond seditiously. To some extent, the question of whether Laud was truly a tyrant in Burton's eyes raises a moot point, since his criteria for obedience have to do far more with what he is bound by decree to do than with the legal foundations of the ruling institution. He accepts an expedient resolution to potential conflict—conflicts similar to the French civil wars and the ongoing war on the continent, which more than once catch his attention—even if, in the process, that meant accepting a status quo that reproduced much of the same irrationalism that he regarded as a key source of the nation's woes.

All of this also could be taken as an attempt, on Burton's part, to reach a practical resolution to a crisis of attitude toward ceremonial practices, a crisis motivated by the extreme skepticism that has been at work throughout the *Anatomy*.[50] Burton's acceptance of a church that may be tyrannical aims at holding together two antithetical positions regarding the relation between melancholy and reform; while the poetic commonwealth had permitted Burton to freely tyrannize over his imaginary populace, the Church of England faced a similar task, albeit with more at stake. That being the case, Burton responds to what Achsah Guibbory describes as "irreparably polarized" tensions between the Laudian Church and puritan ministers.[51] Since no other solution presented itself that wasn't accompanied by some form of false worship, accepting one that upheld the status quo would have been just as well as any other—so long as it keeps the peace.

Of course, what had motivated Burton to devise a poetic commonwealth to begin with had been such intense dissatisfaction with the status quo as to raise the doubt it would ever be worth serious reform. In that regard, the notion that he would have kept to the middle of the road, as Babb suggests, or that he was content with the ruling party regardless of its bias, as Stachniewski proposes, seems a bit unsatisfying.[52] Such a notion also suggests an attitude of practical indifference, which is certainly not the case. For if Burton accepts the tenets of the Church of England on the authority of its decree, rather than its claim to true worship, conversely he assumes a particularly aggressive posture when denouncing radical religious enthusiasts, whether as sects or as self-appointed prophets. Indeed, to an extent they strike him as a special case altogether—one that he would rather get rid of than discuss. As he suggests in his description of superstitious practices, their own behavior does not even correspond to conventional beliefs as to what constitutes proper superstition. Hence, when he asserts, "As a dam of water stopped in one place breaks out into another, so doth superstition," he follows it immediately with the remark, "I say nothing of Anabaptists, Socinians, Brownists, Barrowists, Familists, etc." (III.4.1.1, 324). Likewise, when discussing cures for his readers, he reserves the psychiatric hospital exclusively for "prophets, dreamers, and such rude silly fellows, that through fasting, too much meditation, preciseness, or by melancholy are distempered . . . We have frequently such prophets and dreamers amongst us, whom we persecute with fire and fagot; I think the most compendious cure, for some of them at least, had been in Bedlam" (III.4.2.1, 378–9). As for the fate of the ones not even fit for Bedlam, absolutely nothing is indicated; but as the remark that immediately follows it suggests, "*sed his satis,*" the question is not really Burton's to answer. More likely, they represent the only case for which Burton doesn't have an answer; so absurd are their habits, Burton can do little more than turn a deaf ear to them

What is it about enthusiasts and pseudo-prophets that drives Burton to such extreme hostility toward them? For starters, their behavior amounts to a particularly threatening version of mimetic identification: "What greater madness can there be for a man to take upon him to be a god, as some do? to be the Holy Ghost, Elias, and what not?" (III.4.1.3, 371). Wanting to become as much like Christ as possible, the individual who falls into madness finally imagines that he is Christ; at some stage of the process, that person actually forgets that he is imagining, and thus no longer can distinguish the representation from the thing that is being represented. The condition resembles what is known as psychosis in contemporary psychological terms, insofar as it entails the denial of a difference between fantasy and reality.

However, Burton also shows clear disgust for members of the artisan classes, combined with an equal disgust for their extraordinary attempts to assert power directly over their associates. While Burton may be critical of the ruling powers, the prospect of the laboring classes taking their place remains, for him, unthinkable. Such disdain is not initially obvious, since his complaint resembles that of someone as mainstream as Richard Hooker:

> Some call God and His attributes into question, as Vorstius and Socinus; some princes, civil magistrates, and their authorities, as Anabaptists, will do all their own private spirit dictates, and nothing else. Brownists, Barrowists, Familists, and those Amsterdamian sects and sectaries, are led all by so many private spirits. (III.4.1.3, 371)

It is only as he elaborates, recollecting the actual recent cases of prophets who rely on their own private whimsies, that his descriptions take on a decidedly elitist tone:

> In Poland, 1518, in the reign of King Sigismund, one said he was Christ, and got him twelve apostles, came to judge the world, and strangely deluded the commons. One David George, an illiterate painter, not many years since, did as much in Holland, took upon him to be the Messias, and had many followers . . . We need not rove so far abroad, we have familiar examples at home: Hacket that said he was

> Christ; Coppinger and Arthington his disciples; Burchet and Hovatus, burned at Norwich. We are never likely seven years together without some such new prophets that have several inspirations, some to convert the Jews, some fast forty days, go with Daniel to the lions' den; some foretell strange things, some for one thing, some for another. Great precisians of mean conditions and very illiterate, most part by a preposterous zeal, fasting, meditation, melancholy, are brought into those gross errors and inconveniences. (III.4.1.3, 371)

Whether Burton simply holds conflicted loyalties, or whether he despises these false prophets precisely because their radicalism does what he himself could barely dream of, it is clear he would rather accept a tyrant than live with whatever fantasy of liberation they themselves promised.

There is one final characteristic common to most of these prophets, and this may in turn throw some light on Burton's conservatism. As a rule, the enthusiasts Burton inveighs against do not know how to read. At any rate, they do not know how to read books and treatises with the scrutiny that Burton himself devotes to them—which, in this case, amounts to the same thing. In a book that is driven largely by the author's ability to collect references from other writers, that reserves a section for the miseries of scholars, and that reaches its conclusions about religious despair by instructing readers not to spend too much time puzzling out the mysteries of spiritual writings, the charges of illiteracy that he levels against religious enthusiasts seem especially significant. If reading always poses the risk of endless reading, and of falling into a trap in which the words on the page no longer point to a stable, knowable truth, the opposite trap—the pretense to knowledge that is *not* grounded in perpetual reading—is worse. On the level of self-interest, their success would pose a very real threat for an obsessive project, such as the *Anatomy*, namely the threat of rendering it irrelevant. On a deeper level though, what pseudo-prophets offer is the false promise that reading no longer is necessary, that the perpetual rearrangement of texts into new forms—such as Burton recommends as a cure for melancholy—ultimately does not work, since through prophecy all mysteries of the divine will be comprehended. To that extent, the madness of the prophet is the futile attempt to render analysis and interpretation obsolete; and in the process, they end their miseries too quickly.

The objections Burton raises against religious enthusiasts as illiterates in turn reveal a great deal about Burton's own project as a whole. For Burton, the problems involving ceremony as an adequate form of representing God's glory, while vexing and infinite, have their parallel in the problems that concern writing as a tool of description. If the *Anatomy* purports to be an attempt to say something meaningful about various social patterns, it is always mindful that these statements may be akin to idols of speech. Rather than accurately describe the problems he sets out to understand, then, each effort to do so becomes a misstatement of sorts, but a misstatement which is not in itself open to any analysis or understanding because it always leaves open the possibility that, as a statement, it does not refer to anything. Faced with this awareness, the temptation for Burton seems to have been—at least part of the time—to write without the promise of making a definitive statement about what melancholy is, but to write all the same; hence the text does tend to read as a modern novel, insofar as it incorporates, more or less indiscriminately, styles and texts from whatever suits the author. But writing for the sake of writing, and writing without more than the barest of formal limitations, is not without its merits. In the end, the suspicion that Burton's text is about writing for the sake of expansion may say more about melancholy than anything within the text itself. Melancholy is not necessarily a substance, a condition, or even a fashionable pose. It is, instead, the infinite expanse that Burton repeatedly characterizes metaphorically as the ocean or water, and it calls to mind not Democritus (whom Burton self-consciously imitates) but Heraclitus (who Burton catches himself resembling when he writes about things closest to home). To that extent, the title of the book, *Anatomy of Melancholy,* must be read as a double entendre. It is, on the one hand, analysis of a corpus, or corpse, broken down into its essential parts, just as Vesalius, the inventor of modern anatomy, would have understood the term. Given the nature of the thing being analyzed, however, we may suppose that it is the attempt to give melancholy an anatomy, to impose a shape on it in order to be able to anatomize it—even if, in the end, it turns out to be nothing more than a lapse into idolatry and a perpetuation of the melancholy symptoms that ruin commonwealths and destroy the land. It is in this latter sense that Burton finds himself capable of criticizing the institutions that surround him and at the same time guarantee that his criticism remains, in the fullest sense, the expression of madness. And it is in this latter sense that the question at the core of the *Anatomy*—is melancholy dead?—must remain, for Burton, unanswerable.

Section III
The Distractions of the Times

Chapter Six
The Distractions of the Times: Ideologies of Madness and Disease During the Civil War and Interregnum

INTRODUCTION

Any survey of madness during the turbulent years of civil war, revolution, and interregnum, runs the risk of itself becoming a maddening endeavor—all the more so as the question of madness during this period becomes entangled with disputes over the nature of religious enthusiasm. As Daniel Fouke has commented, the enormous outpouring of writings ultimately leaves contemporary historians with a picture that is anything but clear: "The anti-enthusiasm of the seventeenth century has been extremely difficult for scholars to characterize... Clear battle-lines fail to emerge, and any portrait of the typical 'enthusiast' never gets so far as a bare outline"; hardly an improvement on Michael MacDonald's remark that "The history of mental disorder in early modern England is an intellectual Africa."[1] While the period saw a tremendous production of pamphlet literature that made reference to madness, this does not mean that all writers operated according to a widespread understanding of what madness was.

Part of the reason for the sense of cacophony is that the participants in the struggle tended to write at cross-purposes. As Jonathan Sawday puts it, there are at the very least two versions of madness at work during the period:

> Two discourses of madness, both of which have political implications, are thus available. In one form the charge of madness acts to silence the deviant or aberrant voice. In the other, paradoxically, madness is discovered

> as a means of investing the word with divine authority and power. We can see these two contrasting discourses of madness struggling with one another in the revolutionary period, reflecting the ideological confrontations of the war itself.[2]

As the description suggests, these two versions were radically different. It is not simply that they were opposed to each other, on a more fundamental level they had nothing to do with each other. For those who operated under the one set of assumptions, the other must not have made sense.

Contemporary literary and historical criticism has had a difficult time showing if and how these two versions of madness indeed have anything in common. Very often scholars focus on one while ignoring or downplaying the other; and while legitimate, it has led to distinct schools of thought. One, represented by historians such as Christopher Hill and Nigel Smith, has concentrated on people who feigned madness to advance their authority.[3] Borrowing from the traditional notion of holy Christian madness,[4] writers such as James Nayler, Abiezer Coppe, and Thomas Webb understood madness not as an inhibition, but the necessary precursor to speech itself. Since the present worldly conditions are completely backward, to be perceived as mad by the prevailing social order becomes a sure sign that one is doing something right. Meanwhile, another group has concentrated on madness as a concept defined in the context of various power struggles. During the mid-seventeenth century, political radicalism had come to be understood as pathological in a decisively new way. The most immediate effect was what Fiona Godlee refers to as an effort to "disqualify and invalidate the claims" of individuals or groups who advocated more extreme versions of political and social reform. For as soon as a radical statement is reinterpreted as a symptom of disease, its truth content does not need to be evaluated: "The extraordinary manifestations of conviction displayed by religious enthusiasts were perhaps reason enough—once such things were viewed in more secular terms—to elicit the charge of insanity."[5] It is, in short, everything Freud found so appalling about psychologists and their refusal to listen to their patients.

In the course of this so-called redefinition of political radicalism, something new ostensibly happens to religious enthusiasm—it too becomes a sign of madness, and more often than not, melancholy madness. What had previously been treated as a matter of theological concern suddenly reveals itself as a secular one; it becomes more useful to refer to physical malfunctions than to describe errors in the way that, for instance, the Quakers interpret Scripture.

For the better part of the twentieth century, historians and literary critics have argued that basis for this change was largely an intellectual one, with a handful of writers being responsible for bringing it about. In a few broad strokes, Robert Burton, followed by the Cambridge Platonists Meric Casaubon and Henry More, transformed enthusiasm from a state of divine rapture to a pathological condition, recognizable to anybody who understands activities of the Logos (a term Casaubon himself relies on especially heavily). By the time Jonathan Swift sat down to write his invective against enthusiasts in *A Tale of a Tub*, self-proclaimed prophets hardly stood a chance.

A brief survey of this sub-field reveals that, despite some fairly sharp disagreements over the significance of the change, several basic assumptions are agreed upon with remarkable consistency. These include the notion that the change in the status of enthusiasm was overwhelming and also, it follows, this overwhelming change may be viewed as a pattern. Beginning with George Williamson, whose 1933 article about the replacement of imagination and emotion with the classical temper surveys a large share of seventeenth century intellectual developments, we find the two crucial points:

> The revolt against Enthusiasm, which is the immediate cause of this change of temper, is itself the culmination of the thought of the first half of the century, however its manifestation may vary in religious, scientific, or literary style.[6]

This is later followed by his claim that:

> In 1655 and 1656 two books were leveled at Enthusiasm, one by Meric Casaubon and the other by Henry More; in fact, one may say that hostility toward Enthusiasm then became quite general.[7]

Similarly, John Sena identifies Casaubon and More as the two figures whose intellectual authority created a watershed in the Augustan conception of madness:

> Anti-Puritan attacks for the next one hundred years followed the pattern established by Casaubon and More. The view that enthusiastic phenomena were the natural result of vapors or overheated melancholy became a standard assessment of the sectaries, and the terminology of Casaubon and More, long familiar in medical treatises, became the conventional rhetoric of attack.[8]

More recent critics have turned to Burton's *Anatomy* as the cornerstone text since, in Michael Heyd's words, "historically, he may have been—at least in England—the first to incorporate systematically the medical literature on melancholy for the purpose of religious polemics."[9] Thomas Canavan notes a trend that links Swift's *Tale of a Tub* directly with Burton: "Moreover, the ideas presented in their works suggest an intellectual relationship between Burton and Swift and a continuity in the approach of anti-Puritan writers."[10] Clement Hawes, who describes the transformation less as the triumph of either reason or physiology, lists Burton as something of a prophet, even invoking a Biblical term for chosen-ness to color his point:

> After its publication . . . Anglican pamphleteers began to rework Robert Burton's famous argument about religious pathology in *The Anatomy of Melancholy* into a 'ruling class shibboleth.' . . . It must be added, however, that this elite equation of enthusiasm with madness soon infiltrated circles well beyond the drawing rooms of the indisputably privileged. The pathologizing of enthusiasm thus became part of a broader elite hegemony. It is obvious enough that the pathologizing of manic rhetoric served to denigrate it and eventually to justify 'shutting up,' in all possible senses, its users. The label of madness, retroactively buttressed by medical authority, then served to naturalize and universalize this persecution, concealing its basis in historical conflict.[11]

Even critics who do not place the burden of intellectual changes entirely on the shoulders of Burton, Casaubon, or More, continue to describe the mid-seventeenth century as a period that ushered in an essentially new epoch, characterized by a novel distinction of enthusiasm as something distinct from Reason itself.[12]

What is striking about the above arguments is that the so-called historical developments they refer to are not actually as new or dramatic as their advocates have claimed. In fact, when someone like John Locke asserts that melancholy is the source of enthusiasm, seems to rely on the belief that this is old hat, rather than a radically new cultural episteme:

> Immediate revelation being a much easier way for men to establish their opinions and regulate their conduct than the tedious and not always successful labour of strict reasoning, it is no wonder that some have been very apt to pretend to revelation, and to persuade themselves that they are under the peculiar guidance of heaven in their actions and opinions, especially in those of them which they cannot account for the

ordinary methods of knowledge and principles of reason. Hence we see that in all ages men, in whom melancholy has mixed with devotion, or whose conceit of themselves has raised them into an opinion of a greater familiarity with God, and a nearer admittance to his favour, than is afforded to others, have often flattered themselves with a persuasion of an immediate intercourse with the Deity, and frequent communications from the Divine Spirit.[13]

Recent attempts to identify Burton as the writer who inaugurates a transformation in the general popular understanding of religious enthusiasm therefore seem open to a number of fundamental questions. Among others, what (if anything) did take place during the troubled and turbulent decades under examination?

To be sure, it is all too easy to show that changes from one era to the next always are marked by a greater sense of continuity than historians acknowledge. It is only partly helpful to point out that many sixteenth century writers understood quite well the connection between melancholy and enthusiasm. In the cases of physician Andre du Laurens and philosopher-magician Giordano Bruno, for instance, melancholy had been identified as the chief source of pseudo-prophecy;[14] and more generally, the dual nature of melancholy meant that writers always had to make the distinction between actual genius and what Hooker refers to as "minds possessed."[15] Similarly, we can note that Burton himself drew his material on religious enthusiasm from the Church of England's official policies against various dissenters, all of Burton's innovations notwithstanding. While Burton may have taken the point to new ends, he clearly modeled his survey of religious enthusiasm on such statements as the following by Archbishop Abbott:

> You are therefore to know, that his majesty being much troubled and grieved at the heart to hear every day of so many defections from our religion to Popery and Anabaptism or other points of separation in some part of this kingdom, and considering with much admiration what might be the cause thereof, especially in the reign of such a king who doth so constantly profess himself an open adversary to the superstition of the one and madness of the other.[16]

Ultimately, though, such facts as these merely show that the discourse of invective against enthusiasm merely drew its material from its historical antecedents. They do not necessarily refute the claim that "the first English works which described enthusiasm solely as a physical and mental abnormality caused chiefly by melancholy appeared in the mid-seventeenth century."[17] In fact, if they accomplish anything, they show that contemporary historians had the dates wrong, while in principle they were correct: a widespread rewriting of enthusiasm from divine inspiration to physical pathology more or less did occur.

However, this principle is questionable on two additional grounds, namely that there was a definite widespread consensus of opinion at the intellectual level, and that the disenchantment of enthusiasm among some intellectuals meant that writers stopped mythologizing the condition altogether. Terms like continuity and tradition, such as we have seen above, are misnomers, and they tend to obscure what took place among the Cambridge Platonists more than they explain it. The differences between Burton and Casaubon, and then between Casaubon and More, deserve more attention than they previously have received. What they show, ultimately, is that insofar as melancholy was used as an explanatory device at all, it was an incredibly poor one; if anything, it marked a regression to a conservative intellectual tradition grounded in classical authorities rather than an original innovation.

The first section provides a brief survey of lesser-known writers who discussed madness during the mid-seventeenth century. As it turns out, if there was a transformation in the arguments about enthusiasm, it was not sudden but slow and tremendously uneven; popular books and pamphlets reflected a wide range of viewpoints, of which many are discussed below. Moreover, to the extent that a secularization of enthusiasm did take place, it is incorrect to characterize it by saying that more and more people can to regard it exclusively as a symptom of madness or melancholy. The second section reviews the case for placing Burton at the origin of a new approach to religious enthusiasm and glances briefly at the two Cambridge Platonists who occupy the place of key transitional figures, namely Casaubon and More.[18] A reexamination of their works suggests that the continuity between them is less secure than previous critics have acknowledged.

A better way to characterize what happened to melancholy during the period would be to call it a casualty of empiricism; both melancholy and enthusiasm would become meaningless as writers began to search for new standards of probability in argumentation. As J. F. McGregor and others have shown, one of the most salient features of enthusiastic discourse is its radically anti-authoritarian standpoint:

> The disparate range of enthusiastic doctrines, not obviously tied to any model of ecclesiastical discipline, created and continues to pose considerable problems of interpretation. Enthusiasm may be defined as the

immediate guidance of the Holy spirit superseding any worldly or scriptural authority. It was intrinsically individualist, anarchic, and generally incompatible with the common discipline of church or sect.[19]

While there certainly is something exhilarating about complete disregard for authority, the downside is that it quickly loses any sense of authority of its own. For in all dialogues, even if they manifest themselves as conflicts, it is necessary to establish some measure of authority, if only to serve as a common ground. Without a standard that all participants can accept as axiomatic (which is not the same thing as true), it is not possible to engage in a meaningful dispute. For indeed, it is difficult to respond adequately to a writer who proclaims, at the outset to be writing, "Divine Inspiration and Immediate Illumination [by God Himself] Asserted," as George Whitehead did in a 1674 defense of Quakerism.[20] It is all the more difficult when the literary conventions that defined the so-called voice of sincerity were themselves undergoing drastic changes, changes which demanded greater verifiability through external evidence.[21]

At any rate, such appears to be the course that many writers took in order to move beyond the impasse that the debates over enthusiasm had led to. A sermon published in 1653 gives us a hint. Its author, Joseph Sedgwick, complains: "A confident boasting of dictates from above is not sufficient warrant that the doctrine is heavenly. Without better evidence than their bare word, we may modestly suspect that they are nothing but the distempers of a disaffected brain."[22] What troubled Sedgwick was not the content of prophecy, but the unsubstantiated claim to authority that personal testimony confers. After all, what exactly can one say to another in response to the proclamation that his authority is the divine light? Although Sedgwick does not articulate it in quite these terms, his demand calls for what Giorgio Agamben refers to as the expropriation of experience. Making reference to Francis Bacon's "founding project of modern science," Agamben argues:

> The scientific verification of experience which is enacted in the experiment—permitting sensory impressions to be deduced with the exactitude of quantitative determinations and, therefore, the prediction of future impressions—responds to this loss of certainty by displacing experience as far as possible outside the individual: on to instruments and numbers.[23]

According to this model, experience is transformed from something that had been, by definition, unique to the individual who has undergone a "crossing-over through danger," to something that must be shared by everybody.

STRANGE RAPTURES

As Michael MacDonald notes in his magnificent study of early modern psychology, the seventeenth century developed an astonishing vocabulary for madness: "During the late sixteenth and early seventeenth centuries, the English people became more concerned about the prevalence of madness, gloom, and self-murder than they had ever been before, and the reading public developed a strong fascination with classical medical psychology."[24] While precedents certainly were available—the world turned upside down was a well-known biblical topos, and the image of the diseased body-politic still circulated widely—seventeenth century pamphleteers from all professions really took advantage of the new language, placing it in an overtly political context. Thus, as Jonathan Sawday remarks, "The language with which insanity is described is, in the seventeenth century, a consciously political language."[25] Rather than describe an individual's mental disposition, madness referred explicitly to the way one conducted affairs within society.

A brief survey of pamphlets, speeches and sermons from the 1640s gives a sense of the multiple ideological functions that the term "madness" played. As the concept's relative popularity suggests, at least part of the purpose was to place political turbulence in a familiar language, if not a universally agreed upon one. In his satirical poem, "Mad Fashions Od Fashions, Alls out of Fashion,"[26] John Taylor invokes the themes of universal madness and metamorphosis to account for what he calls "these distracted times." The title page contains an emblem of the world-turned-upside down motif. A man, whose head sticks out of his breeches, feet swinging wildly through the air, occupies the center. He is surrounded be various images of backwardness, including a rabbit chasing a fox, a mouse chasing a cat, a horse whipping a cart, and a plow pushing a tiller. As though the image required further explanation, he begins:

> The Picture that is Printed in the front
> Is like this Kingdome, if you look upon't:
> For if you well doe not it as it is,
> It is a Transform'd metamorphosis.
> This Monstrous Picture plainly doth declare
> This land (quite out of order) out of square.[27]

As the poem progresses, it becomes clear whom Taylor really wants to hold accountable:

> For Now, when as a Royall Parliament,
> (With King, and Peers, and Commons whole consent)
> Have almost sate two yeeres, with paines and Cares,
> And charge to free us from our Griefes and Fears,
> For when may a worthy Lord and knight
> And good Esquire (for King and Countreys Right)
> Have spent so much time with Great Toyle, and Heede,
> All Englands vicious Garten how to weed.[28]

Similarly, in an anonymous pamphlet entitled, *Englands Mad Petition to the Right Honourable, The, &c.*, the author makes a plea for the expansion of Bedlam hospital to accommodate the twelve million new patients who surely will require admittance. The cause, it maintains, is the assault on an "unequalled virtuous King"; and if the title page is sincere, it is all the more audacious in that it was "Presented to Both Houses" for their consideration. The text itself reads as follows:

> Have wee not been so franticke, that without any legall consideration or suspition of eyes or thoughts; we have madly dislocated a principall Joynt of our Parliament (and indeed next to the head) and yet we are so consoperated in our Lethargy, that wee have not so much as mention'd it for a fault, and that is the Places and Voices of the Bishops, for ever since Parliaments have beene used in *England*, all till this present have consisted of Lords Spirituall and Temporal, and the House of Commons, but not these spirituall Lords (which are the Bishops) are not once nam'd (nor thought on) and yet wee pretend for a legal and compleat Parliament, is not this extreame madnesse?[29]

In both cases, madness serves as little more than a convenient handle with which to describe ongoing political turmoil—we can just as easily imagine each writer complaining about the same social troubles without making recourse to it.

Other writers could couch political arguments about madness within a more overtly theological framework. Thomas Croft's Spiritual handbook, *Paradise Within us: Or, The happie Mind* rehearses well-known theories about the humors, as well as the diseases they cause:

> That the humours of the body are an occasion of Passions and perturbations of the mind, is a received ground among all Physitians and

> Philosophers. It is well knowne in Philosophy, that the affections of the mind, doe follow the apprehensions of the phansie; And Physitians doe well know, that the apprehensions of the Phansie are conformable to the dispositions of the body and the humours that predominate therein.[30]

Just as he concludes, however, he reminds his readers that personal diseases do have potentially public ramifications:

> To the body these Intemperate voluptuous and luxurious courses, doe often cause many evill corrupted Humour, strange Maladies, Griefes, and distempers. From whence spring the common Diseases of our Times, but from Intemperate voluptousness . . . To the Mind also, these vices does often so besot the same, as it becomes, very unfit for any good thoughts or actions either Humane or Divine; And the Spirites being thereby distempered, the Mind becometh prone to evill thoughts and desires, and the Passions so enthralled that a multitude of perturbations, discontents, and vexations are thereby caused.[31]

On occasion, specific grievances resembled descriptions that might be found in Burton's *Anatomy*, though they did not necessarily originate from it. As a result, there was one sense in which the designation of melancholy might indeed have been an appropriate characterization of what such a political salvo as the 1640 petition of twelve peers refers to as "your whole Kingdom become full of fear and discontent."[32] This was that the particular grievances often mentioned by the people coincided with conditions that Burton had identified as the signs of a nation overrun with melancholy. In the petition itself, the writers point to excessive warfare, a decline in revenue, the "heavy charges of merchandise to the discouragement of trade,"[33] and the corruption of the church. Similarly, the famous "Roots and Branches Petition," which called for the abolishment of the present system of ecclesiastical government, cited, "The multitude of monopolies and patents . . . the large increase of customs and impositions upon commodities, the ship money, and many other great burdens upon the Commonwealth, under which all groan."[34] The same petition noted that "Trading is decayed, many poor people want work, seamen lose employment, and the whole land is much impoverished, to the great dishonour of this kingdom and blemishment to the government."[35] Walter Bridges picked up on the implications of complaints such as these, himself assailing the house of commons in a Sermon of Six false reasons for civil war:

> The fifth consideration is a sullen Melancholy one, trading's dead, our money goes, never so many payments, &c. This man is not worth the answering, I shall onely desire him to learne, if he be learnable, what Iob sayes, Iob 2.10. Shall we receive good at the hands of God, and not evil also?[36]

As these and other documents suggest, though, the corporealization of the commonwealth could work just as much in their own interests as it could in the interests of the crown's defenders. The Petition of Twelve expresses concern over the "great distempers and dangers now threatening the church and state,"[37] while a Speech of Lord Digby's to the House of Commons reinvokes the image of ruler as physician, "Let him purge away our grievances never so efficaciously."[38] As had been the case regarding the theoretical articulations of the body-politic,[39] its actual deployment in a political milieu proved to serve little more than self-interest.

By no means is the above survey exhaustive. Nor does it intend to simply accumulate specific cases, since the point is to suggest that the rhetoric of madness had a normative objective. To identify, say, a Roundhead in the manner Taylor does elsewhere, as, "a man (though cut within a quarter inch to the skill) hath more hair then wit, and according to his daily distractions, may be titled *Hair brain'd*,"[40] is useful insofar as it refers to a network of texts that do more or less similar things. But while repetition of such accusations may have made the accusations themselves more recognizable, it does not necessarily follow that the seventeenth century had a better understanding of what exactly madness consisted of.

The use of madness as a normative device is no less evident during the decades that followed—the turbulent years of such radical sects as the Quakers, and pseudo-movements as the Ranters.[41] As MacDonald points out:

> For more than a century after the English Revolution, the governing classes assailed the religious enthusiasm of the sects. Anglican propagandists declared that the visions and inspirations of radical Dissenters were insane delusions based on false perceptions and diseased imaginings. The earliest opponents of religious enthusiasm argued that it was caused by melancholy, but during the eighteenth century orthodox controversialists followed Swift in claiming that it was a kind of madness.[42]

MacDonald contends that the repetition of this charge eventually hastened a new skepticism toward enthusiasm. While many writers, particularly of the lower classes, continued to rely on witchcraft and demonology, among the intellectual elite melancholy and madness presented themselves as more reliable explanations.[43]

All the same, the second half of the seventeenth century may also be read as a collective search for new ways to articulate arguments against radical sects as traditional ones became ineffective and as their intended targets grew unfazed by the charges. Writers who did invoke melancholy often tended to embed it within a series of explanations, to which they often seemed indifferent. Thomas Comber's 1678 text, *Christianity no Enthusiasm* provides a clear example of this method. While he does acknowledge the possibility of melancholy as a cause for religious enthusiasm, it is embedded in a list that clearly diminishes its importance:

> And having observed these and the like things: viz. That Bad men, Evil Designs, Inward Heats, Melancholy Fancies, Satans Suggestions, the want of better Arguments, or the like, have frequently in all the Ages of the Church, taken Sanctuary under so Sacred a cover, (as by the Catalogue given Chapter the Sixth, doth sufficiently appear: which (if necessary), might be inlarged in those several Periods downward, to our own late licentious times, when Inspirations and Heavenly Impressions were made the common stale for many purposes).[44]

For the rest of the lengthy treatise, however, the charge of melancholy delusion does not enter the treatise, concentrating on biblical exegesis to show his opponents how they had misunderstood the scripture. If melancholy was an effective device for attacking Quakers, Comber seems largely unaware of it.

Numerous tracts written against the Quaker and Ranter sects suggest that while Burton may have had an impact in terms of shaping the discourse of anti-enthusiasm, it was considerably more modest than recent critical attention has suggested. In fact, accusations of madness were part of a larger attack more appropriately described as theological than psychological. As J. F. McGregor reminds us, Ranterism was treated as the ultimate heterodoxy; it prompted the Blasphemy Act of 1650 rather than immediate calls for hospitalization.[45] The same holds true for attacks on the Quakers. Thus, when Francis Higginson wrote his *Irreligion of the Quakers*, his primary concerns were heresy and blasphemy:

> In the meanwhile the uncurb'd Licentiousness of many evil men, and blasphemous heretical seducers through the Nation, makes many honest Christians now look upon the present times as ill boding times, who

a few years ago were raised in their expectations, to see better dayes then any age ever produced, since the time that our Savior Christ and his Apostles were living on earth.

If the Quakers presented a danger to the Commonwealth, what they said seems to have outweighed what mental state they were in when they said it:

> The more therefore the blasphemy against the God of Heaven abounds among the Apostates of this Generation, the more we should (and if we fear God indeed, we shall) labor to glorify him, the more we should be grieved for the dishonour done to his sovereign Majesty, and the more earnestly should we pray, that this bloody sin may not be imputed to the nation.[46]

Likewise, when W. Allen launched his attack on enthusiasm in 1674, his charges consisted of "New Notions and new affected Modes and Phrases,"[47] rather than any sense they were deluded. In fact, most of Allen's treatise consists of extensive biblical interpretation, in order to demonstrate, finally:

> That Heresie is one of those works of the Flesh, which shut Men out of the Kingdom of God, Gal. 5.20,21. And considering the Nature and bad influence of several of your opinions, and with what pertinaciousness you persist in them, its greatly feared, not to say confidently believed by such as are jealous over you with a Godly jealousie, that many of you at least, lye under no less guilt than that of grand Heresie.[48]

To the extent that such arguments were even possible, such writers needed to presuppose that the Quakers' errors began at the level of interpretation.

To the extent that writers did perceive Quaker writers to be out of possession of their own faculties, it was typically the devil they identified as the source of blame. When John Gilpin wrote the testimony of his experience with a handful of Quaker meetings, particularly the enthusiastic fit which left him crawling on his belly and licking the dust before falling into a catatonic state for a day, he concludes:

> I was fully resolved that it was the Devils power that had acted me all along formerly, and was perswaded that I really was possesst with a Devil, which must be ejected, & in the morning I verily thought that a Devill went out of me, at which instant I roared very hideously, certing *now is the Devill gone out of me,* at which instant I and my family heard

it thunder (though none in the Towne besides heard it) which made me thinke it was the Devil, *he being the Prince of the power of the Air.*[49]

If melancholic despair does play a role in Gilpin's testimony, it is because he cannot seem to shake the devil: "Thus I apprehended my selfe wholly under the power of the devil, and had no power to recover my selfe out of that bad condition" (11). Thomas Underhill was particularly attuned to Satan's influence on the Quaker sect, using (among others) Gilpin's testimony to verify it. When he writes of the Anabaptists, whom he considers direct predecessors to the Quakers, he explains their emergence as follows:

> When Satan perceived that he could no longer keep up the Tyranny and Errors undisturbed, but that Christ would send out such a light, as should disgrace and dispel his darkness; he renewed his old attempts again, and setteth upon Christ in his own Kingdome, and falls upon the Reformation in its own quarters, to disgrace it by the diversity of *evil Doctrines and practices of those,* who pretended to be Reformers.[50]

Again, to the extent that Underhill did see Quakerism as madness, he took it as a symptom of demonic possession, even leaving some doubt as to whether their truly mad acts were authentic:

> Suitable to this is the Story that I had from one that I am sure tells the truth: That coming once into a great Assembly of them at *Glasiers* Hall *London* (their then meeting place) he found some trembling, others howling, others crying out, and violently moving their bodies just like mad folks, who were (to his appearance) forcibly held by the more sober, just as mad folks are, and all this for many minutes together, the like carriage he affirms, he thought he had been nowhere on this side hell. But when he dealt with their Speaker, endeavouring to prove him a *Seducer,* they were so vexed, that they left their Bedlam carriage, and like the pictures of the Witches in the *Fortune-Book* fell upon him with dreadfull denunciations and impudent censures, until he charged them with hypocrasie and voluntariness and called upon them to howl again, and to let him alone with that fellow their Speaker.[51]

One gets the sense that mental delusion would have been the preferable explanation.

Ranters and other radical groups regularly were accused of consorting with the devil—unsurprising, given that they were known to make outrageous oaths against God on a regular basis—and popular pamphlets went to great lengths to expose them as Satan-Worshippers. The title page to Gilbert Roulston's *Ranters Bible* makes reference to "their blasphemous opinion of our Lord and Saviour Jesus Christ, and their burning of his blessed WORD, and Sacred Scriptures; the names of their new gods, and worshipping of the Sun, and three black clouds; with the manner of their idolizing them, North, West, East, and South; their drinking of healths to the Devill, and disposing of places in Hell," and so forth. In a short comedy called, "The Joviall Crew, or, The Devill turn'd RANTER," the author subsumes his charges of madness under the notion of demon worship. The play's title page includes the following stanza:

> *Bedlam* broke loose? yes, *Hell* is open'd too:
> *Mad-men,* & *Fiends,* & *Harpies* to your view
> We do present: but who shall cure the *Tumor?*
> All the world now is in the *Ranting Humor.*

Meanwhile, in scene two, the Devil makes an appearance and lays claim to "These mad pranks of these our Jovial crew."[52]

On occasions, pamphleteers would use religious turmoil as the pretext for more scurrilous purposes. Such was the case with Thomas Bray's *A New Sect of Religion Descryed, Called Adamites,* in which the author recounts a recent trip of his to one of the more unsavory London neighborhoods. Thus he writes:

> For I, the *Author,* walking in *Moore-fields* (as may custome is to take the fresh Ayre) met with a *brother* in a great melancholy, he went a slow pace, his hat over his eyes, & his eyes fixed on the ground, his arms were locked one within the other, with all the postures of a male-content as possible could be. I noted his carriage a great while, at last being desirous to know something from him, stroke him upon the shoulder with this salute, well overtaken, brother.[53]

As if on cue, the malcontent unloads his deep concerns about a new religious group he has become acquainted with, which inevitably the author winds up visiting. It is there that the elaborate dress of the malcontent gives way to the scene of a room filled with naked women and men, the latter struggling—unsuccessfully—to beat down their erections. At a time when the notions of private delusion and madness were available to writers, such descriptions of Satan's influence—or in the case of Bray, Venus' influence—nevertheless remained by far the preferable solution to the question of anti-social behavior.

If the Royal Society had indeed done its work, to a large extent that work had gone unnoticed beyond its own domain.

In short, the charge of melancholy as the source of enthusiasm no longer was meaningful; at any rate, it was no more meaningful than the claim to divine inspiration that provoked the charges of melancholy madness in the first place. Since the pathologization of enthusiasm was stuck in the same dogmatic trap as its counterpart, both enthusiasts and the critics would be stuck repeating the same arguments indefinitely. And to the extent that charges of melancholy did persist into the Restoration, it may be understood as much the effect of inertia as anything else.

ENTHUSIASM IN JEST

Amid this outpouring of documents appeared two writers who gave full consideration to the problem of enthusiasm, and who have in turn received considerable critical attention in contemporary histories of enthusiasm: Meric Casaubon and Henry More. Often these two writers have been revered for delivering the initial blow against seventeenth century prophecy. Just as often, they have been mistaken as writers who shared a common objective; since both sought to demystify the supernatural origins of contemporary enthusiasts, it is thought they shared certain beliefs about the nature of the phenomenon they wrote about. In fact, the assumptions behind their works were very much at odds with each other. These differences become evident when we consider the way More and Casaubon actually discuss melancholy; while both refer to the condition as a cause of enthusiasm, and while both make reference to the famous Aristotelian problem as the ground for their "discoveries" about contemporary prophets and their own published experiences (such as *The Life of Sister Katharine of Jesus, Nunne of the Order of our Lady, &c.*, the alleged inspiration behind Casaubon's study), ultimately they employ it for radically different purposes.

In the case of Casaubon (the earlier of the two), melancholy is mentioned only briefly, just long enough to let his readers know how little it serves his objectives. After all, he contends, it is already among the better known causes for inspiration:

> First then we shall observe a concurrence of Naturall Causes. This is granted by all Physicians and Naturallists. *Melancholici, maniaci, ecstatici, phrenetici, epileptici, hystericae mulieres:* All these be diseases naturally incidentall to all both men and women; the last only proper to women as naturally incidentall to all, so curable by naturall means and

The Distractions of the Times 169

> remedies. Nobody doubts of that. To all these naturall diseases and distempers, enthusiastick divinatatory fits are incidentall. I do not say that it doth happen very often: that is not materiall, whether often of seldome. But when it doth happen, as the disease is cured by naturall means, so the Enthusiasms go away, I will not say by the same means, but at the same time.[54]

Nor does the physiological argument preclude a theological one. Thus, at the moment when he finally does make reference to Aristotle, it is precisely in order to demonstrate how unsuitable Aristotle is for explaining enthusiasm in physical terms alone:

> Except we shall say, that *Aristotle* intended to assign a double cause: the one naturall in preparing the body, without which preparation nothing would be done; the other supernaturall, the formall & immediate cause of the operation. And if this were his meaning, then he is much wronged by them who lay to his charge, as though he made Melancholy the onely cause; whereas themselves also allow of some previous preparation and disposition (in such cases) as necessary.[55]

Beyond these comments though, Casaubon does not have much to say about the humors.

What does interest Casaubon is the idea that all aspects of divination can be explained by natural causes, even if those causes cannot be known, as he indicates midway through chapter two of his examinations. It is a peculiar passage, regarding a case that really leaves Casaubon stumped: the illiterate individual who, without any access to it, suddenly speaks in a foreign tongue, such as Hebrew or Aramaic. (He acknowledges, for instance, that the cause might be a combination of distempered humors and the Devil—who takes advantage of the imbalance.)[56] Recognizing the problem such an individual presents, Casaubon makes an astonishing reply:

> The question is not (so properly) whether any manifest, or very probable naturall cause can be shewed; but whether it be against all reason, whether manifest of probable, to believe that some kind of enthusiastick Divination may proceed from causes that are naturall, though it be beyond the reach of man to find them, as in many other things whereof no question is this, I say, being the true state of the Question, before we come to the consideration of particular reasons and causes, I think it necessary for their sakes that are not used to the speculation of Nature and her secrets,

to insist a while upon some such things as are certainly known (though from causes to most men unknown and incomprehensible,) to be naturall: and some such things also which in themselves, if well considered, deserve no lesse admiration, though the causes be not unknown.[57]

What is so striking about this remark is not just that it rejects supernatural causes in favor of natural ones. More important, Casaubon really has no compelling reason to make it, since it would have been just as easy—if not easier—to conclude that there are some things that simply cannot be demonstrated one way or the other.

The word that gives trouble in this passage is "beyond," since it can be taken as either a preposition or the statement of a rule. On the one hand, the natural cause may not be known at this moment. In time, however—perhaps as the great march of intellect reaches a new territory—the cause will present itself. On the other, the natural cause may belong to a class of things that the human mind simply is not capable of apprehending, since it can only know things that it can observe and measure in some sense. The point here is not to decide though, since it is unclear just how Casaubon can be so sure of either case. While he is no less convinced that the contemporary enthusiast mistakes a supernatural cause for a natural one, and while the purpose of his book is to try to show that, in fact, all phenomena can be explained by natural causes, as he indicates by the conclusion:

> From those generall instances, not lesse to be wondered at, though certainly known and acknowledged to proceed from causes that are naturall, whether known or unknown, That it is possible, if not probable, that some Enthusiastick Divination may proceed from naturall causes[58]

in the end he does not show how these conclusions themselves can be shown. In the act of stating the rule of causality, Casaubon ends up on what Martin Heidegger refers to as a "sure path to ruin," in reference to Casaubon's contemporary Leibniz.[59] At any rate, while he is determined that a natural cause for enthusiasm must exist, he is unable to state what it is.

If Casaubon is concerned with advocating a rationalist approach to knowledge about enthusiasm, and if he subsequently becomes troubled with the question of how to adequately establish the foundations for such knowledge, More by contrast simply writes propaganda. Or rather, More is completely untroubled with making the assertion that melancholy is the cause of enthusiasm, if not the only cause one needs to know about:

The Distractions of the Times

> We shall now enquire into the *Causes* of this Distemper, how it comes to passe that a man should be thus befooled in his own conceit. And truly unlesse we should offer lesse satisfaction then the thing is capable of, we must not onely treat here of *Melancholy,* but of the *Faculties of the Soul* of man, whereby it may the better be understood how she may become obnoxious to such disturbances of *Melancholy,* in which she has quite lost her own Judgement and freedome, and can neither keep out nor distinguish betwixt her own Fancies and reall Truths.[60]

For all his talk about inquiring into causes, though, the basis for his study is almost entirely textual; it is difficult to imagine how the treatise could have been written were it not for the Aristotelian problem, which he refers to in section eleven:

> We will name something now more generall, whose nature notwithstanding is so various and *Vertumnus*-like, that it will supply the place of almost all particulars, and that is *Melancholy;* of which *Aristotle* gives witness, that according to the severall degrees and tempers thereof men vary wonderfully in their constitutions.[61]

More also refers to Democritus Jr. and Laurentius, not because he has anything to add about them, but precisely because they relieve him of the task of providing examples:

> *Aristotle* affords us no Examples of this kind; others do. *Democritus junior,* as he is pleased to style himself, recites severall Stories out of Authours to this purpose. As out of *Laurentius* one concerning a French Poet, who using in a feaver *Unguentum pouleum* to anoint his temples to conciliate sleep, too such a conceit against the smell of that ointment, that for many yeares after he imagined every one that came near him to sent of it.[62]

Indeed, as we read through the incredibly terse document—of the fifty-seven sections, not one runs more than a page or so—we get the sense that More has missed Burton's point. While Burton compiles, digresses and assimilates without necessarily bringing his thoughts to a conclusion, More takes for granted that melancholy is already understood, both as a substance and as a cause.

In the context of writers like Burton or Casaubon, More's treatise reads like a reactionary impulse to reaffirm conventional beliefs rather than make an original statement about anything at all. Precisely because he treats melancholy as a foregone conclusion, More launches an attack against the contemporary problem of "Quaking." For More, this action amounts to "deluded souls take to be an infallible sign they are inactuated by the Spirit of God, that it may be onely an Effect of their melancholy."[63] Further, of the Quaker sect he writes, "as it often happens in that Sect they call *Quakers,* who undoubtedly are the most *melancholy Sect* that ever was yet in the world."[64] To be sure, such remarks pathologize enthusiasm and radical religious sects, perhaps more emphatically than anything we have seen before. And as critics have pointed out, this opinion held sway well into the eighteenth century, not only because More's voice "was one of the most authoritative in his time,"[65] but because the argument itself offers an irresistible temptation—namely, to believe that one knows something about religious enthusiasm, as well as something about the body to back it up. That such knowledge about the body was itself beginning to lose ground gives the lie to More's entire project—and perhaps he acknowledges this inadvertently when he describes the difference between poetry and enthusiasm:

> From this Complexion are *Poets,* and the more highly-pretending *Enthusiasts:* Betwixt whom this is the great difference, That a *Poet* is an *Enthusiast in jest,* and an *Enthusiast* is a *Poet in good earnest;* Melancholy prevailing so much with him, that he takes his no better then *Poeticall* fits and figments for divine Inspiration and reall Truth.

Has melancholy already begun to pass over from an actual physical ailment to a mood that poets imitate in the course of their poetic designs? If so, is More himself even aware that it is happening?

Rather than amount to a continuous campaign or pattern, the Cambridge Platonists' investigation into the causes of enthusiasm revealed a fundamental conflict—Casaubon and More were completely opposed over what could be known about the condition. On one side, Casaubon remained suspicious about any claims to divine inspiration precisely because such claims could not be demonstrated to others; the radically idiomatic character of divine inspiration thus rendered it unknowable. On the other side, religious enthusiasm was simply madness—melancholy madness, to be exact. More thus perpetuated a traditional belief, and he did so precisely because it was traditional. To that extent More falls short of rendering an accurate account of enthusiasm, and in the long run it may not be his point to do so. Meanwhile, the dilemma that emerges from these two writers becomes clear enough. One can either falsely explain the mental state of another, or one can declare it entirely off limits to rational explanation; but neither can adequately describe what goes on in the experience they are both concerned with. For Casaubon and More, the problem of divine inspiration remains unsolved.

It is in the context of this dilemma that the chapter that follows will turn John Milton's dramatic poem, *Samson Agonistes*. As readers know, Milton is deliberately silent about the role divine inspiration plays in Samson's final act of violent destruction—if, indeed, inspiration plays a role at all. The text itself does not offer many clues for interpretation, and unsurprisingly, critics are sharply divided over how to interpret the action. Particularly vexing is Samson's inner state as he heads off to the temple—has he been restored from the despair and/or melancholy that critics have noted to heroic strength, or does his departure mark the ultimate plunge into madness, precisely because there is no way to verify? While this division exists among critics, it is safe to say that there is very little in the text itself that guarantees a resolution to our doubts. Unlike Book Three of *Paradise Lost*, there is no scene in Heaven, no voice of the Father. Instead, this is a poem about experiencing the divine from a world from which the Divine will has thoroughly veiled itself. It is little wonder then that readers have been divided over whether Samson's final act is a demonstration of faith or of madness, since both involve a certain foregoing of reason in order to proceed.

One of the curious ways the play undercuts Samson's claim to inspiration is through the repeated use of the term experience. In his brilliant study of Ranter writings, Nigel Smith demonstrates the deep affinity between experience and prophecy among mid-seventeenth century radicals.[66] As Smith shows, experience was widely understood as a form of testimony, with is own genre characteristics—just as prophecy had been—which Puritans used to narrate "upon the events, often deeply emotional, which lead to eventual regeneration."[67] While Milton must have been cognizant of this practice, it is evident that he uses the term "experience" for entirely different purposes, namely to undermine the authority of prophecy within the dramatic poem. In the course of the poem Samson refers to his experience as a way to re-orient his sense of destiny; rather than turn him into a full fledged empiricist though, Samson's recourse to experience ultimately leads him to commit himself to a Divine will that cannot be known. To that extent, Samson's iconoclasm sets itself against what the chorus refers to as "vain reasonings." As the poem suggests though, accepting Samson's motives as radically unknowable and giving in to the necessary demand to render accounts for it anyway ultimately are inseparable. Both responses in turn are components of a shift that may be truly novel after all—as Milton suggests, madness is located not in Samson's conduct itself, but in the simultaneously futile and necessary attempts to comprehend it.

Chapter Seven

"Tell us the Sum": Milton's Accounts of Melancholy and Madness in the 1670s

> "Monstrous indeed is the madness of men who desire thus to subject the immeasurable to the puny measure of their own reason."
>
> –John Calvin, *Institutes of Christian Religion*

INTRODUCTION

From its first audience in the 1670s until the present age, many readers of John Milton's dramatic poem *Samson Agonistes* have suspected that this text somehow engages with the idea of melancholy, as it had come to be understood during the Restoration, though it is far less clear just how this engagement actually works. Ironically, this has as much to do with what Milton says as to what he leaves out. In the course of the text, he makes only two remarks. Each refers to melancholy as a physical substance, and neither one turns out to offer very satisfying explanations, either for what happens within the text itself or the experience of reading it. The first (and only explicit) statement appears in his description of tragedy, which reworks Aristotle's concept of *catharsis*. There, he notes that the function of tragedy is:

> therefore said by Aristotle to be of power by raising pity and fear, or terror, to purge the mind of those and such like passions, that is to temper and reduce them to just with a kind of delight, stirr'd up by reading or seeing those passions well imitated. Nor is Nature wanting in her own effects to make good his assertion: for so in Physic things of melancholic hue and quality are us'd against melancholy, sowr against sowr, salt to remove salt humours.[1]

Granted, this passage does not in the least suggest that Milton privileges the melancholy humors—any more than salt—if anything, the description suggests that Milton's primary concern is with pity and fear. Meanwhile, within the poem itself, we find a less explicit, but no less important reference to the black humors that were associated with melancholy disorder. During the first exchange between Samson and Manoa, the father tries to console the son by suggesting that his despair is physiological in origin (and thus amenable to medicinal cures):

> Man. Believe not these suggestions which proceed
> From anguish of the mind and humours black,
> That mingle with thy fancy. (599–601)

Samson's response, however, is to reject his father's explanation on the grounds that recourse to physiological disorders does not sufficiently characterize the extent of his grief. Instead he describes his grief as a condition of the mind, a condition which is no less powerful merely for being insubstantial:

> O that torment should not be confin'd
> To the bodies wounds and sores
> With maladies innumerable
> In heart, head, brest, and reins;
> But must secret passage find
> To th' inmost mind,
> There exercise all his fierce accidents,
> And on her purest spirits prey,
> As on entrails, joints, and limbs,
> With answerable pains, but more intense,
> Though void of corporal sense. (606–16)

By this point in the tragedy, the concept of black humors starts to sound rather more like a red herring. In contrast to the famous companion lyrics "L'Allegro" and "Il Penseroso," especially with the latter's appeal to contemplative genius, and even in contrast to the lazar houses that Michael reveals to Adam in Book Eleven of *Paradise Lost,* the melancholy in *Samson* is alluded to only to be dismissed. Perhaps Milton rejected it as an outdated physiological disorder, or perhaps as a sign of what goes wrong when human behavior is reduced to a series of physical operations.

Given its highly dubious status in *Samson,* it is something of a wonder that readers would have considered melancholy to be much of an issue at all.

Nevertheless, a number of critics have found it to be very significant, recognizing that while conventional Renaissance descriptions of an upsurge of black bile may not offer useful accounts of Samson's state of mind and behavior, a more subtle version does perhaps appear. It would be difficult to retrace, point for point, the entire history of literary criticism as it pertains to this topic, though there are three dominant trends that deserve consideration. These roughly break down as follows. To begin with, Samson's miserable condition has been interpreted as an expression of Milton's own sense of political defeat and even greater sense of outrage at his countrymen for returning to the bondage of monarchy that he himself had fought so hard to destroy. What better way for a defender of the Good Old Cause to both acknowledge one's recent defeats and simultaneously encourage his audience of "fit though few" to continue the fight—violently, if necessary—than to appeal to a Biblical figure who embodies that very spirit of militancy even while in the throes of bondage?[2] Certainly, using the historical example of Samson for the sake of contemporary political allegory was not implausible—as Sharon Achinstein argues, many of Milton's readers would have regarded the Biblical figure as a hero worthy of imitation.[3] Meanwhile, Samson iconography had been immensely popular during the civil war period, and neither his popularity nor his credibility as an exemplary figure was the least bit damaged when his story of divine vengeance was appropriated by exultant Royalists and unyielding Puritans alike.[4] For his part, whatever general suspicions he may have held toward allegorical poetry, Milton did not shy away from making explicit reference to the Samson episode in his prose writings; in more than one sense, Samson's tragic heroism was instrumental for Milton's own political engagement. If we accept these premises, then, a dramatic representation of Samson's conversion from despair to violent revenge against his idolatrous oppressors could easily serve either as wish-fulfillment or what passes—in modern parlance—under the troubling term, "incitement."

More often though, Samson's own state of mind is placed under scrutiny. The central issue revolves around the question of his state of mind during the final moments of his life, when he allows himself to be led to the Philistine festival in honor of the fish-god Dagon. One of the more animated debates surrounding Milton's text concerns the question whether these final moments represent what Milton elsewhere calls "regeneration," or whether instead his murder-suicide amounts to no more than irrational violence that says more about his waste of potential than its fulfillment. Over the course of this debate, such terms as "melancholy" and "despair," have played a small role, but a noticeable one all the same. The controversy may be said to begin with Don Cameron Allen's claim that the text "Centers on the regeneration of a desperate man and includes in its circular scope all of the theological dicta on the genesis and cure of despair."[5] It continues with questions of whether or not Allen's claim is accurate; in particular, whether Samson's self-destructive violence can truly be said to be a sign of overcoming despair, or, as Irene Samuel suggests—more sensibly, given the way Samson dies—tragic irony.[6] Indeed, in many ways the text seems to invite claims that, in the end, the poem is about the difficulties inherent to the interpretive process itself, as Daniel Lochman, Henry MacDonald and others suggest.[7] And as Stanley Fish has suggested on a number of occasions, what Samson's tragic ending finally shows is that his experience is radically incommunicable—even to Samson himself—and to impose rational interpretations is to misunderstand the divine will, which resists such interpretations by nature.[9] These aspects may render Samson's final act "radically ambiguous," but they do not necessarily reduce the dramatic poem to a document about indeterminacy; despite the fact that, as witnesses, we cannot know Samson's inner nature, there are any number of ways to resolve our questions about him. As Mary Ann Radzinowicz and Anthony Low have demonstrated, for instance, the presence of irony does not necessarily preclude readers from asserting structural patterns within the work, and thereby concluding in favor of Samson's recovery and God's providential justice by the end.[8]

The controversy is complicated still further by an enigmatic declaration that Samson makes to the chorus moments before he departs to the Philistine's festival, where he performs his destructive act. As he announces:

> Be of good courage, I begin to feel
> Some rouzing motions in me which dispose
> To something extraordinary my thoughts . . .
> If there be aught of presage in the mind,
> This day will be remarkable in my life
> By some great act, or of my days the last. (1381–89)

Samson thus hints at renewed strength, and divinely sanctioned strength at that; unfortunately, it could just as easily have signaled a private delusion—mistaking one's inner turmoil for divine inspiration—as evidently it have been during previous episodes of Samson's less than prestigious career. To that end, Samson's use of the word "or" in line 1389 is of little help, as it suggests that, in the end he not only does not know what lies in store for him, but what its significance will be. Thus by the end of the dramatic poem two competing pictures begin to emerge: either Samson is an agent of Providence, and his violent destruction is satisfying; or he is sick. The striking thing is that both pictures are mutually unsatisfying. The source of Samson's inspiration being unknowable, any attempt to explain it becomes a form of delusion, if not outright madness; and as it turns out, the characters within the play who do offer an interpretation of Samson tend to come across as disturbingly off-base.

It is the seemingly inscrutable nature of Samson's announcement that calls to mind the third important critical trend to be considered here. This consists of examining Samson's alleged recovery and vengeance in the context of ongoing debates about religious enthusiasm and religious melancholy, such as Karen Edwards does in her recent article, "Inspiration and Melancholy in *Samson Agonistes*."[10] These debates had taken on renewed urgency during the 1650s, when England witnessed the emergence of several radical religious sects who engaged in various sorts of disruptive behavior, including rhetorically violent lay prophecies. These debates were hardly settled by the 1670s when *Samson Agonistes* appeared in print. Of central concern was the question of distinguishing a genuine prophet from a mere heretic or impostor, on the one hand, and a person afflicted with religious melancholy on the other. As we have seen in the previous chapter, it was the Cambridge Platonist Henry More who wrote the most definitive, it not the most reductive statement to that effect. His book *Enthusiasmus Triumphatus* offered a scathing critique of religious enthusiasm, ultimately taking for granted what other seventeenth century writers (including Burton and Casaubon) were at least willing to subject to further inquiry. Samson's assertion that providence itself has entered into him in the form of a divine vibration may therefore feel suspicious. For even if one assumes that the character reports a genuine sensation, there is no guarantee that readers would have been able to distinguish it from illness. For his part, Milton offers suggestions for comparison to both prophets and religious melancholics of the later seventeenth century, but he provides nothing that would allow us to resolve the issue definitively.

These positions are worth bearing in mind, not for the sake of summary—in fact, the critical controversies surrounding *Samson* are far too extensive to afford a summary as brief as the one above[11]—but because they reveal a set of assumptions that do recur frequently whenever readers accept that the early modern tradition of melancholy may provide an important context for Milton's tragic poem. Such critical assumptions maintain that if melancholy explains anything, it directs attention to the poem's title character (and/or author) as though the point were to show that Samson could be adequately analyzed either by humoral terminology, the continental tradition of quasi-divine inspiration, or any one of its variants. In other words, it is to determine whether Samson's conduct during the final episode of his life is consistent with symptoms associated with melancholy illness. And while such attention is not by any means misplaced, it does potentially overlook one crucial aspect of the way that Milton had come to make use of the term by the end of his career.

As will become clear through a reexamination of the final year or so of his publishing career, Milton's sense of melancholy took on new significance as it helped clarify his position regarding proper forms of public worship. For Milton, the question of whether or not an individual was melancholy no longer was sufficient; what mattered was to distinguish melancholy from the sorts of public conduct that he had come to identify with the less flattering terms, madness and delusion. Just as important, the question of melancholy became less a matter of aesthetics and much more substantially a matter of collective experience—the term came to designate a condition that was central to the individuals concerned with their own salvation. Under that context melancholy is no longer simply an instrument for the explaining character motivation (literary or otherwise), and by asking whether or not Samson bears melancholy characteristics, on a very fundamental level we as readers miss this point. And in doing so, we risk losing sight of why, at the end of Milton's own career, the concept of melancholy continued to matter.

UNSPEAKABLE MELONCHOLY

In order to see how this transformation took place, it may be helpful to consider Edwards' argument more closely. It is a particularly helpful contribution, not only because her treatment of melancholy in Milton's tragedy is so extensive, but because she herself is sensitive to the subtle variations in terminology that had been underway during the period when Milton was composing his text.[12] According to this argument, Milton's sense of melancholy underwent a profound change in usage, if not exactly in meaning or significance. Thanks in large part to the polemical denunciations that had become popular by the 1650s, to refer to inspiration as the effect of melancholy no longer would have held the same resonance as it had during the early stages of Milton's career, when he could write a poem like "Il Penseroso" with comparatively few reservations. If Samson's state of mind is so radically inscrutable then, it is because Milton took pains to avoid a term that had become too badly tainted by the likes of More; if he had used it, it would have served no other purpose than to generate unnecessary squabbling over words. Thus she writes that:

> To represent melancholy as it was traditionally understood, Milton cannot call Samson a melancholic. The term had become, for Milton's purposes, unspeakable. The brave new discourse of the Restoration had stripped melancholy of its ancient grandeur; melancholic *enthusiasmos*

cannot be taken seriously after 1660. The poet who had hailed "divinest Melancholy" in his youth is able to make use of the traditional concept for the hero of *Samson Agonistes* only by withholding the name.[13]

As this assessment suggests, Milton was just as eager to seek out what he describes in "Il Penseroso" as "Something like prophetic strain"; only he was less willing to identify it in those terms. By the time he had published *Samson Agonistes,* he found himself in a position where he was forced, yet once more, to call upon the meaning, not the name.

It is always a thankless critical task to account for an *absence* in a text. In that regard, Edwards is as compelling as one can be when she explains why melancholy does not appear in *Samson* when Milton could just as well made more explicit use of it. The strength of the argument notwithstanding, it does require some modification, for in point of fact Milton does invoke the name itself on more than one occasion during the later stages of his career. Indeed, the year 1673 saw the republication of his early poems, including "L'Allegro" and "Il Penseroso"—if Milton had come to hold reservations about melancholy as a legitimate source of inspiration, it was not made evident by this gesture. More important, melancholy plays a small but decisive role in his arguments concerning religious toleration, which appear the same year in his pamphlet *Of True Religion.*

The question of religious toleration had become an especially knotty problem by the 1670s, and indeed the mere fact that Milton decided to intervene in the public debates is itself a sign just how intensely the passions were flaring. (Milton had been tactfully silent on matters political during the Restoration; and while certainly everything he published during his later years—including his *Art of Logic*—may have carried both direct and indirect references to public controversies, he was no longer the audacious pamphleteer he had been during the 1640s and 1650s.) The question on toleration had been revived during recent parliamentary sessions, and Milton's specific concern lay with the Crown's position, which implied (among other things) a more lax approach to Roman Catholicism. Milton's pamphlet intended to warn his readers of the dangers that would inevitably befall England should it backslide to ceremonial forms of worship that pre-dated the Reformation itself: or as he puts it, with customary graciousness, "the worst of superstitions."[14]

Significantly, it is in response to his fear of public superstition that Milton makes reference to melancholy, and as he describes it in the pamphlet's final paragraphs, rather than lead to fantastic delusions of the mind, melancholy may in fact be his readers' only sure defense against them. Thus he warns:

> There is no man so wicked, but at sometimes his conscience will wring him with thoughts of another world, & the Peril of his soul: the trouble and melancholy which he conceives of true Repentance and amendment he endures not; but enclines rather to some carnal Superstition, which may pacify and lull his Conscience with some more pleasing Doctrin. (439)

Certainly, this does not sound much like the sage wisdom of that divinest goddess whom the youthful poet had depicted in his early lyric. Instead, Milton has moved away from his desire for prophetic inspiration, and toward something like an anxiety of existence that he characterizes, borrowing a passage from Phillipians, as "fear and trembling," with which the individual works out one's salvation.[15]

Meanwhile, in the course of making shifting attention from inspiration to anguish, Milton also abandons what might be considered a naïve pretense to apprehend the universe as an entirety. In his youthful poem, he had expressed such a desire by the optimistic lines:

> Dissolve me into ecstasies,
> And bring all heaven before mine eyes . . .
> Where I may sit and rightly spell
> Of every star that heaven doth shew,
> And every herb that sips the dew. (165–74)

What is implicit here, through the repeated use of the word "every" (as well as the "all" in line 166), is that the universe is potentially knowable, if not quantifiable. Moreover, it is through the pensive contemplation brought about in melancholy ecstasies that one attains this ability. Such an outlook is entirely absent by the end of his career. The contemplative individual who can know the stars for what they are—and whose pensiveness implies, above all else, orientation within an otherwise mysterious cosmos—gives way to its evil twin, the person who attempts to:

> bribe God as a corrupt judge; and by his Proctor, some Priest or Fryer, to buy out his Peace with money, which he cannot with his repentance. (439)

If the prophet in "Il Penseroso" had hoped to count the stars, the person of bad faith counts coins, vainly supposing his sins can be expressed in economic terms. So much for enumeration. It is this pretense that God demands a price for human conduct that in turn prompts Milton's final—and most urgent—warning to his readers:

> The last means to avoid Popery is to amend our lives: it is a general complaint that this Nation of late years, is grown more numerously and excessively vitious then heretofore: Pride, Luxury, Drunkenness, Whoredom, Cursing, Swearing, bold and open Atheism every where abounding: Where these grow, no wonder if Popery also grow a pace. (438–39)

As dangerous as Roman Catholicism strikes Milton, then, in one sense it is incidental; a far more urgent concern is the widespread frivolousness that has virtually stifled the public concern for the more painful aspects of searching for the "scattered limbs of Osiris" (so to speak). It is almost as though the turbulent decades of the 1640s and 1650s had come to belong to a past so distant—or at any rate, a past so widely repressed—that England had become indifferent. And while Milton may have despised Roman Catholicism for promoting the wrong doctrine, at the very least it promoted something; but to dismiss such controversies altogether as irrelevant is to court real disaster. It is in response to this threat that Milton finally advocates a program of internal struggle that is both perpetual and uncertain, fundamentally incompatible with computations of any sort.

The pleasure that melancholy comes to offer—if in fact it can be called a pleasure—is that of struggling with one's salvation on an individual level. One cannot make recourse to prefabricated solutions, there is no genuine formula for repentance that one can simply apply. Above all, nobody can rely on the acts of another—hero or otherwise—to assure themselves of their own redemption. Ultimately, if Milton does see room for religious tolerance, it is because there is always room for doubt, and even more room for accepting responsibility for one's own fate.[16] It is an uncomfortable existence, albeit one that is infinitely preferable to the kinds of false solutions that his Roman Catholic adversaries would establish as alternatives. For as Milton points out, again making recourse to Scripture, alternatives such as ceremonlialism and recourse to formulas fall squarely into the realm of delusion. Thus, he writes:

> Idolatry brought the Heathen to hainous Transgressions, *Romans 2 d.* And hainous Transgressions oft times bring the slight professors of true Religion, to gross Idolatry: 1 Thess. 2.11, 12. *For this cause, God shall send them strong delusion that they should believe a lye, that they all might be damnd who believe not the truth, but had pleasure in unrighteousness.*

And Isaiah 44.18. Speaking of Idolators, *They have not known nor understood, for he hath shut their Eyes that they cannot see, and their hearts that they cannot understand.* (439–440)

It is difficult to overestimate Milton's disdain for the delusion that God sends as the punishment for idol worship. For Milton, this would have been a real concern, since the threat of idolatry was pervasive. As Barbara Lewalski reminds us, Milton's sense of idolatry extended to capture any "disposition to attach divinity or special sanctity to any person—pope or king or prelate, or any human institution or material form."[17] The passage Milton cites from Thessalonians (incorrectly, it turns out) is immediately followed by a description of the more horrifying aspects of divine vengeance and destruction. (If Milton held idolatry in scorn, he would have thought himself in good company.) Inasmuch as Milton responds to questions about the nature of religious melancholy and enthusiasm at all, his response is to reassess the terms of the debate altogether—melancholy not only is distinct from delusion, but when used as the spur to true Repentance, it is the rational individual's only defense.

SHAMEFUL GARRULITY

Although it would be a stretch to say that *True Religion* and *Samson Agonistes* were companion pieces, nevertheless it is clear that Milton had similar concerns in mind when he composed his tragic poem. Samson's fundamental struggle consists of a series of attacks against similar types of false presumptions that give rise to superstition and idolatry, not only among the Philistines but also the Israelites, whose own misconduct had given rise to the need for his heroism in the first place. Indeed, on one important level Samson's conflict with the Philistines becomes a vehicle for redirectng the reader's attention to another, more fundamental conflict with the Israelites themselves. From one end of the tragedy to the other, Samson's associates—represented both by Manoa and the chorus of Israelites who accompany him—demonstrate a pattern of behavior that shares many of the characteristics of bad conscience that Milton would come to describe two years later. These range from figurative (and in some ways sensible) attempts to narrate Samson's fate as an exemplary story—to render an accurate account of it, as it were—to more crude gestures, such as bribery and potentially superstitious ceremonies. Taken together, they suggest a community that has designed the conditions for its survival around a set of false practices and beliefs. And to that extent the rhetorical force of the tragedy is not only to draw attention to the death of the hero, but to illustrate what occurs when the significance of that hero's death fails to take hold among the very people for whom it is most urgently meant.

As we shall see, this failure takes many forms throughout the course of the text. It becomes particularly urgent during the last 500 lines or so, when the chorus exults over Samson's death in a manner that even Milton's more sympathetic readers have referred to as "spin control."[18] However, even during the tragedy's opening moments, these same characters suggest they are well on their way toward rendering disastrously false judgments of Samson's fate. It begins with what is probably an unanswerable question for most of us: to what extent can Samson, as individual, be brought into alignment with a written narrative of Samson as hero, or Judge? But in searching for the way to situate Samson's life within a recognizable narrative pattern of divinely inspired heroism, the chorus ultimately risks perpetuating the very activity that had incapacitated Samson in the first place. To borrow the words Samson himself uses to explain his tragic error, they commit the act of "shameful garrulity" (491).

In the course of answering this question, the characters end up making several references to various forms of imprinting—notably, writing and coinage—as though in order to assess Samson's public status one had to be certain about the values that fit words could obtain. To be fair, Samson shows as much concern over his place in history as anyone else in the poem, though as he converses with the other characters, that concern seems to grow less important for him. When he first appears, he struggles not only to find a spot to rest, but to arrange the events of his life into some kind of recognizable order—in both a physical and moralistic sense, he seeks *orientation*. Gradually, his thoughts come to him like a swarm of hornets, and in the process of sorting them out he complains in terms that specifically invoke images of language and writing:

> O wherefore was my birth from Heaven foretold
> Twice by an Angel, who at last in sight
> Of both my Parents all in flames ascended
> From off the Altar, where an Off'ring burn'd,
> As in a fiery column charioting
> His Godlike presence, and from some great act
> Or benefit reveal'd to Abraham's race?
> Why was my breeding order'd and prescrib'd
> As of a person separate to God,
> Design'd for great exploits? (23–32)

Samson's sense of defeat has its root primarily in what he believes had been told to him, and that had been told to him precisely because it had already been written out in advance, or (as in line 230) pre-scribed. But in the course of his first conversations with the Chorus and later Manoa, Samson suggests that he is already in the process of moving away from both assumptions. Hence his word "prescribed" gives way to another, more deceiving form of writing, which he invokes while he compares the chorus' friendship to a counterfeit coin. In sarcasm, he says:

> Your coming, Friends, revives me, for I learn
> Now of my own experience, not by talk,
> How counterfeit a coin they are who friends
> Bear in their Superscription (of the most
> I would be understood) in prosperous days
> They swarm, but in adverse withdraw their head
> Not to be found, though sought. (187–93)

By contrast, and almost as if they had heard Samson's private ruminations, it is the chorus that retains the word "prescript" in their advice:

> As if they would confine th' interminable,
> And tie him to his own prescript,
> Who made our Laws to bind us, not himself . . . (307–09)

The early stages of the dramatic conflict can be seen to obtain around this cluster of terms. Samson differentiates as one who has come to invoke various images of *imprinting,* if not to call providence into question, then to question whether following providence must entail recognizing one's "place in history," or understanding the significance of one's acts with respect to what God disposes. In contrast, the chorus, which invokes it precisely insofar as it restores that divine order to the level of mystery: they affirm it when they least expect it, and paradoxically the fact that it happens by surprise is what assures them it is at work after all.

Meanwhile, the word "prescript" suggests an additional meaning, namely a formula, or even formulaic statement, offered in the direction of restoring one to health. As Milton's use of the word may suggest, the statements made with respect to Samson's historical condition in turn carry real implications for the Israelite's overall benefit. On that subject, the chorus and Samson again are clearly divided. The chorus remains convinced that words can quite literally serve as healing devices. Indeed, it is this very belief that prompts them to address Samson directly in the first place:

> We come thy friends and neighbours not unknown
> From Eshtaol and Zora's fruitful Vale
> To visit or bewail thee, or if better,
> Counsel or Consolation we may bring,
> Salve to thy Sores, apt words have power to swage
> The tumors of a troubl'd mind,
> And are as Balm to fester'd wounds. (180–86)

In turn, they assure him that "Just are the ways of God, and justifiable to man," (294–95) a proposition which emphasizes not only divine justice, but more importantly our ability to put it into words. Hence, in urging Samson to remain patient, the chorus makes recourse to ancient *sentences,* as if to suggest that such knowledge already is available in abundance:

> Many are the sayings of the wise
> In antient and in modern books enroll'd;
> Extolling Patience as the truest fortitude . . . (652–54)

Such appeals to wisdom have the intention of reinforcing Samson's belief in the communicative power of language, and as it happens their concerns are not entirely unfounded. For Samson, human language repeatedly strikes him as mere noise: when he first appears, he seeks to retire from the "popular noise" of the Philistines—and significantly, whoever the mysterious guide is who leads him to his place of rest, that character is completely silent. When the chorus does appear, Sasmon disappoints them, either by failing or refusing to recognize their speech as meaningful language. Thus he complains:

> I hear the sound of words, their sense the air
> Dissolves unjointed ere it reach my ear. (176–77)

As inconsolable as Samson may come across, however, his resistance has its merits as well. Ironically, it is Manoa who provides the grounds for suspicion when he couples adages with bribes:

> I however
> Must not omit a Fathers timely care
> To prosecute the means of thy deliverance
> By ransom or how else: mean while be calm,
> And healing words from these thy friends admit. (601–05)

This is not Manoa's most flattering moment, to be sure, but in the process of establishing a connection between wise sayings and monetary ransom, he suggests that such a connection may have existed all along. To the extent that language has ceased to function for Samson, it is largely insofar as the proper function of language already involves the calculation of things that were never meant to be figured in such terms to begin with.

To be sure, the conflict over the public functions of language operates on many levels throughout Milton's text. For Samson, a series of failures in interpreting God's will, the last of which leads to his final imprisonment, raises profound doubts over the reliability of allegedly divine proclamations. Meanwhile, as the passages noted above indicate, Samson and the Chorus are at odds over whether language on its own is enough to relieve suffering— whether there is such a thing as a "talking cure," after all. But perhaps most important is the question of language's role in the shaping of Samson's public reputation, and on this level the controversy is not whether Samson is truly a hero or not, but more fundamentally, whether it is wise to cultivate public fame in the first place. For in doing so, the Israelites risk participating in a type of discourse that is, at its best, unstable. Indeed, Samson may have had reasons from the very start to be suspicious about the advantages of securing his public reputation. If not, Dalila provides him with one when she parts ways with him. As she explains:

> Fame if not double-fac't is double-mouth'd,
> And with contrary blast proclaims most deeds,
> On both his wings, one black, th' other white,
> Bears greatest names in his wild aerie flight.
> My name perhaps among the Circumcis'd
> In Dan, in Judah, and the bordering Tribes,
> To all posterity may stand defam'd,
> With malediction mention'd, and the blot
> Of falshood most unconjugal traduc't.
> But in my countrey where I most desire,
> In Ecron, Gaza, Asdod, and in Gath
> I shall be nam'd among the famousest
> Of Women, sung at solemn festivals,
> Living and dead recorded, who to save
> Her countrey from a fierce destroyer, chose
> Above the faith of wedlock-bands, my tomb
> With odours visited and annual flowers. (971–87)

It is an embarrassing moment, not because it exposes Samson as a failure, but because it suggests that Samson's conflict had been essentially a mimetic rivalry all along. Even if Samson had been successful, his success would be uncomfortably close to his adversaries. For his part, Milton had learned through bitter experience what Dalila states in precept. Following the execution of Charles I, Milton had engaged in an impassioned defense of the emerging republic's cause, only to witness the counterfeit autobiography *Eikon Basilike* capture the attention of the reading public. In the course of a mere few pages, the deposed tyrant and enemy of the people had been reframed as a martyr and saint. During the years that followed, Milton engaged in a series of bitter disputes over the various details of his own life, including the moral significance of his blindness. In his polemics, Milton expressed disdain for the populous "rabble," which, in his mind, was too easily seduced by cheap propaganda, at the cost of truth (which can be distorted as easily as one's eyes follow the words on a page). Likewise, with respect to *Samson Agonistes*, Milton would have insisted that the difference between Samson and Dalila is substantial rather than arbitrary. Behind Dalila's remarks about fame seems to lurk an even deeper concern that in the end, it is less about truth and falsehood than about one's relation to certain more or less arbitrary symbols; ultimately though, Milton seems to entertain this dangerous thought only to dismiss it as insignificant in the face of truth.

Still, if Milton would have been quick to dismiss Dalila's farewell as a clear invitation to idolatry, when it comes to defending the Israelite's responses to Samson's final act the matter is very much a matter of doubt. Milton may well have been of two minds about the Israelites; if the Book of Judges offers any hint, the most remarkable feature of Samson's heroism was its failure to reform their conduct. Over the course of his public career, Milton repeatedly expressed deep admiration for Samson's heroism, while sparing little criticism for the Israelites in the process. But, as is well known, his admiration for Samson could be tempered by qualifying statements. In *A Defence of the People of England* for instance, he cautions against worrying too extensively over the precise nature of Samson's motivation. In the end, what matters is what one can know, not what one can speculate about interminably, and in this instance Milton is certain which is which:

> Even the heroic Samson, though his countrymen reproached him saying, Judges 15, "Knowest thou not that the Philistines are rulers over us?," still made war single-handed on his masters, and, whether prompted by God or by his own valor, slew at one stroke not one but a

host of his country's tyrants, having first made prayer to God for his aid. Samson therefore thought it not impious but pious to kill those masters who were tyrants over his country, even though most of her citizens did not balk at slavery.[19]

As Milton suggests, what makes Samson so admirable is not simply his conduct itself. More important is his autonomy—he is not answerable to human norms, customs, or laws. His piety is thus put forth as a foil for the remaining Israelites, who know all too well what it means to submit to the rules of other men. In the final sections of *Samson Agonistes,* Milton raises similar concerns, although there the intention very much seems to be to force his reader's into endless speculation. Gradually, the poem's hero becomes increasingly ambiguous—the last speech of his is a declaration of intentions, but it is a declaration that could mean just about anything. His most important act takes place "off-stage" (if it can be put this way). As the catastrophe unfolds, though, both Manoa and the Chorus filter his conduct through a series of interpretive gestures with the aim of situating Samson within a larger historical narrative. To put it less elegantly, they *talk* about Samson's death as though doing so had been his purpose all along. Meanwhile, their talking has the effect of reducing Samson's conduct into a series of readable texts—they turn him into a legend. While Samson himself had characterized his intentions in deliberately indeterminate language, using the phrase "some great act" to announce his plans, the remaining characters go to great lengths to affix the nature of that act to determinate, measurable bounds. As the concluding remarks of this chapter will suggest, it is within this difference that we can start to discern what might rightly be called the emerging madness of the Israelites. For in their glorification of Samson's death as an act of heroism, the surviving Israelites show the signs of the public delusion that emerges as the product of public superstition.

During the moments when Samson performs his feats of strength, Milton presents his action to us through a series of auditory images. At first glance, this series appears to convey a sense of progress. It begins with a pair of literally meaningless noises, which leave the chorus and Manoa at a relative loss for understanding:

> What noise or shout was that? it tore the Skie.
> Chor. Doubtless the people shouting to behold
> Thir once great dread, captive, & blind before them,
> Or at some proof of strength before them shown. (1472–75)

The only moment of comprehension consists in noting the differences in volume and tone between the first and second noise:

> O what noise!
> Mercy of Heav'n what hideous noise was that!
> Horribly loud unlike the former shout.
> Chor. Noise call you it or universal groan
> As if the whole inhabitation perish'd,
> Blood, death, and deathful deeds are in that noise,
> Ruin, destruction at the utmost point. (1508–14)

It is not until the messenger arrives at line 1540, or so, that these noises are translated into articulate statements. The mere fact that the messenger can put an account of Samson's death into words suggests a major step forward, though what turns out to be most striking about the messenger's story is its extraordinary number of shortcomings. From the start, and in a way that reminds us all too poignantly that Samson's death occurred at a performance designed to look like a sporting event, the messenger makes note of his bad view:

> The building was a spacious Theater
> Half round on two main Pillars vaulted high,
> With seats where all the Lords and each degree
> Of Sort, might sit in order to behold,
> The other side was op'n, where the throng
> On banks and scaffolds under Sky might stand;
> I among these aloof obscurely stood. (1606–12)

As he admits, his position prevents him from determining several crucial details, and the result is an account that bears only the vaguest resemblance to the version one finds in the book of Judges. As he concludes we realize that there is virtually no difference between what he sees and what he merely thinks he sees; meanwhile, we recognize that the alleged transition from noise to articulate statement offers only the semblance of progress, not progress itself.

Indeed, if the chorus and Manoa had been listening to the messenger's story carefully, the would have recognized that the messenger was not a true witness to Samson's death, since the only ones who witness it properly are also destroyed in the process. The fact that they do not owes more to what they are listening for than with what the messenger actually says. We happen to recognize this because of the way that Manoa prompts him to tell it. Impatiently, he says:

> Tell us the sum, the circumstance defer. (1557)

While the conventions of classical tragedy do require an elaborate account of the hero's death, in light of Manoa's previous conduct it inadvertently becomes a request of extraordinary bad taste. Manoa reminds us of the several moments when he thought to offer ransom for his son, an option he continues to seek right up until very the moment that the messenger arrives, and which is perhaps reinforced by the chorus' response immediately following: "Oh dearly bought revenge, yet glorious!" (1660) When we recall that Samson's final promise to the Israelites had been that he would perform, on that very day, "some great act," we cannot help but wonder further whether Manoa heard the sound of the words without quite catching how they were intended.

To be fair, Manoa's demand can be understood as a legitimate desire to end the suspense that the messenger has placed him under since his arrival; but in his enthusiastic response afterwards, his impatience becomes magnified. In making preparations to commemorate Samson's death as an act of heroism, Manoa makes a series of remarks that imply an all out rush to final judgment, beginning with an assertion most remarkable for its abruptness:

> Come, come, no time for lamentation now,
> Nor much more cause, Samson hath quit himself
> Like Samson, and heroicly hath finish'd
> A life Heroic, on his Enemies
> Fully reveng'd, hath left them years of mourning,
> And lamentation to the Sons of Caphtor
> Through all Philistian bounds. To Israel
> Honour hath left, and freedom, let but them
> Find courage to lay hold on this occasion,
> To himself and Fathers house eternal fame;
> And which is best and happiest yet, all this
> With God not parted from him, as was fear'd,
> But favouring and assisting to the end.
> Nothing is here for tears, nothing to wail
> Or knock the breast, no weakness, no contempt,
> Dispraise, or blame, nothing but well and fair,
> And what may quiet us in a death so noble. (1708–24)

"Tell us the Sum"

Many critics have made note of Manoa's suggestive use of a similitude—Samson hath quit himself *like* Samson—but just as peculiar is the sense of finality that Manoa imposes on the discussion. If the first line suggests a sense of hastiness, words such as "quit," "end," and "finished" recur throughout his exultation. Most important, he proposes to celebrate Samson's death by rendering it readable for once and future generations in the most literal manner possible. He announces:

> There I will build him
> A monument, and plant it round with shade
> Of laurel ever green and branching palm,
> With all his trophies hung, and acts enrolled
> In copious legend, or sweet lyric song. (1733–37)

As an object that anyone could point to—and just as important, as one that conveys a sense of visibility, of solidity, and of permanence—the monument that he proposes would enable him to define, and thus delimit, the significance of Samson's final gesture with a finality of its own.

Ironically, while the legends and songs would not fulfill the desires of Samson, they do recall those of Dalila, whose parting shot to her estranged husband had been to alert him to all the songs her nation would sing about her in future ages. As she had boasted:

> I shall be nam'd among the famousest
> Of Women, sung at solemn festivals,
> Living and dead recorded, who to save
> Her country from a fierce destroyer, chose
> Above the faith of wedlock-bands, my tomb
> With odours visited and annual flowers. (982–87)

To that end, Manoa's rush for closure take on characteristics that bear a striking similarity to the very forms of idolatry that Samson had been placed in this world to destroy. Ostensibly, Manoa's greatest concern is that certain elements of Samson's death might not be resolved, and this would entail constant re-examination, even periods of occasional doubt. His flaw is not simply that he manipulates, or spins, Samson's death in as favorable a light as he can—anyone might be expected to do that, especially during a period of warfare. More fundamentally, his mistake is to believe that has gestures can establish Samson's public disposition once and for all.

For his part, Manoa recognizes that this monument will have to exist in time, but the only way this registers is through a series of images that ceremonial repetitions. He dreams of a future when youthful Israelites will try to imitate Samson's valor, and when virgins shall cover flowers on his grave during "feastful days," as he describes them, in language that again carries unmistakable echoes from Dalila's final speech. The chorus contributes by likening Samson to a Phoenix, a creature whose very nature is to revive and re-flourish. Taken together, these images have the effect of placing Samson within a recognizable historical framework. Nevertheless, these same images hint at a sense of delusion on the part of the Israelites, for it is the same chorus that draws our attention to the onset of madness at the public level. Significantly, the madness that they speak of, and which they attribute to the Philistines, occurs right in the middle of a public festival. To that end, they observe:

> While thir hearts were jocund and sublime,
> Drunk with Idolatry, drunk with Wine,
> And fat regorg'd of Bulls and Goats,
> Chaunting thir Idol, and preferring
> Before our living Dread who dwells
> In Silo his bright Sanctuary:
> Among them he a spirit of phrenzie sent,
> Who hurt thir minds,
> And urg'd them on with mad desire
> To call in hast for thir destroyer;
> They only set on sport and play
> Unweetingly importun'd
> Thir own destruction to come speedy upon them. (1669–81)

While there are clear differences between this festival and the sort of holiday celebrations that Manoa describes—among all the things Manoa imagines taking place, at Samson's grave a Bacchanalian orgy hardly is one of them—in the end it is not those differences that matter. The flowers and songs he imagines may be enough for the two simple reasons that they divert attention from God to Samson, and that they direct attention from Samson to a visual aid. Such customs therefore introduce the possibility that future generations may paradoxically forget the very things their acts are supposed to commemorate. As these speeches come to a close, we are in a position to be mistrustful of the Israelites' intentions. Even without making recourse to the book of Judges, where we find that they do not give up idol-worship, we have reasons to remain uncertain about their redemption. And indeed, that experience of uncertainty might well have been Milton's point. For by drawing conclusions too quickly, readers run the risk of giving way to false comforts, and these would ultimately deprive us of the melancholy that obtains whenever we work out our salvation on our own, with fear and trembling, and without recourse to the predetermined formulas that others have devised.

CONCLUSION

Part of what makes *Samson Agonistes* such a compelling text is that it stages the fantasies and anxieties, not only of Milton's age, but of subsequent ages as well. At its most basic level, Samson embodies characteristics that critics have identified with both melancholy discontent and divine vengeance that takes on apocalyptic proportions in the end. But more important, Milton's Samson is compelling because of what he reveals about madness, and to that end, he was addressing his readers on a particularly crucial matter. During the seventeenth century the Biblical character had come to register an astonishing array of ideological positions concerning various questions: what was the role of divine vengeance and martyrdom in a post-Apostolic age; to what extent could biblical narratives apply to contemporary public events; and what assurance did England have that God would indeed protect His chosen nation from bondage. Much as Milton admired Samson throughout his own public career, he also recognized that Samson's story did not lend itself to interpretations that in turn sanctioned violent acts as examples of divine vengeance for subsequent ages to imitate. Or rather, he recognized that the story lent itself all too easily. Thus rather than give us clues to determine whether Samson was divinely inspired or simply beset with private delusions, his text shows that the location of madness may lie in the unsatisfying attempts to explain Samson's conduct beyond what the surface events tell us. Finally, to the extent that he participated in a society that was deeply concerned with the nature of religious enthusiasm—and that had increasingly come to identify it as a physiological disorder—Milton seems unwilling to accept the notion that a mere diagnosis would explain Samson effectively. But for that matter, he is just as reluctant to affirm that what lies behind it really is divine infusion. What truly motivates the prophet—particularly those prophets whose accounts we read about in the Bible—may not be accessible to explanation after all. For Milton, one enters the realm of madness only when one believes that their mystery can somehow be made more transparent through explanations that attempt to do the work of renewed examination. To that end, rather than abandon melancholy, Milton invites us to embrace it. For in the course of doing so, we can perhaps feel that we have understood his own last public demand to his readers, perhaps the only demand which Milton believed there was no time for delay: "We must amend our lives."

Notes

NOTES TO THE INTRODUCTION

1. A concise synopsis of the Hippocratic theory of the humors, as well as its significance for Renaissance medicine, can be found in Nancy G. Siraisi, *Medieval and Early Renaissance Medicine: An Introduction to Knowledge and Practice* (Chicago and London: University of Chicago Press, 1990), 104–06.
2. In fact, this book is being published very shortly after Douglas Trevor's study, *The Poetics of Melancholy in Early Modern England* (Cambridge: Cambridge University Press, 2004); so recently, I have not had time to sufficiently respond to his arguments within this book.
3. Richard Younge, *The Prevention of Poverty, Together with the Cure of Melancholy, Alias Discontent. Or the best and surest way to Wealth and Hapiness: being Subjects very seasonable for these Times; wherein all are Poor, or not pleased, or both; when they need be neither* (London, 1655). Other texts are listed in the Works Cited section.
4. As it turns out, these pamphlets lent support to Christopher Hill's claim that, as the seventeenth century wore on, more and more people came to recognize lay prophecy as a symptom of illness, as opposed to heresy or blasphemy. See Christopher Hill, "John Mason and the End of the World," *Puritanism and Revolution: Studies in Interpretation of the English Revolution of the 17th Century* (New York: St. Martin's Press, 1997), 290–302.
5. Anon., *The Melancholy Visioner, or, The Factious Citizen* (London 1685).
6. A significant portion of this terminology derived from classical sources, such as Lucan's unfinished *Pharsalia*. Lucan repeatedly uses the term *furor* to describe the cause for the conflict between Caesar and Pompey; and likewise, to the extent that Lucan served as a model for texts such as Cowley's unfinished account of the English Civil war, *furor* provided the necessary explanation for what drove the conflict forward. In contrast, some playwrights often described melancholy as the effect of civil war; see, for instance, Thomas

197

Lodge's *The Wounds of Civil War,* and the anonymous university play, *Caesar and Pompey.*

7. For the sake of convenience, I will refer to this author and text as pseudo-Aristotle and the pseudo-Aristotelian *Problems* respectively.
8. Raymond Klibansky, Erwin Panofsky and Fritz Saxl, *Saturn and Melancholy: Studies in the History of Natural Philosophy, Religion and Art* (New York: Basic Books, 1964).
9. A fuller discussion of psychoanalysis and melancholy appears further below.
10. Friedrich Niezsche, "The Utility and Liability of History," *Unfashionable Observations,* (Stanford: Stanford University Press, 1995).
11. Lawrence Babb, *The Elizabethan Malady: A Study of Melancholia in Literature from 1580 to 1642* (East Lansing: Michigan State College Press, 1951), 74–82; L. C. Knights, *Drama and Society in the Age of Jonson* (London: Chatto and Windus, 1937): Appendix 2; Bridget Gellert Lyons, *Voices of Melancholy: Studies in Literary Treatments of Melancholy in Renaissance England,* Ideas and Forms in English Literature (London: Routledge & Kegan Paul, 1971), 34–44; Jonathan Dollimore, *Radical Tragedy: Religion, Ideology and Power in the Drama of Shakespeare and his Contemporaries* (Durham: Duke University Press, 1993), 49–50; James Biester, *Lyric Wonder: Rhetoric and Wit in English Renaissance Poetry* (Ithaca: Cornell University Press, 1997), esp. chapter two.
12. Babb, *Elizabethan Malady,* 80.
13. Lyons, *Voices of Melancholy,* 58–70.
14. In addition to those mentioned at other points of this Introduction, as well as subsequent chapters, I refer to Duncan Salkeld, *Madness and Drama in the Age of Shakespeare* (Manchester and New York: Manchester University Press, 1993); Carol Thomas Neely, *Distracted Subjects: Madness and Gender in Shakespeare and Early Modern Culture* (Ithaca: Cornell University Press, 2004). Erik Midelfort has written fascinating studies of the political dimensions of madness in sixteenth century Germany. See H. C. Erik Midelfort, *Mad Princes of Renaissance Germany* (Charlottesville: University Press of Virginia, 1996).
15. Winifreid Schleiner, *Melancholy, Genius, and Utopia in the Renaissance* (Wiesbaden, 1991), 12.
16. For Porter and Godlee, see *The Anatomy of Madness: Essays in the History of Psychiatry in Three Volumes,* vol. 2, eds. W. F. Bynum, Roy Porter, and Michael Shepherd (London and New York: Tavistock Publications, 1985); Clement Hawes, *Mania and Literary Style: The Rhetoric of Enthusiasm from the Ranters to Christopher Smart* (Cambridge: Cambridge University Press, 1996). A fuller indication of authors who discuss the social function of madness during the civil war appears in chapter six.
17. Debora K. Shuger, *Habits of Thought in the English Renaissance: Religion, Politics, and the Dominant Culture,* reprinted by the Renaissance Society of America (Toronto: University of Toronto Press, 1997), 14.

18. In related fashion, writing about melancholy can lead to an obsession with precise and "accurate" definitions just as easily as to the most dilatory prose treatises that the period saw.
19. See Klibansky, et al., *Saturn and Melancholy: Studies in the History of Natural Philosophy, Religion and Art* (New York: Basic Books, 1964); Erwin Panofsky, *The Life and Art of Albrecht Dürer* (Princeton: Princeton University Press, 1943), 158–71; Rudolf and Margot Wittkower, *Born Under Saturn: The Character and Conduct of Artists, A Documented History from Antiquity to the French Revolution* (New York and London: W. W. Norton & Co., 1963), 98–108.
20. Panofsky, *Dürer*, 167.
21. Panofsky, *Dürer*, 160.
22. Klibansky, et al., *Saturn and Melancholy*, 42.
23. Klibansky, et al., *Saturn and Melancholy*, 114.
24. Cf. Schleiner, *Melancholy, Genius and Utopia*, 10–12. While Schleiner has argued that the genial concept of melancholy was not dominant during the Elizabethan and Stuart periods, in fact this point had already been anticipated by the Warburg writers.
25. Klibansky, et al., *Saturn and Melancholy*, 248.
26. One can only imagine what they would have thought about the following passage from Lynn Enterline's, *Tears of Narcissus*, 7: "Though I pay careful attention to the appearance of the word 'melancholia' in early modern writing and to the kinds of problems historically associated with it—from dreams and phantasms to the strange psychosomatic ravages of lycanthropy—I do not require that the term be used as a diagnosis before reading a figure as melancholic."
27. For a good study of this legend and its interpretation in the Renaissance, see Thomas H. Cain, "Spenser and the Renaissance Orhpeus," *University of Toronto Quarterly* 41 (1971): 24–47; 25.
28. Freud, "Mourning and Melancholia," 248.
29. Freud, "Mourning and Melancholia," 248.
30. Kristeva, *Black Sun*, 11. Kristeva herself departs from this model in order to focus on "another form of depression," one that analysts encounter among narcissistic patients; it is this form of depression that provides the basis for both her study as well as Enterline's. It is necessary to bear in mind that Freud's melancholy patients possessed an irrepressible urge to confess their guilt and shame, whereas the depression Kristeva describes refers to an inexpressible grief; in light of this difference, it is easy to conclude that Freud and Kristeva make reference to different conditions. Kristeva's successes in clinical settings and her demonstration of an essential connection between narcissistic melancholy and aesthetic activity notwithstanding, my own work returns to the cannibalistic hostility of early psychoanalytic theory in order to parse out ideas which hitherto have not been developed.

31. Without wishing to dwell too long on the point here, one thinks of Brutus who intends to carve Caesar "as a dish fit for the gods"; alternately, one might include Samson, who kills the Philistines at a feast from which he has been both excluded and invited.
32. See Mark J. Curtis, "The Alienated Intellectuals of Early Stuart England," *Crisis in Europe 1560–1660: Essays from Past and Present,* Ed. Trevor Aston (London: Routledge and Kegan Paul, 1965), 295–316.
33. Such arguments tend to explicitly follow Foucault's thesis on the "Great Confinement," which he expresses almost aphoristically with the charge, "No longer a ship [of fools] but a hospital." Michel Foucault, *Madness and Civilization: A History of Insanity in the Age of Reason,* trans. Richard Howard (New York: Vintage Books, 1965), 35, 38–64.
34. John N. King, *English Reformation Literature: The Tudor Origins of the Protestant Tradition* (Princeton: Princeton University Press, 1982); Norbrook, *Poetry and Politics,* 56–58; Louis Montrose, "Of Gentlemen and Shepherds: The Politics of Elizabethan Pastoral Form," *English Literary History* 50 (1983): 415–59.
35. Norbrook, *Poetry and Politics,* 58.
36. Julia Kristeva, *Black Sun: Depression and Melancholia,* trans. Leon S. Roudiez (New York: Columbia University Press, 1989), 33–36; n. 1, 265
37. Jacques Hassoun, *The Cruelty of Depression: On Melancholy,* foreword by Michael Vincent Miller (Reading, MA: Addison-Wesley, 1997), ix-x.
38. "Melancholy? Marry gup, is melancholy a word for a barber's mouth? Thou shouldst say heavy, dull and doltish: melancholy is the crest of courtiers' arms, and now every base companion, being in his muble fubles, says he is melancholy." Quoted in Michael MacDonald, *Mystical Bedlam: Madness, Anxiety, and Healing in Seventeenth-Century England,* Cambridge History of Medicine (Cambridge: Cambridge University Press, 1981), 151.

NOTES TO CHAPTER ONE

1. Timothy Bright, *A Treatise of Melancholie,* The English Experience: Its Record in Early Printed Books, Published in Facsimile, no. 212 (New York: Da Capo Press, 1969); M. Andreas Laurentius, *A Discourse of the Preservation of the Sight: of Melancholike Diseases; of Rheumes, and of Old Age,* trans. Richard Surphlet, Shakespeare Association Facsimiles no. 15, (Oxford: Oxford University Press, 1938). All subsequent citations from Bright and Laurentius refer to these editions, respectively.
2. Lawrence Babb, *The Elizabethan Malady: A Study of Melancholia in English Literature from 1580 to 1642* (East Lansing: Michigan State University Press, 1951). While Babb defines melancholy as a disease that became popular, even faddish, during the Elizabethan reign, the present study argues that discussions

Notes to Chapter One

about melancholy emerged in the midst of a more widespread interest over what attributes would best characterize Elizabethan culture as such.

3. For a survey of this text, along with extensive commentary about its historical significance, see Klibansky et al., *Saturn and Melancholy.*
4. For this particular use of Bright and Laurentius, see Babb, *The Elizabethan Malady;* Lily Campbell, *Shakespeare's Tragic Heroes: Slaves of Passion* (London: University Paperbacks, 1930); Bridget Gellert Lyons, *Voices of Melancholy: Studies in Literary Treatments of Melancholy in Renaissance England* (London: Routledge & Kegan Paul, 1971). Famous applications of Bright to Shakespeare include A. C. Bradley, *Shakespearean Tragedy* (London: Macmillan, 1905); J. Dover Wilson, *What Happens in Hamlet,* third edition (Cambridge: Cambridge University Press, 1951), appendix E.
5. A single reference to this document appears in the "October" episode of *The Shepherdes Calender;* a more detailed consideration of this text will appear further below.
6. It is a mistake to assume that melancholy conferred a privileged status upon anyone who suffered from its effects. Even in the classical version of melancholy, as put forth by Dürer and interpreted by Panofsky, the price of genius was torment and ineffectual torpor.
7. These presuppositions become clear when we reflect on the actual manner in which early modern medical treatises on melancholy have been preserved and disseminated. For many years, Bright's *Treatise* has been studied precisely for the clues it provided toward diagnosing Hamlet's mental disorders—a critical operation that even William Carlton, Bright's foremost contemporary biographer, could not avoid. William J. Carlton, *Timothe Bright: A Memoir of "The Father of Modern Shorthand"* (London: Elliot Stock, 1911), 55–7. To his credit, Carlton rejects the conclusions of his predecessors who had falsely assumed that Bright provided "the key" to Shakespeare, and who had imagined a young unemployed aspiring playwright poring over Bright's *Treatise* like they offered recipes for poundcake. Carlton, whose tone is almost never ironic, addresses the Shakespeare-Bright connection out of professional obligation rather than deep conviction, and it is the reserve that perhaps provides the best clue for future scholarship, when it comes to characterizing the relation between poetry and medicine in early modern culture. Similarly, if Laurentius has retained significance for twentieth century readers, the clue lies in the name of the series in which his text has been preserved: "Shakespeare Association Facsimiles." (Such critical maneuvers become all the more striking when we consider that, in all probability, Shakespeare himself did not read either physician, much less use them as sources for his own melancholy figures.)
8. If there is a playwright who escapes this pattern, it is Ben Jonson, but only at the expense of turning his characters into literary mouthpieces who give

pedantic lectures on behalf of the author; Jonson's use of melancholy and humor theory will be considered more extensively in the following chapter.
9. With regard to Spenser, one can only surmise. It is only the mysterious EK, whose identity has managed to resist everybody's best hypotheses, who claims to have read the treatise in the first place; meanwhile, it is only on the basis of his own furtive remarks that the classical notion of enthusiasm formed the basis for Spenser's theories of poetry.
10. Bright, *Treatise*, 129.
11. Bright, *Treatise*, 130.
12. Bright, *Treatise*, 115.
13. Bright, *Treatise*, Introduction. One may wonder whether Bright designed his treatise in part as a response to a treatise, *On Heroical Frenzies*, written by Giordano Bruno in 1585; while Bruno had been living and writing in England, his *Italian* language treatise, which defends precisely the kind of sacred enthusiasm that Bright leaves to one side, seems diametrically opposed to the *Treatise on Melancholie*. In similar fashion, one may suspect whether the English translation of a Huegenot French author was not timed to redress the Jesuit Thomas Wright, whose *Passions of the Mind in Generall* went into manuscript circulation in 1598.
14. See Richard Helgerson, *Forms of Nationhood: The Elizabethan Writing of England* (Chicago and London: University of Chicago Press, 1992).
15. Timothy Bright, *A Treatise* (London, 1580).
16. Bright, *A Treatise*, 16.
17. Bright, *A Treatise*, 17.
18. Bright, *Characterie*, Introduction.
19. See, for instance, G.B., *Rarities: Or the Incomparable Possibilities in Secret Writing* (1665), 2: "I conceive it cannot be prejudicial to matters of State for every ordinary person to be able to conceal his own Concerns in a Character only legible to himself, and that no man in a condition where the managery of the Pen is requisite, but may have occasion to lay by something secretly to prevent intrusion into his private affairs."
20. Bright, *Melancholie*, Introduction.
21. Robert Wakefield, *On the Three Languages*, Medieval and Renaissance Texts and Studies (Binghamton, NY: SUNY Press at Binghamton, 1989).
22. See Sarah Stever Gravelle, "The Latin-Vernacular Question and Humanist Theory of Language and Culture," *Renaissance Essays II*, ed. William J. Connell (Rochester: University of Rochester Press, 1993), 110–29. As she observes, 110: "Several other humanists shared [Lorenzo Valla's] understanding that linguistic difference is a cause of the differences in the character and mind of cultures."
23. Bright, *Melancholie*, Sig. A. See Bridget Gellert Lyons, *Voices of Melancholy* (London: Routledge & Kegan Paul, 1971), 143–45. According to Lyons, 144: "[Bright's] initial proposition that the word 'melancholy' has many

applications—his first chapter is entitled 'Howe Diverslie the word Melancholie is taken'—is an introduction of complications that he intends to resolve."

24. Bright, *Melancholie*, 2.
25. Bright, *Melancholie*, 187.
26. Some historical criticism has traced the origins of melancholy to the patristic concept of *acedia,* sloth or despair. See Giorgio Agamben, *Stanzas: Word and Phantasm in Western Culture,* trans. Ronald L. Martinez, Theory and History of Literature, vol. 69 (Minneapolis: University of Minnesota Press, 1993), 3–21; Eric Rothstein, "Et in Acedia Ego," in *Madness, Melancholy, and the Limits of the Self,* eds. Andrew D. Weiner and Leonard V. Kaplan, Graven Images, vol. 3 (Madison: University of Wisconsin Law School, 1996), 65–91; John Stachniewski, *The Persecutory Imagination: English Puritanism and the Literature of Religious Despair* (New York: Oxford University Press, 1990), 60–62. By the late sixteenth century, many writers drew a distinction between the two conditions in order to emphasize the medical dimensions of the one and the spiritual dimensions of the other. Surprisingly enough, it was Robert Burton who was able to put it most succinctly: "But melancholy and despair, though often, do not always concur." *The Anatomy of Melancholy,* ed. Holbrook Jackson (New York: New York Review of Books, 2001), vol. III, 396.
27. See the Table of English Words in *Characterie.*
28. Bright, *Melancholie*, 52.
29. Edmund Spenser, *The Works of Edmund Spenser: A Variorum Edition,* eds. Edwin Greenlaw, C. G. Osgood, et al., 11 vols. (Baltimore: Johns Hopkins University Press, 1932–1957), 10.16.
30. Thomas Cain, "Renaissaince Orpheus," 32: "'October' seems to depict Colin's alienation from the Orphic strain, in the end this amounts to an affectation of modesty." See also John Steadman, *Moral Fiction in Milton and Spenser* (Columbia: University of Missouri Press, 1995), chapter one; Anthea Hume, *Edmund Spenser: Protestant Poet* (Cambridge: Cambridge University Press, 1984); Richard Danson Brown, *'The New Poet': Novelty and Tradition in Spenser's "Complaints"* (Liverpool: Liverpool University Press, 1999). Hume appeals to what she refers to as English readers on the whole in order to maintain that Orpheus represents, 51: "a figure of triumph—the ideal artist, lover and civiliser," even in "October." Richard Danson Brown suggests that Spenser viewed Orpheus through the lens of Christian allegorization; thus what was significant about the figure was his rescue of Eurydice, or harrowing of Hell.
31. Edmund Spenser, *The Shorter Poems,* ed. William A. Oram et al. (New Haven: Yale University Press, 1989). Subsequent references to Spenser's lyric poetry, hereafter given parenthetically, refer to this edition.
32. Patricia Vicari, "The Triumph of Art, the Triumph of Death: Orpheus in Spenser and Milton," *Orpheus: The Metamorphosis of a Myth,* ed. John Warden (Toronto: University of Toronto Press, 1982), 207–30, 210.

33. Anne Lake Prescott, "Spenser (Re)Reading du Bellay: Chronology and Literary Response," *Spenser's Life and the Subject of Biography*, eds. Juduth H. Anderson, Donald Cheney, and David A. Richardson (Amherst: University of Massachusetts Press, 1996), 134–45. As Prescott suggests through her examination of du Bellay's influence on Spenser, 131, not only does the French poet cause Spenser to "escape a Virgilian career path," but on a more fundamental level compromises the very notion of biographical "linearity as such."
34. Paula Blank, *Broken English: Dialects and the Politics of Language in Renaissance Writings* (London and New York: Routledge, 1996), 12.
35. As subsequent chapters will show, however, what was suitable for poetry would prove disastrous in other domains; during the mid-seventeenth century, pamphlet writers lashed out against illiterate preachers with increasing frequency and alarm.
36. Patrick Cheney, *Spenser's Famous Flight: A Renaissance Idea of a Literary Career* (Toronto: University of Toronto Press, 1993), 30.
37. Cf. Steadman, *Moral Fiction*, 30.
38. Cheney, *Famous Flight*, 31. To some extent, Cheney qualifies his sense of what Orpheus represented for Spenser, arguing along premises Angus Fletcher lays out in his book on Spenserian prophecy. See Angus Fletcher, *The Prophetic Moment: An Essay on Spenser* (Chicago: University of Chicago Press, 1971).
39. See Andrew Hadfield, "Was Spenser a Republican?" *English: The Journal of the English Association* 47 (1998): 169–82; Graham L. Hammill, "'The thing/Which never was': Republicanism and *The Ruines of Time*," *Spenser Studies* 18 (2003): 165–83. As Hammill proposes, 170: "In the 1590s, as Spenser became increasingly frustrated with Elizabethan domestic and foreign policy, not only did he engage in alternative forms of political thought like republicanism, but also his poetry intensified its readers' responsibilities for political and historical thought."
40. See J. G. A. Pocock, *The Machiavellian Moment: Florentine Political Thought and the Atlantic Republican Tradition* (Princeton: Princeton University Press, 1975), 83–113.
41. Sean Kane, *Spenser's Moral Allegory* (Toronto: University of Toronto Press, 1989), 55. Kane's remarks are reminiscent of Harry Berger's descriptions of Phaedria, Mammon and Acrasia's Bower as forces that replace life with an illusory imitation of life. See Harry Berger, *The Allegorical Temper: Vision and Reality in Book II of Spenser's "Faerie Queene"* (Handon, CT: Archon Books, 1967), 67–68.
42. Edmund Spenser, *The Faerie Queene*, in *The Works of Edmund Spenser: A Variorum Edition*, vol. 2, eds. Edwin Greenlaw, Charles Grosvernor Osgood, Frederick Morgan Padelford, Ray Heffner (Baltimore: Johns Hopkins University Press, 1947), Book II, canto ix, stanza 1. All further references to Book, canto and stanza numbers, which will be noted in the text parenthetically, refer to this edition.

43. Bright, *Treatise*, 51.
44. I discuss the ambiguous nature of the body-politic image more extensively in chapters two and five.
45. Michel Foucault, *The Order of Things: An Archaeology of the Human Sciences* (New York: Vintage Books, 1970), 32, 23–24.
46. James Nohrnberg, *The Analogy of "The Faerie Queene"* (Princeton: Princeton University Press, 1980), 351; Jonathan Gil Harris, *Foreign Bodies and the Body-Politic: Discourses of Social Pathology in Early Modern England* (Cambridge: Cambridge University Press, 1998); David Read, *Temperate Conquests: Spenser and the Spanish New World* (Detroit: Wayne State University Press, 2000), 83–91. For a fuller account of Maleger as a melancholic, see Berger, *The Allegorical Temper*, 84; David Lee Miller, *The Poem's Two Bodies* (Princeton: Princeton University Press, 1988), 185; Michael Schoenfeldt, *Bodies and Selves in Early Modern England: Physiology and Inwardness in Spenser, Shakespeare, Herbert, and Milton* (Cambridge: Cambridge University Press, 2000), 51.
47. Angus Fletcher, *Allegory: The Theory of a Symbolic Mode* (Ithaca and London: Cornell University Press, 1964), 189–219.
48. Schoenfeldt, *Bodies and Selves*, 61.
49. Schoenfeldt, *Bodies and Selves*, 66; cf. Nohrnberg, *Analogy*, 351.
50. Schoenfeldt, *Bodies and Selves*, 69.
51. Mark Breitenberg, *Anxious Masculinity in Early Modern England* (Cambridge: Cambridge University Press, 1996), 5: jealousy on the early modern stage was "largely a projection of the husband's own fears translated into a story about his wife's inevitable infidelity of concupiscence."
52. Jonathan Sawday has argued that what makes the castle an uncanny encounter is Guyon's inability to recognize it as his own body. Similarly, David Lee Miller has argued that, as a description of the body, canto ix represses mention of the genitalia, thereby drawing attention to its anxious condition. Jonathan Sawday, *The Body Emblazoned: Dissection and the Human Body in Renaissance Culture* (London: Routledge & Kegan Paul, 1995), 162–63; cf. Miller, *Poem's Two Bodies*, 165–83.
53. Berger, *Allegorical Temper*, 30–33. As Berger has shown in his interpretation of the Cave of Mammon episode, such a discrepancy is precisely the thing that has given readers trouble in understanding why Guyon collapses when he returns to the surface.
54. Walter Benjamin, "On Language as Such and the Language of Man," *Selected Writings: Volume One, 1913–1926* (Cambridge, MA: Harvard University Press, 1996), 73.

NOTES TO CHAPTER TWO

1. See Lawrence Babb, *The Elizabethan Malady*, 73–75. Babb identifies the years 1580–1642 as the period when melancholy went from being virtually

nonexistent in dramatic texts to becoming perhaps the most well known stage figure of the period. Needless to say, these years correspond roughly to the permanent playhouses themselves.

2. Edmund's remark, "My cue is villainous melancholy, with a sigh like Tom O'Bedlam."
3. See, for instance, Frances Yates, *The Occult Philosophy in the Elizabethan Age,* reprinted (New York: Routledge Press, 2001), chapters 13–14. Yates is particularly sensitive to the problems that genial melancholy held for Elizabethans, in the wake of counter-Reformation propaganda.
4. Lawrence Babb, *The Elizabethan Malady* 75 ff.; Bridget Gellert Lyons, *Voices of Melancholy,* 17; Jonathan Dollimore, *Radical Tragedy,* 50.
5. Babb, *The Elizabethan Malady,* 74: "Apparently the disgruntled or seditious traveler had become well established as a social type by 1580. apparently he was the original malcontent." Lyons adds that malcontents could just as easily be associated with Puritan doctrine, though in both cases the point is to connect the malcontent with potentially seditious religious doctrine.
6. Babb for his part seems to have been writing in response to an overly political version of the melancholy malcontent, as characterized by L. C. Knights, *Drama and Society in the Age of Jonson,* (London: Chatto and Windus 1937), 315–32.
7. Jonathan Haynes, *The Social Relations of Jonson's Theater,* (Cambridge: Cambridge University Press, 1992), 51–2.
8. L. C. Knights, *Drama and Society in the Age of Jonson,* 130–39, 131.
9. Dollimore, *Radical Tragedy,* 155.
10. Erica Fudge, *Perceiving Animals: Humans and Beasts in Early Modern English Culture* (New York: St. Martin's Press, 2000); Nicholas McDowell, *The English Radical Imagination: Culture, Religion, and Revolution, 1630–1660* (Oxford: Clarendon Press, 2003), 55–61; Gail Kern Paster, "Melancholy Cats, Lugged bears, and Early Modern Cosmology: Reading Shakespeare's Psychological Materialism Across the Species Barrier," in *Reading the Early Modern Passions: Essays in the Cultural History of Emotion,* eds. Gail Kern Paster, Katherine Rowe, and Mary Floyd-Wilson (Philadelphia: University of Pennsylvania Press, 2004), 113–29. Paster's essay is especially intriguing in pointing out that Falstaff's melancholy consists of identifying himself with animals, a characteristic shared by the melancholy Jaques, who I consider below. While Paster argues that Falstaff's identification had its basis in a fundamental similarity between human and animal bodies, my own argument adds that malcontents' identification with animals occurs in the process of their increasing marginalization from their respective societies.
11. I borrow the sense of the term bestial, if not the term itself, from Fudge, 136: "The bestialist lost his claim to human-ness when he performed an act

which destroyed the boundaries between the species." While the term may have had explicitly sexual connotations, it was not limited by them.
12. The need for such a distinction may well have been more urgent in light of the famous bear baiting arenas, with which the public playhouses were in competition for public attention.
13. Ben Jonson, *Every Man Out of His Humour,* The Complete Plays of Ben Jonson, volume one, ed. G. A. Wilkes (Oxford: Oxford University Press, 1981); William Shakespeare, *As You Like It,* ed. Agnes Latham, The Arden Shakespeare Second Series, Reprinted (London: Thomson Learning, 2001). All subsequent citations from these plays, given parenthetically, refer to these editions, unless otherwise noted.
14. Shakespeare's motto had read "Non Sans Droict," to which Jonson has his vainglorious buffoon Puntarvolo offer the following suggestion, when he looks upon a shield that an associate of his has recently obtained: "Let the word be "Not without mustard" (3.4.74). While Jonson lampoons lines from Shakespeare's plays, Puntarvolo's crack targets the playwright himself. For his part, Shakespeare's brilliantly foolish Touchstone comments upon the general absence of honor in the modern world by reminiscing "Of a certain knight, that swore by his honour they were good pancakes, and swore by his honour the mustard was naught." For a fuller account of the rivalry between Jonson and Shakespeare, including this exchange of gibes, see Katherine Duncan-Jones, *Ungentle Shakespeare: Scenes from his Life* (London: Arden Shakespeare, 2001), 122–8.
15. See Vito R. Giustiniani, "Homo, Humanus, and the Meanings of Humanism," *Renaissance Essays,* volume two, ed. William J. Connell (Rochester: University of Rochester Press, 1993), 29–57. More recent accounts of the importance of learning and humanity include Fudge, *Perceiving Animals,* 64–65, McDowell, *English Radical Imagination,* 69.
16. Pico's fable has been exhaustively scrutinized by writers across various disciplines, ranging from philosophers to literary critics and historians. My own argument owes much to a number of individuals who have observed that Pico's accomplishment was not to identify the human as a fixed and stable category, but precisely the opposite—to define him by suspending categories altogether and replacing them with virtually unlimited potentiality. Among them, see Ernst Cassirer, *The Individual and the Cosmos in Renaissance Philosophy* (Philadelphia: University of Pennsylvania Press, 1973); Dollimore, *Radical Tragedy,* esp. 169–70; Giorgio Agamben, *The Open: Man and Animal* (Stanford: Stanford University Press, 2004).
17. Giovanni Pico della Mirandola, *Oration on the Dignity of Man,* trans. A. Robert Caponigri (Washington, D.C: Regnery Gateway, 1956), 7.
18. Agamben, *The Open,* 30: "The humanist discovery of man is the discovery that he lacks himself, the discovery of his irremediable lack of *dignitas.*"

19. Pico, *Oration*, 8.
20. Michel de Montaigne, *The Complete Essays*, trans. Donald M. Frame (Stanford: Stanford University Press, 1957), 318–457. All citations of Montaigne's essay refer to this edition.
21. Montaigne, "Apology," 336.
22. Montaigne, "Apology," 331.
23. Giorgio Agamben, *The Open*, 26–27: "In Linnaeus's optical machine, whoever refuses to recognize himself in the ape, becomes one."
24. In this sense, Jonson revisits the character Sir Stephano, from *Every Man In His Humor*, who looks for a chair that he might be melancholy on, thereby literally reducing his humoral disposition to a series of postures that anybody—especially anybody with sufficient income—might acquire.
25. As Anne Barton suggests, Jonson did not want to bother with a cat, though in the course of leaving it off stage he draws attention to the differences between "ens" and word that preoccupies him at the outset.
26. See Mark S. R. Jenner, "The Great Dog Massacre," *Fear in Early Modern Society*, William G. Naphy and Penny Roberts eds. (Manchester and New York: Manchester University Press, 1997), 44–61. As Jenner suggests, dogs may have been interpreted as the cultural symbols of excessive social promiscuity, particularly as their social status intersected with the conditions that determined social standings among humans. In that context, the dog in Jonson's play may suggest ambivalence about its owner's social standing.
27. Barton, *Jonson*, 72. Cf. Helen Ostovich ed., *Every Man Out*, (Manchester: Manchester University Press, 2002), 82: "Macilente's betrayal of Carlo, like his other betrayals including the murder of the dog, places Macilente in a dubious position. He is a renegade, disregarding the social bonds which restrain or modify most socially aberrant behaviour. On the other hand, he defends himself by taking a moral stand against socially accepted corruption in a world in which the vilest person, provided he has money enough, 'shall not only pass, but pass regarded' (3.3.11–14). As Ostovich maintains, while Macilente rejects his world, it does not necessarily follow that Jonson uncritically advocates his methods.
28. Andrew Gurr, *The Shakespearean Stage 1574–1642* (Cambridge: Cambridge University Press, 1980), 97–8.
29. See Helen M, Ostovich, "'So Sudden and Strange a Cure': A Rudimentary Masque in *Every Man Out of His Humour*, *English Literary Renaissance* 22 (1992): 315–32. Ostovich describes the process of personation well, with respect to Buffone, 323: "With his running commentary in asides to the audience, he seems to occupy a position halfway between dramatic actor and clown, never completely absorbed in the action, always conscious of the audience and violating dramatic illusion."
30. Cf. Harold Jenkins, "As You Like It," *Shakespeare: Modern Essays in Criticism* (revised), ed. Leonard F. Dean (London and New York: Oxford University

Press, 1967), 114–33, 122: "And there is also Jaques to point out that the natural life in Arden, where men usurp the forest from the deer and kill them in their "native dwelling place," while deer, like men, are in distress abandoned by their friends, are as cruel and unnatural as the other."

31. C. L. Barber, *Shakespeare's Festive Comedy: A study of Dramatic Form and its Relation to Social Custom* (Princeton: Princeton University Press, 1959), 228–29; Devon L. Hodges, *Renaissance Fictions of Anatomy* (Amherst: University of Massachusetts Press, 1985), 50–66. Barber suggests that Jaques' ineffectiveness is a deliberate effort on Shakespeare's part to distance his play from the sordid settings of Jonson's comedies. Hodges offers a less sympathetic view, arguing, as the character's name suggests, that Jaques represents little more than the "debris" or waste products of Arden forest.

32. See, for instance, Robert N. Watson, "As You Liken It: Simile in the Wilderness," *Shakespeare Survey* 56 (2003): 79–92.

33. This is not atypical of Shakespeare's melancholy characters. Take, for instance, Falstaff's melancholy, which is partly grounded in his status as an impoverished nobleman who can expect certain prerogatives, but who nevertheless must inhabit a social world that gradually has less and less room for him.

NOTES TO CHAPTER THREE

1. William Shakespeare, *Julius Caesar*, The Arden Shakespeare Third Series, ed. David Daniell (London: Thomas Nelson, 1998). All further citations, hereafter listed in the text parenthetically, refer to this edition.

2. When William Scott wrote his comprehensive study of Shakespeare's melancholics, for instance, he neglected the play altogether; it is doubtful that, were this fact pointed out to him, he would have thought of it as an oversight. W. I. D. Scott, *Shakespeare's Melancholics* (London: Mills & Boon, 1962). More recently, when Charles and Elaine Hallett refer to *Julius Caesar*, it is precisely in order to note the problems it raises in their attempt to define the mad-revenger genre. Charles and Elaine Hallett, *The Revenger's Madness: A Study of Revenge Tragedy Motifs* (Lincoln and London: University of Nebraska Press, 1980), 265–66.

3. If contemporary literary criticism is correct about the affinity between discontent and madness, *Julius Caesar* would have been an ideal play for staging the typical malcontent. Thomas McAlindon and W. Nicholas Knight have argued that Brutus does exhibit many of the traditional characteristics of the melancholy malcontent. More recently, Duncan Salkeld has argued that the vocabulary of madness was inflected greatly with political terminology, suggesting that madness was expected to have political implications as a rule. Thomas McAlindon, *Shakespeare's Tragic Cosmos* (Cambridge: Cambridge University Press, 1991), 76–101; W. Nicholas Knight, "Brutus'

Motivation and Melancholy," *The Upstart Crow* 5 (1984): 108–24; Duncan Salkeld, *Madness and Drama in the Age of Shakespeare* (Manchester: Manchester University Press, 1993), 1–5.

4. Richard Wilson, "A Brute Part: *Julius Caesar* and the Rites of Violence," *Cahiers Elisabethans: Late Medieval and Renaissance English Studies* 50 (1996): 19–32; 29: "[*Julius Caesar*] Became the most quoted play of the English Revolution," albeit no documentary evidence backs his claim.

5. David Norbrook, *Writing the English Republic: Poetry, Rhetoric and Politics, 1627–1660* (Cambridge: Cambridge University Press, 1999), 12: "Students would be encouraged to compose speeches in which Brutus justified the assassination of Caesar to save the republic." See also J. P. Sommerville, *Politics & Ideology in England, 1603–1640*, 2d. ed. (London and New York: Longman, 1999), 10–11.

6. Knights, *Drama & Society*, 324. As Knights argues, melancholy underwent a sudden shift from affectation to sign of real social discontent, following the death of Elizabeth. More often than not, the cause of discontent was frustrated ambition.

7. James I, *Political Writings,* Cambridge Texts in the History of Political Thought (Cambridge: Cambridge University Press, 1994), 64.

8. James I, *Political Writings,* 70.

9. See North's translation of Plutarch's *Lives,* in Geoffrey Bullough, ed. *Narrative and Dramatic Sources of Shakespeare,* vol. 5 (New York: Columbia University Press, 1964), 116–17; anon., *Caesar and Pompey, or, Caesar's Revenge;* Robert Burton, *The Anatomy of Melancholy,* vol. 1, eds. Nicholas K. Kiessling, Thomas C. Faulkner and Rhonda L. Blair (Oxford: Clarendon Press, 1990), 319. Taken together, these references suggest that at least a minor tradition of representing Brutus as a melancholic did exist. In all likelihood, this was a variation of what Manfredi Piccolomini identifies as a more typical characteristic of Brutus as archetype, namely a tendency toward intellectualism. *The Brutus Revival: Patricide and Tyrannicide During the Renaissance* (Carbondale and Edwardsville: Southern Illinois University Press, 1991), 95–97.

10. Cf. Knight, "Brutus' Motivation," 109. It should not be forgotten, however, that Hamlet identifies himself as another Brutus in a meta-theatrical exchange with Polonius that must have referred to the previous season's performance of *Julius Caesar* at the Globe.

11. See chapter one of this study.

12. Ronald Berman, "A Note on the Motives of Marcus Brutus," *Shakespeare Quarterly* 23 (1972): 197–200; 199: "The irony of *Julius Caesar,* of course, consists of the failure of Marcus Brutus to 'imitate' the virtue of his ancestors."

13. Perhaps an allusion to Nashe's "Terrors of the Night," which describes many similar wondrous signs as symptoms of melancholy insanity. Thomas

Nashe, "The Terrors of the Night," *The Unfortunate Traveller and Other Works* (London: Penguin Books, 1972), 208–50.

14. Robert Miola, "*Julius Caesar* and the Tyrannicide Debate," *Renaissance Quarterly* 38 (1985): 271–89; Rebecca Bushnell, *Tragedies of Tyrants: Political Thought and Theater in the English Renaissance* (Ithaca and London: Cornell University Press, 1990).
15. Sharon O'Dair, "Social Role and the Making of Identity in *Julius Caesar*," *Studies in English Literature 1500–1900,* 33 (1993): 289–307; 298.
16. Indeed, this sort of melancholy only seems possible once the meaning of the term humor itself shifts from a physical substance to something that denotes mood or interest.
17. Hallett and Hallett, *Revenger's Madness,* 58: "The era also differentiated madnesses of passion that result when the individual is asked to bear too much."
18. Edward Forset, *The Body Natural and Politique,* The English experience, its Record in Early Printed Books Published in Facsimile, no. 520 (New York: Da Capo Press, 1973), iii
19. Forset, *Body Natural,* 72.
20. Forset, *Body Natural,* 15.
21. "A Homily Against Disobedience and Wylfull Rebellion, " *Divine Right and Democracy: An Anthology of Political Writing in Stuart England* (London: Penguin Books, 1986), 94–98; 98: "What a perilous thing were it to commit unto the subjects the judgement which prince is wise and godly, and his government good, and which is otherwise. As though the foot must judge of the head: an enterprise very heinous, and must need breed rebellion. For who else be they that are most inclined to rebellion but such haughty spirits? From whome springs such foul ruin of realms?"
22. John Ponet, *A Short Treatise of politique power; and of the true obedience which subjects owe to Kings, and other civill governours* (London, 1556), Sig. C8. See also J. P. Somerville, *Royalists & Patriots: Politics and Ideology in England, 1603–1640* (London and New York: Longman, 1986), 264.
23. Francis Bacon, "The Essays or Counsels, Civill and Morall," The Oxford Francis Bacon, vol. 15, ed. Michael Kiernan (Oxford: Clarendon Press, 1985), 46.
24. Bacon, *Essays,* 46.
25. James I, *Political Writings,* 10–11, 25. King James adopted a similar position, at least to the extent that he imagined the king as the realm's physician.
26. David G. Hale, *The Body Politic: A Political Metaphor in Renaissance English Literature* (The Hague: Mouton, 1971), 69. Significantly, it is Shakespeare whom he singles out, as Shakespeare made more use of the analogy than any other playwright during the period.
27. Hale, *Body-Politic,* 81.
28. Jonathan Gil Harris has argued that one of the dangers to the traditional images of body as commonwealth—at least as far as apologists for absolutist

theories of government were concerned—was that the very terminology used to articulate the image of a stable political hierarchy often was used for subversive ends. Jonathan Gil Harris, *Foreign Bodies and the Body-politic: Discourses of Social Pathology in Early Modern England*, Cambridge Studies in Renaissance Literature and Culture, no. 25 (Cambridge: Cambridge University Press, 1998), 36–40. See also Kevin Sharpe, *Remapping Early Modern England: The Culture of Seventeenth-Century Politics* (Cambridge: Cambridge University Press, 2000), 112–13.

29. See Harris' discussion of Thomas Starkey in *Foreign Bodies*, 38.
30. Forset, *Body Natural*, 65.
31. Sigurd Burkhardt, *Shakespearean Meanings* (Princeton: Princeton University Press, 1968), 6–9; Daniell ed., *Julius Caesar*, "Introduction," 16–22. Both discuss the parallel between Julius Caesar and James I, regarding their introduction of new calendars during their reigns.
32. Linda Woodbridge, *The Scythe of Saturn: Shakespeare and Magical Thinking* (Urbana and Chicago: University of Illinois Press, 1994), 289–90; Naomi Conn Liebler, *Shakespeare's Festive Tragedy: The Ritual Foundations of Genre* (London and New York: Routledge, 1995), 85–111; Richard Wilson, "'Is this a Holiday?': Shakespeare's Roman Carnival," *English Literary History* 54 (1987): 31–44. Richard Wilson has argued that the elements of festivity and holiday are present precisely in order to be mastered by an emerging bourgeois class, coercive in nature. In Wilson's words, 41: "By syphoning the subversiveness of popular festivity in the representation of a deflected and contained rebellion, the Shakespearean text anticipates the counter-revolution of the Cromwellian Commonwealth and faithfully enacts the coercive strategy of those subtle London masters who "stir up servants in an act of rage" (2.1.176) the better to control them." Wilson quotes a speech from Brutus that will be discussed further below. As that analysis will suggest, it is difficult to imagine just how it could be taken as the representation of the coercive class-based forces Wilson has in mind.
33. This is a variation on the critical belief that Cassius' complaint is directed against Caesar's destruction of traditional republican values. See, for instance, Anson, "Hardened Heart," 26; Kahn, *Roman Shakespeare*, 86; Liebler, *Festive Tragedy*, 97–99.
34. See Paster, *Body Embarrassed*, 94, 107–09; Kahn, by contrast, locates what she calls "the feminine" as that which is excluded in the signifier Rome. *Roman Shakespeare*, 77–79. Rebecca Bushnell, makes an parallel argument, arguing that the conspirators use antithesis to figure Caesar as both monstrous and divine. *Tragedies of Tyrants*, 147–49. Cf. Liebler, *Festive Tragedy*, 98: "Cassius's complaint that 'this man/Is now become a god' is entirely justified." Liebler's argument comes closer to my own, as she notes that what is at stake in the opening scenes is a wide-scale subversion of the meaning and

significance of traditional ceremonies. The effect is widespread ambiguity, as well as the distortion of traditional political roles.

35. When the play was read largely as Shakespeare's character study, critics often examined Brutus in terms of the errors he committed, and what he should have done. See, for instance, William Bowden, "The Mind of Brutus," *Shakespeare Quarterly* 17(1966): 57–67; D. J. Palmer, "Tragic Error in *Julius Caesar*," *Shakespeare Quarterly* 21 (1970): 399–409; Myron Taylor, "Shakespeare's *Julius Caesar* and the Irony of History," *Shakespeare Quarterly* 24 (1973): 301–08. Without turning this into another character study, we can reconsider Brutus' flaws while bearing in mind they are hardly exclusive to Brutus.

36. Burkhardt, *Shakespearean Meanings*, 3.

37. Paster, *Festive Tragedy*, 111: "Particularly telling in this context, then, is Antony's use of the trope of putting a tongue into Caesar's wounds, a figure that seems to oppose mute femaleness to a phallicized image of speech." In one sense, this argument builds upon Paster's reading of these two passages. For Paster, what is at stake is whether Antony can "reify" Caesar's femininity in order to control it, much as a Petrarchan lover manipulates his mute beloved. I depart from Paster's reading insofar as I regard the issue to be whether Antony and Caesar alike can be properly "rhetoricized" according to a stable rendition of the body-politic.

38. Similarly, Brutus finds himself at a loss to inscribe himself within the patrilineal tradition that would have made him the logical guardian of liberty against tyranny. While he is all too aware of what his ancestry had done to the Tarquins, he far less certain of what that knowledge should entail. I am grateful to the participants of the University of Wisconsin colloquium March, 2001, for pointing this out. Cf. Liebler, *Festive Tragedy*, 106: "Unfortunately Brutus misses *his* current (in both senses of tide and immediate moment): his *hamartia* is literally a "missing of the mark." Similarly, Liebler has argued that, while Brutus recognizes his role both within his family's tradition and history's essentially "repetitive, if not altogether cyclical" patterns, he is unable to translate this recognition into a successful strategy.

39. Little wonder then that critics such as Liebler and Woodbridge have noted a ritualistic dimension to the assassination. That Caesar takes on the traditional characteristics of the *pharmakos* seems indisputable the moment Brutus portrays him as a divine meal: "Let's carve him as a dish fit for the gods." It is here, I think, that we find an unacknowledged basis for the Freudian fable of the primal murder, as he describes it in *Totem and Taboo*. (See Introduction.)

40. Burkhardt, *Shakespearean Meanings*, 4; John Sutherland and Cedric Watts, "The Watch on the Centurion's Wrist," *Henry V, War Criminal? & Other Shakespeare Puzzles* (Oxford: Oxford University Press, 2000), 7–13. While

Burkhardt assumes that Shakespeare's anachronism was deliberate, John Sutherland and Cedric Watts have suggested that it may not have been quite as much as previously thought.

41. Blaise Pascal, *Pensées*, trans. Honor Levi (Oxford: Oxford University Press, 1995), 16: "This mistress of error and falsehood, and all the more treacherous because it is not consistently treacherous. For it would be an infallible rule of truth if it were an infallible one of lies. But while it is more often false, it gives no indication of its quality, indicating in the same way both truth and falsehood. I am not speaking of mad people, I am speaking of the wisest, and it is amongst them that imagination has the overriding right to change their minds."

NOTES TO CHAPTER FOUR

1. Quoted in *The Sermons of John Donne*, vol. 7, eds. George R. Potter and Evelyn M. Simpson (Berkeley and Los Angeles: University of California Press, 1954), 74.
2. Donald Roberts, "The Death Wish of John Donne," *Publications of the Modern Language Association* 62 (1947): 959; R. G. Siemens, "'I haue often such a sickly inclination': Biography and the Critical Interpretation of Donne's Suicide Tract, *Biathanatos*," *Early Modern Literary Studies* 7: p. 5 (2001)
3. I discuss Donne's treatise more extensively in "Paradoxical Donne: *Biathanatos* and the Problems with Political Assimilation," *Prose Studies* 24 (2001): 1–17. As I argue there, in the course of presenting his argument for suicide, Donne explores the more basic conflicts between civil laws and what he perceives to be natural human instinct. He further suggests that they are fundamentally incompatible, and that the historical evidence of suicide demonstrates the inevitable disjunction between state structures and the human instincts they are designed to govern.
4. An extraordinary article by Marjory Lange points out Donne's elaborate, if not inconsistent use of melancholy as not only a personal illness but also the sign of sin and political rebellion. Like Robert Burton, John Donne's contribution to the early modern notion of melancholy was to *complicate* it to the point where it no longer could be used as a simple term of diagnosis. See Marjory E. Lange, "Humourous Grief: Donne and Burton Read Melancholy," *Speaking Grief in English Literary Culture: Shakespeare to Milton*, eds. Margo Swiss and David A. Kent, (Pittsburgh: Duquesne University Press, 2002), 69–97.
5. John Donne, *The Sermons of John Donne*, vol. 3, eds. George R. Potter and Evelyn M. Simpson, (Berkeley and Los Angeles: University of California Press, 1957). It is worth noting, in passing, that the same passage makes reference to the Lord's responsibilities as well. For God to exclude members of

His church would itself constitute tyranny; by extension, it would seem, so too would exclusion from the Church of England constitute a breach of responsibility. For a more extensive development of Donne's use of illness as a metaphor in the sermons, see Winifred Schleiner, *The Imagery of John Donne's Sermons* (Providence: Brown University Press, 1970), 68–85. As Schleiner points out, 74: "Donne's sermons were about man's condition in this world, about sin, and the ways to remedy it. Therefore there could be a place for melancholy only as a disease."

6. *The Sermons of John Donne,* vol. 7, 91.
7. In the Preface, James apologizes for his brevity, declaring, "If I in this Booke haue beene too particularly plaine, impute it to the necessitie of the subject, not so much being ordained for the institution of a Prince in generall, as I haue said, as containing particular precepts to my Sonne in speciall: whereof he could haue made but a generall vse, if they had not contained the particular diseases of this kingdome, with the best remedies for the same, which it became me best as a King, hauing learned both the theoricke and practicke thereof, more plainely to expresse, then any simple schoole-man, that onely knowes matters of kingdomes by contemplation." King James, *Basilicon Doron,* in *Political Writings,* Cambridge Texts in the History of Political Thought, ed. Johann P. Sommerville (Cambridge: Cambridge University Press, 1994), 9–10.
8. For an assessment of King Charles' early ecclesiastical policy, see Jeanne Shami, "Labels, Controversy, and the Language of Inclusion in Donne's Sermons," in *John Donne's Professional Lives,* ed. David Colclough (Cambridge: D. S. Brewer, 2003), 135–57; Peter McCullough, "Donne as Preacher at Court: Precarious 'Inthronization,'" in *John Donne's Professional Lives,* 179–202; Achsah Guibbory, "Donne's Religion: Montagu, Arminianism, and Donne's Sermons, 1624–30," *English Literary Renaissance* 31 (2001): 412–39. McCullough notes that Donne's immediate appeal to King Charles was precisely that his position on an inclusive church made him relatively non-controversial. As Achsah Guibbory points out, however, Laud and his supporters would increasingly use the rhetoric of inclusion as a distinctly exclusionary tactic, setting their sights on Calvinists who preached too rigorously on the doctrine of predestination.
9. John Donne, *Devotions Upon Emergent Occasions* (Ann Arbor: University of Michigan Press, 1997), 57. All subsequent page numbers, hereafter given in the text parenthetically, refer to this edition.
10. See Louis Martz, *The Poetry of Meditation* (New Haven and London: Yale University Press, 1954), 135–44.
11. Robert M. Cooper, "The Political Implications of Donne's *Devotions,*" *New Essays on Donne,* ed. Gary A. Stringer (Salzburg: Institut für Englische Sprache und Literatur, 1977), 192–210, 192; cf. Jonathan Goldberg, *James*

I and the Politics of Literature: Jonson, Shakespeare, Donne and Their Contemporaries (Stanford: Stanford University Press, 1989), 81–82.

12. Indeed, to argue for an endless web of political imagery is to overlook the truly endless web of spiritual metaphors that really do predominate the text. See, for instance, N. J. C. Andreasen, "Donne's *Devotions* and the Psychology of Assent," *Modern Philology* 63 (1965): 207–18; Martz, *Poetry of Meditation*, 138–40; Joan Webber, *Contrary Music: The Prose Style of John Donne* (Madison: University of Wisconsin Press, 1963), 183–201. As Andreasen shows, 208: "[The *Devotions*] Follow a pattern characteristic of devotional literature, a pattern based on the psychology of religious assent." While Webber notices the political imagery, she notes, 187, that the images of disease and rebellion tend to appear in the meditations, which have the following theme: "Both man and nature are bound toward annihilation, which is their center and their end." Do relatively infrequent references thus mandate what might be called a political reading?

13. Mary Arshagouni Papazian, "Politics of John Donne's *Devotions Upon Emergent Occasions:* or, New Questions on the New Historicism," *Renaissance and Reformation/Renaissance et Reforme* 27 (1991): 233–48; 242. As Papazian claims, the *Devotions* presents Donne "Turning away from the world of politics and turning toward a world that transcends everyday weariness." For by situating the treatise in the context of James' recent failure to intervene in the crumbling Palatinate affair, rather than of Charles' recent fiasco with the Spanish Infanta, Papazian concludes that the overall political tone of the work is one of renunciation over failure to influence royal policy rather than one of active engagement.

14. Donne refers to his disease as a hieroglyph, *Devotions*, 80.

15. Rumor itself was hardly a new concern among writers, with representations of Fama dating back to classical literature, including Virgil's *Aeneid,* and with public gossip always presenting itself as a public nuisance. Literary representations of rumor were common during Queen Elizabeth's reign. More well-known examples include William Shakespeare's allegorical representation of Rumor in the induction to *The Second Part of Henry IV,* and Edmund Spenser's depiction of The Blatant Beast in Book VI of *The Faerie Queene.* But by the 1620s, changes in the forms of public discourse—particularly, the emergence of news separates and newsmongers, people who thrived more or less on a culture of scandal—both transformed and in turn raised new concerns about public discourse.

16. Elena Levy-Navarro, "John Donne's Fear of Rumours in the *Devotions upon Emergent Occasions* and the Death of John King" *Notes & Queries* 245 (December 2000): 481–83.

17. For an assessment of the impact of news on the political culture of London, see Richard Cust, "News and Politics in Early Seventeenth Century England," *Past and Present* 112 (1986): 60–90; Nigel Smith, *Literature and Revolution in*

England, 1640–1660 (New Haven and London: Yale University Press, 1994), 54–70; Dagmar Freist, *Governed by Opinion: Politics, Religion and the Dynamics of Communication in Stuart London, 1637–1645* (London and New York: Tauris Academic Studies, 1997), 177–238. While Smith perhaps overstates his case when he asserts, 54: "In the 1640s the newspaper, or newsbook, as it was then called, happened for the first time," it nevertheless is clear that the development of newsbooks contributed fundamentally to the dissemination of anti-monarchal viewpoints during the period of civil war. While many pamphleteers did in fact adapt a distinctly Royalist slant, in retrospect King Charles seems to have been notoriously unskilled at conducting public relations propaganda.

18. Thomas Cogswell, *The Blessed Revolution: English Politics and the Coming of War, 1621–1624* (Cambridge and New York: Cambridge University Press, 1989), 281.
19. Dagmar Freist, *Governed by Opinion: Politics, Religion and the Dynamics of Communication in Stuart London 1637–1645* (London and New York: Tauris Academic Studies, 1997), 178–79.
20. James, *Basilicon Doron*, 28.
21. *Pace* Jeanne Shami, whose own scholarship diligently points out the dangers of the so-called "sounds like" argument. See Jeanne Shami, "Donne's Sermons and the Absolutist Politics of Quotation," in *John Donne's Religious Imagination: Essays in Honor of John T. Shawcross*, eds. Frances Malpezzi and Raymond-Jean Frontain (Conway, AR: University of Central Arkansas Press, 1995), 380–412; Shami, "Labels, Controversy, and the Language of Inclusion in Donne's Sermons," 139–42. While I do concede the somewhat crude nature of my comparison here, I hope to avoid the more egregious fault of using this single passage as the index of Donne's political identity.
22. See, for instance, the seventh, ninth, and eleventh meditations.
23. For a fuller explanation of the doctrinal significance of the bells, see Richard Strier, "Donne and the Politics of Devotion," *Religion, Literature, Politics and Post-Reformation England, 1540–1688*, eds. Donna B. Hamilton and Richard Strier (Cambridge: Cambridge University Press, 1996), 93–114; cf. Andreasen, "Psychology of Assent," 217: "In Meditation Sixteen, he recognizes that he is bound to other men in a community of sin and, like all men, deserves death when judged according to his merits . . . After this insight, another follows, inevitably in the following meditation; all men, bound together by sin, must also be bound by love for one another."
24. Virgil, *The Aeneid*, tr. Allen Mandelbaum (New York: Bantam Books, 1981), Book Four, lines 238–52.

NOTES TO CHAPTER FIVE

1. For a survey of melancholy as the butt of ridicule, see Babb, *Elizabethan Malady*, chapter four; Lyons, *Voices of Melancholy*, 27–34.

2. Theodore Spencer, "The Elizabethan Malcontent," *Joseph Quincy Adams Memorial Studies,* ed. James G. McManaway (Washington, D.C.: Folger Shakespeare Library, 1948), 523–35.
3. Incidentally, Burton's *Anatomy* was published during the same year when Donne proclaimed, in sermon. "For to exclude others from that Kingdom, is a tyrannie, an usurpation; and to exclude thy selfe is a sinfull, and a rebellious melancholy." I discuss this remark in chapter four.
4. Robert Burton, "Democritus Jr. to the Reader," *The Anatomy of Melancholy,* ed. Hobrook Jackson, New York Review Books Classics (New York: New York Review of Books, 2001), 39. Subsequent references to this section will be noted in the text as "Preface." References to additional sections of the *Anatomy* also will be noted in the text parenthetically, listing volume, section, member, subsection (when applicable), and page number.
5. For a description of the topic of universal madness or sickness, both as a classical literary topic and as a manifestation of baroque style, see Ernst Robert Curtius, *European Literature and the Latin Middle Ages,* trans. Willard R. Trask, Bolingen Series no. 36 (Princeton: Princeton University Press, 1953), 94–98; José Antonio Maravall, *Culture of the Baroque: Analysis of a Historical Structure,* trans. Terry Cochran, Theory and History of Literature, vol. 25 (Minneapolis: University of Minnesota Press, 1986), 150–56.
6. For favorable analyses of Burton's reformist aspirations, see Hugh Trevor Roper, "Robert Burton and *The Anatomy of Melancholy,*" *Renaissance Essays* (Chicago: University of Chicago Press, 1961), 249–50: "He is not only a student of man: he is a would-be reformer of society. He is deeply conscious of the disorders of his age, and he believes that those disorders can be cured. They cannot be cured by public debate, religious controversy, war or politics. Those have never made anything better. They can be cured only by a change in human psychology, in the heart of man"; Mueller, *Robert Burton's England,* 33: "Democritus Junior is intensely interested in the study not only of the melancholy person but also of the melancholy kingdom, particularly England. He sees a definite relationship between the two, and he is seeking a national, as well as individual salvation."
7. Wolf Lepenies, *Melancholy and Society,* trans. Jeremy Gaines and Doris Jones (Cambridge: Harvard University Press, 1992), 15: "If all are mad, then madness is but a quality all can be accused of having—that is, the accusation has little effect. Equally, if all are melancholic, then melancholy can no longer really be regarded as a disease." In his remarkable examination of Burton's utopianism, Lepenies points out the futility of the argument that the entire world has gone mad, for madness loses its force if there is nothing to distinguish it.
8. I base this distinction upon a similar type that David Norbrook discusses in his survey of republicanism during the 1620s and 1630s: an otherwise healthy commonwealth presently run by corrupt rulers, versus a commonwealth

whose rulers are corrupt because of a fundamental flaw in the system of government. See David Norbrook, *Writing the English Republic: Poetry, Rhetoric and Politics, 1627–1660* (Cambridge: Cambridge University Press, 1999), 80–83.

9. Rosalie L. Colie, *Paradoxica Epidemica: The Renaissance Tradition of Paradox* (Princeton: Princeton University Press, 1966), 430–31: "To begin with the most obvious element of all, Burton's material was by medical and philosophical tradition contradictory . . . Again and again, as Burton points out, cases of melancholy display contradiction: the same thing may, in different cases, be cause and symptom, cause and cure; or, the cure of one may be the cause of another."

10. Lyons *Voices of Melancholy,* 148: "The most strikingly artistic feature of the *Anatomy,* however, is its conscious creation of unity out of diversity."

11. Eleanor Patricia Vicari, *The View From Minverva's Tower: Learning and Imagination in "The Anatomy of Melancholy"* (Toronto: University of Toronto Press, 1989), 31–42. As Vicari notes, 35, cartography was Burton's favorite among all the geographical sciences, particularly insofar as it contributed to a cure for melancholy.

12. Cf. William R. Mueller, *The Anatomy of Robert Burton's England* (Berkeley and Los Angeles: University of California Press, 1952), 1. Mueller argues that the history of Burtonian criticism suggests "at least three Robert Burtons," which he identifies as follows: an antiquarian collector of knowledge; a "quaint literary stylist [and] curious museum piece"; and "a man concerned primarily with his expressed purposes of showing the causes, symptoms and cures of melancholy." Mueller acknowledges that each Burton reflects the interests of the critical reader; to that observation, we should add that our attempts to organize various strands of criticism reflect a similar historical bias.

13. Many critics have in fact noticed the utopian strain in Burton's Preface. See William R. Mueller, "Robert Burton's Economic and Political Views," *The Huntington Library Quarterly* 11 (1948): 341–59; Mueller, *Robert Burton's England,* 33–52; J. Max Patrick, "Robert Burton's Utopianism," *Philological Quarterly* 27 (1948): 345–58; Hugh Trevor Roper, "Robert Burton and *The Anatomy of Melancholy,*" *Renaissance Essays* (Chicago: University of Chicago Press, 1961), 239–74. More skeptical accounts of Burton's utopianism include Fox, *The Tangled Chain: The Structure of Disorder in the "Anatomy of Melancholy"* (Berkeley: University of California Press, 1976); Robert Appelbaum, *Literature and Utopian Politics in Seventeenth-Century England* (Cambridge: Cambridge University Press, 2002), 81–88. For a description of Burton as a defender of the conventions of the Church of England, see Lawrence Babb, *Sanity in Bedlam: A Study of Robert Burton's "Anatomy of Melancholy"* (East Lansing: Michigan State University Press, 1959), 83–84. As Babb points out, and as will become clearer below, there is very little that

Burton says regarding religion that does not find echoes among people as prominent as Archbishop Abbot.

14. This is not to suggest that critical interest in Burton's utopianism has been abandoned; rather, that the prevailing critical assumption is that his discussion of religious enthusiasm had a more decisive impact on England's political climate.

15. George Williamson, "The Restoration Revolt Against Enthusiasm," *Studies in Philology* 30 (1933): 571–603; Thomas L. Canavan, "Robert Burton, Jonathan Swift and the Tradition of Anti-Puritan Invective," *Journal of the History of Ideas* 34 (1973): 227–42; John F. Sena, "Melancholy Madness and the Puritans." *Harvard Theological Review* 66 (1973): 293–309; Robert Kinsman, "Folly, Melancholy, and Madness: A Study in Shifting Styles of Medical Analysis and Treatment, 1470–1675," *The Darker Vision of the Renaissance,* ed. Robert Kinsman (Berkeley: University of California Press, 1974), 273–320; Fiona Godlee, "Aspects of Non-Conformity: Quakers and the Lunatic Fringe," *The Anatomy of Madness: Essays in the History of Psychiatry in Three Volumes,* vol. 2, eds. W. F. Bynum, Roy Porter and Michael Shepherd (London and New York: Tavistock Publications, 1985), 73–85; Michael Heyd, "Robert Burton's Sources on Enthusiasm and Melancholy," *History of European Ideas* 5 (1984): 17–44; Clement Hawes, *Mania and Literary Style: The Rhetoric of Enthusiasm from the Ranters to Christopher Smart* (Cambridge: Cambridge University Press, 1996), 8–10; McDowell, *English Radical Imagination,* 99. Often, though not always, such assessments have distinct parallels with Foucault's famous "Great Confinement," an event which takes place within a few decades (and miles) of Burton's text.

16. I discuss this argument more extensively in chapter six.

17. Stanley Fish, *Self-Consuming Artifacts: The Experience of Seventeenth Century Literature* (Berkeley: University of California Press, 1972), 303–52; Jonathan Sawday, "Shapeless Eloquence: Robert Burton's Anatomy of Knowledge," *English Renaissance Prose: History, Language, and Politics,* ed. Neil Rhodes (Tempe: University of Arizona Press, 1997), 173–202. Sawday describes Fish's impact as follows, 174: "Suddenly, the *Anatomy* was revealed as an example of postmodernism *avant la lettre*—a mocking, self-parodic exploration of the disorganized and fragmentary nature of the world in which it refused to be located."

18. Samuel Wong, "Encyclopedism in the *Anatomy of Melancholy,*" *Renaissance and Reformation/Renaissance et Reformation* 22 (1998): 5–22, 16 : "As they multiply, disease and symptoms merge, dissolving into myriad "concepts" that transform each victim into the author of his own inscrutable affliction. Thus symptomatology becomes a sly derangement of the encyclopedia—an ever expanding, collectively composed archive of "signes" where authority is subsumed by a private language of symptom and comprehension undone by an infinite discourse of disease." See also Sharon Cadman Seelig, *Generating*

Texts: The Progeny of Seventeenth-Century Prose (Charlottesville: University Press of Virginia, 1996), 109–10: "Thus the very descent into particulars, which ought to be the stamp of completeness, in fact suggests incompleteness."

19. Fox, *Tangled Chain*, 181.
20. Lepenies, *Melancholy and Society*, 17: "No better word can be found as a superordinate category for these concordant characteristics than "order" . . . With his utopia, Burton counters his concept of prevailing melancholy."
21. Lepenies, *Melancholy and Society*, 6. My argument coincides with Lepenies' description of melancholy behavior in the contemporary world, which consists largely of repetitive diversions intended to take away the sting of boredom.
22. Burton seemed fond enough of Rhasis' sentence to quote it more than once: "And for this disease in particular, 'there can be no better cure than continual business,' as Rhasis holds" (II.2.4, 71).
23. David Hume, *A Treatise of Human Nature*, ed. L. A. Selby-Bigge (Oxford: Clarendon Press, 1978), 269: "Nature herself suffices to that purpose, and cures me of this philosophical melancholy and delirium, either by relaxing this bent of mind, or by some avocation, and lively impression of my senses, which obliterate all these chimera. I dine, I play a game of back-gammon, I converse, and am merry with my friends."
24. Curtius, *European Literature*, 83–85.
25. Lyons, *Voices of Melancholy*, 113: "All of Burton's derogatory remarks about the carelessness of his writing and the raggedness of his form must therefore be interpreted as defining and characterizing the personality that he displays for us in the *Anatomy*, a highly artificial personality."
26. Burton, "Preface," 23: "By which means it comes to pass, 'that not only libraries and shops are full of our putid papers, but every close-stool and jakes.'"
27. Among the many remedies for melancholy, whose sole purpose is to do little more than to occupy the minds of the afflicted, the following seems particularly appropriate: "He may apply his mind, I say, to heraldry, antiquity, invent impresses, emblems; make epithalamiums, epitaphs, elegies, epigrams, *palindroma epigrammata*, anagrams, chronograms, acrostics upon his friends' names; or write a comment on Martianus Capella, Tertullian *de pallio*, the Nubian geography, or upon *Aelia Laelia Crispus*, as many idle fellows have essayed; and rather than do nothing, vary a verse a thousand ways with Putean, so torturing his wits" (II, 97–98).
28. Lord Byron, *The Life, Letters, and Journals of Lord Byron*, ed. Thomas Moore (London, 1901), 48: "The Book, in my opinions, most useful to a man who wishes to acquire the reputation of being well read, with the least trouble, is 'Burton's Anatomy of Melancholy,' the most amusing and instructive medley of quotations and classical anecdotes I ever perused."

29. Sawday, "Shapeless Eloquence," 202. As Sawday shows, Burton's proclivity for endless compilation of language bears a striking resemblance to the discursive methods that emerged in the context of Vesalius' new methods for theoretical anatomy. For Vesalius, and for those who followed him (among whom Burton was not necessarily one, as Sawday points out), knowledge was structured according to a syncretic model; any new bit of information could be added to the preexisting corpus without concern for disrupting its integrity. As Sawday concludes, 202: "The logic of Burton's project (which he followed through with such single-minded determination throughout his life) might remind the twentieth-century reader of a Borgesian fable. For, henceforth, there would only need to be one book, one endlessly redivided and ever-growing anatomy of knowledge." While Sawday is persuasive, the above argument should suggest another way to account for Burton's fondness for "endlesse worke."
30. Appelbaum, *Utopianism*, 81.
31. Georges Canguilhem, *The Normal and the Pathological*, trans. Carolyn R. Fawcett in collaboration with Robert S. Cohen (New York: Zone Books, 1989), 41–42: "It proved difficult to maintain the qualitative modification separating the normal from the pathological in a conception which allows, indeed expects, man to compel nature and bend it to his normative desires. Wasn't it said repeatedly after Bacon's time that one governs nature only by obeying it? To govern disease means to become acquainted with its relations with the normal state, which the living man—loving life—wants to regain. Hence the theoretical need, but a past due technique to establish a scientific pathology by linking it to physiology. Thomas Sydenham (1624–1689) thought that in order to help a sick man, his sickness had to be delimited and determined." It is worth noting here that when Georges Canguilhem introduces his astonishing challenge to the traditional historical assumptions about the character of disease, he uses contemporaries of Burton's to illustrate his claim.
32. Mueller, *Robert Burton's England*, 35: "[Burton] makes a direct criticism of his own country, discusses its economic, political and social weaknesses, and seeks a way to overcome them. His passion for economic improvement parallels Bacon's insistence on scientific reform . . . He looked upon the economic instability of England as one of the principal causes of the melancholy of his day."
33. On Burton's mercantilism, see Mueller, *Robert Burton's England*, 37–39.
34. David Hawkes, *Idols of the Marketplace: Idolatry and Commodity Fetishism in English Literature, 1580–1680* (New York: Palgrave, 2001), 24. See also Appelbaum, *Utopianism*, 83. As Appelbaum suggests, Burton's commitment to industriousness contradicted his endorsement of monarchical order, although the contradiction would not have registered as such for him. These recent arguments are a dramatic departure from critical assessments of Burton's utopianism from the earlier part of the century.

35. Mueller *Robert Burton's England*, 37: "He is saying that his planned community *would* make an excellent state."
36. Fox, *Tangled Chain*, 182; Mueller, *Robert Burton's England*, 87; Stachniewski, *Persecutory Imagination*, 243. Mueller, argues that, while Burton was committed to religious reform as he was to political reform, he felt too close to the church "to maintain objectivity"; Stachniewski, by contrast, suggests that Burton was comfortable with a church policy that "actually suits him quite well," since he had been disinclined to believe in Calvinist theology all along. My own position comes closer to Fox's than Mueller's or Stachniewski's.
37. Fox, *Tangled Chain*, 172: "Burton contradicts the whole rationale of division and subdivision and recreates a picture of man gazing at chaos."
38. Significantly, Burton also designates commodity as a form of idolatry, rebuking it as "the chief thing we respect," 318. While his treatment of the idolatrous nature of commodities may be brief, it is interesting to note that it appears at all.
39. Fox, *Tangled Chain*, 180.
40. See David Renaker, "Robert Burton's Palinodes" *Studies in Philology* 76 (1979): 162–81. For a more general analysis of the schism growing among religious groups, see Achsah Guibbory, *Ceremony and Community from Herbert to Milton: Literature, Religion, and Cultural Conflict in Seventeenth-Century England* (Cambridge: Cambridge University Press, 1998).
41. Stachniewski, *Persecutory Imagination*, 228–29.
42. It should be noted in passing that while Burton clearly has the idea of purification in mind when he uses the term one cannot help but notice that, for Burton, reform cannot occur without leaving its own excremental waste behind.
43. Stachniewski, *Persecutory Imagination*, 243.
44. Babb, *Sanity in Bedlam*, 87–89; Stachniewski, *Persecutory Imagination*, 243; Renaker, "Robert Burton's Palinodes," 172.
45. Walter Benjamin, *The Origins of German Tragic Drama* (London and New York: Verso 1977), 139. As Benjamin points out, Calvinism led "great men" away from conventional melancholy, only to plunge them into a deeper version of nihilism: "Something new arose: an empty world. In Calvinism—for all its gloominess—the impossibility of this was comprehended and in some measure corrected. The Lutheran faith viewed this concession with suspicion and opposed it. What was the point of human life if, as in Calvinism, not even faith had to be proved . . . There was no answer to this except perhaps in the morality of ordinary people—'honesty in small things,' 'upright living'—which developed at this time, forming a contrast to the *taedium vitae* of richer natures."
46. Renaker, "Robert Burton's Palinodes," 177.
47. See for instance, 366, 370–72.

48. As Stachniewski points out, Burton ended his first edition by reluctantly referring his readers to the radical preacher, William Perkins; and while he doesn't explicitly comment on the following, it is worth noting that the expanded and revised editions make a stern admonition against too much reading of these scriptural authorities.
49. *Articles Agreed Upon,* 4–5.
50. Michael McKeon, *Origins of the English Novel, 1600–1740* (Baltimore: Johns Hopkins University Press, 1987), 63–64. I borrow the term "extreme skepticism" from McKeon's study. As McKeon uses it, the term denotes a reaction to the naïve empiricist practices that early modern historians had employed to distance themselves from the allegorical and fantastic conventions of romance fiction. To the extent that Burton's method of collecting fragments of quotations from various sources and presenting them as though they were actual units of data can itself be taken as an anti-empiricist gesture, the *Anatomy* suggests an alternate path; if one response to naïve historicism had been the novel, the other was Burton's sprawling text.
51. Guibbory, *Ceremony and Community,* 42: "As Laudian and puritan positions defined themselves in terms of their differences from each other, tensions and contradictory values that had long existed in the English Church—and that to some extent were indigenous to Christianity—became irreparably polarized. The seventeenth-century conflict over worship thus reflects fundamental tensions within Christianity that had intensified with the Reformation but reached a state of Crisis in England only during the middle decades of the seventeenth century."
52. Renaker, "Robert Burton's Palinodes," 177: "If ever a scholar worked with a noose around his neck, it was an English university man expounding predestination in the 1630s, when Burton was working on the expanded third and fourth versions of the 'Cure of Despair.'" Renaker plausibly suggests that Burton faced an impossible time navigating between the contradictory positions held by crown and parliament.

NOTES TO CHAPTER SIX

1. Daniel Fouke, *The Enthusiastical Concerns of Dr. Henry More: Religious Meaning and the Psychology of Delusion* (Leiden, New York: E. J. Brill, 1997), 11–12; Michael MacDonald, *Mystical Bedlam: Madness, Anxiety, and Healing in Seventeenth-Century England,* Cambridge History of Medicine (Cambridge: Cambridge University Press, 1981), 1.
2. Jonathan Sawday, "'Mysteriously Divided': Civil War, Madness and the Divided Self," *Literature and the English Civil War,* eds. Thomas Healy and Jonathan Sawday (Cambridge and New York: Cambridge University Press, 1990), 127–43; 129.

3. Christopher Hill, *The World Turned Upside Down: Radical Ideas During the English Revolution* (New York: Penguin Books, 1975), 277–86; J. F. McGregor, "Seekers and Ranters," *Radical Religion in the English Revolution*, eds. J. F. McGregor and B. Reay (Oxford: Oxford University Press, 1984), 121–39; 137–38; Nigel Smith, *Perfection Proclaimed: Language and Literature in English Radical Religion 1640–1660* (Oxford: Clarendon Press, 1989), 56–57; David Loewenstein, *Representing Revolution in Milton and his Contemporaries: Religion, Politics, and Polemics in Radical Puritanism* (Cambridge: Cambridge University Press, 2001), 94. While Loewenstein makes reference to feigned madness as a sign of political defiance, his overwhelming concern is with the more charismatic aspects of seventeenth century prophets.
4. M. A. Screech, "Good Madness in Christendom," *The Anatomy of Madness: Essays in the History of Psychiatry in Three Volumes*, vol. 2, eds. W. F. Bynum, Roy Porter, and Michael Shepherd (London and New York: Tavistock Publications, 1985), 73–85.
5. Fiona Godlee, "Aspects of Non-Conformity: Quakers and the Lunatic Fringe," *The Anatomy of Madness*, vol. 2, 73–85; 80.
6. George Williamson, "The Restoration Revolt Against Enthusiasm," *Studies in Philology* 30 (1933): 571–603; 571.
7. Williamson, "Restoration Revolt," 582.
8. John Sena, "Melancholy Madness and the Puritans," *Harvard Theological Review* 66 (1973): 293–309; 300.
9. Michael Heyd, "Robert Burton's Sources on Enthusiasm and Melancholy: From a Medical Tradition to Religious Controversy," *History of European Ideas* 5 (1984): 17–44; 18.
10. Thomas L. Canavan, "Robert Burton, Jonathan Swift, and the Tradition of Anti-Puritan Invective," *Journal of the History of Ideas* 34 (1973): 227–42; 228.
11. Clement Hawes, *Mania and Literary Style: The Rhetoric of Enthusiasm from the Ranters to Christopher Smart* (Cambridge: Cambridge University Press, 1996), 4–5.
12. Robert Kinsman, "Folly, Melancholy, and Madness: A Study in Shifting Styles of Medical Analysis and Treatment, 1450–1675," *The Darker Side of the Renaissance* (Berkeley: University of California Press, 1974), 273–320; Christopher Hill, "John Mason and the End of the World," *Puritanism and Revolution: Studies in Interpretation of the English Revolution of the 17th Century* (New York: St. Martin's Press, 1997), 290–302.
13. John Locke, *An Essay Concerning Human Understanding* (New York: Prometheus Books, 1995), 591.
14. Cf. Sena, "Melancholy Madness," 297. As Sena acknowledges, du Laurens was a major pioneer in modern thought about religious melancholy.

15. Richard Hooker, *Ecclesiastical Polity: Selections*, ed. Arthur Pollard (Manchester: Carcanet, 1990), 21.
16. George Abbott, "Archbishop Abbott's Letter Regarding Preaching," *Records of the Old Archdeaconry of St. Albans: A Calendar of Papers A.D. 1575 to A.D. 1637*, ed. H. R. Wilton Hall (St. Albans, 1908), 150–52; 151.
17. Sena, "Melancholy Madness," 297.
18. As John Sena notes, 297–98: "The first English works which described enthusiasm solely as a physical and mental abnormality caused chiefly by melancholy appeared in the mid-seventeenth century: Meric Casaubon's *A Treatise Concerning Enthusiasme* (1655), and Henry More's *Enthusiasmus Triumphatus* (1656)." Similarly, see Williamson, "The Restoration Revolt," 582–89.
19. McGregor, "Seekers and Ranters," 121; cf. Kristen Poole, *Radical Religion from Shakespeare to Milton: Figures of Nonconformity in Early Modern England* (Cambridge: Cambridge University Press, 2000), 13. Poole notes the affinity between radical religion and social confusion, "Radical religion, with an emphasis on the individual conscience and a disregard for orthodox discursive boundaries, seemed to create an anarchical Babel."
20. George Whitehead. *Enthusiasm Above Atheism: or, Divine Inspiration and Immediate Illumination [by God Himself] Asserted. And the Children of Light Vindicate* (London, 1674).
21. See Michael McKeon, *The Origins of the English Novel 1600–1740* (Baltimore: Johns Hopkins University Press, 1987), chaps. 2–3. As McKeon observes, in his discussion of Locke, 80: "Those who believe in a revelation that is not supported by empirical evidence Locke calls 'enthusiasts' . . . The truth of revelation, then, requires authentication by the truth of empirical knowledge." Incidentally, as McKeon points out, the rift between what he calls metaphysics and epistemology, had its effect on the discourse of enthusiasm as well. Citing Joseph Glanvill, who himself was an active supporter of the Royalist Society, McKeon reminds us, 85: "Glanvill's piety is not to be doubted, for he chastises those more skeptical than he by reminding us that only Satan benefits from the belief 'that the stories of *Witches, Apparations,* and indeed every thing that brings tidings of another world, are but *melancholick Dreams,* and *pious Romances.*'"
22. Joseph Sedgwick, *A Sermon, preached at St. Marie's in the University of Cambridge May 1st, 1653. Or, An essay to the discovery of the spirit of enthusiasme and pretended inspiration, that disturbs and strikes at the Universities* (London, 1653).
23. Giorgio Agamben, *Infancy and History: Essays on the Destruction of Experience,* trans. Liz Heron (London and New York: Verso, 1993), 17.
24. MacDonald, *Mystical Bedlam,* 2.
25. Sawday, "Madness and the Divided Self," 134.

26. John Taylor, "Mad Fashions, Od Fashions, All out of Fashions, or, The Emblems of these Distracted times" (London, 1643).
27. Taylor, "Mad Fashions," lines 1–6.
28. Taylor, "Mad Fashions," lines 21–28.
29. *Englands Mad Petition to the Right Honourable, The, &c.,* (London, 1647).
30. Robert Crofts, *Paradise Within us: Or, the happie Mind.* (London, 1640), 30.
31. Crofts, *Paradise Within,* 68–69.
32. "The Petition of twelve peers for the Summoning of a New Parliament, 1640," *The English Civil War and Revolution: A Sourcebook,* ed. Keith Lindley (London: Routledge, 1998), 57–59; 58.
33. "The Petition of Twelve Peers," 58.
34. "To the Right Honourable the Commons House of Parliament," *Religion and Society in Early Modern England: A Sourcebook,* eds. David Cressy and Lori Anne Ferrell (London: Routledge, 1996), 174–79; 176.
35. "To the Right Honourable Commons House," 178.
36. Walter Bridges, *Joabs Counsell and King Davids Seasonable Hearing it. Delivered in a Sermone Before the Honourable House of Commons, At their late solemne Fast, Feb. 22* (London, 1643), Preface.
37. "Petition of Twelve," 58.
38. "Lord Digby's speech in the Commons to the bill for triennial parliaments," *The English Civil War,* 69.
39. See also chapter two
40. Taylor, *A Medicine For the Times,* 4.
41. McGregor, "Seekers and Ranters," 122: "There is little objective evidence that either Seekers or Ranters formed coherent movements or that they existed in any considerable numbers. An examination of the source and context of the types of surviving evidence for the two sects suggests that they are largely artificial products of the Puritan heresiographers' methodology; convenient categories in which to dispose of some of the bewildering variety of enthusiastic speculation."
42. MacDonald, *Mystical Bedlam,* 170.
43. MacDonald, *Mystical Bedlam,* 11.
44. Thomas Comber, *Christianity no Enthusiasm* (London, 1678), Sig. A2-A2v.
45. McGregor, "Seekers and Ranters," 131–32. McGregor points out that violators faced time in prison or houses of correction, which suggests "the Act was as much an instrument of moral reformation as an attempt to extirpate false doctrine."
46. Francis Higginson, *Irreligion of the Quakers* (London, 1678), Sig. A2.
47. W. Allen, *The Danger of Enthusiasm Discovered* (London, 1674), 118.
48. Allen, *The Danger of Enthusiasm,* 129.
49. Thomas Underhill, *Hell Broke Loose: or An History of the Quakers Both Old and New* (London, 1660), 9.

50. Underhill, *Hell Broke Loose*, 3; cf. anon., *The Phanatiques Creed, or a Door of Safety*, 6: "They are a bloody-minded and trayterous Generation constant in nothing but vileness, contemners of Gods word, and broaching their own Diabolical tenet for true religion: Satan is their Guide, Rebellion their fellow-Souldier, Hypocrasie their Profession, Heresie their captain, their Colours Bloody."
51. Underhill, *Hell Broke Loose*, 1–2.
52. Anon., *The Joviall Crew: Or, the Devil Turn'd Ranter* (London, 1650), 3.
53. Thomas Bray, *A New Sect of Religion Descryed, Called Adamites*. London, 1641, Sig. A2.
54. Meric Casaubon, *A Treatise Concerning Enthusiasme*, A Facsimile Reproduction of the Second Edition of 1656, ed. Paul J. Korshin (Gainesville, FL: Scholars' Facsimiles & Reprints, 1970), 36–37.
55. Casaubon, *A Treatise Concerning Enthusiasme*, 53.
56. As Macdonald reminds us, this was a traditional assumption: "The theory that Satan exploited the weaknesses of people suffering from melancholy even provided an argument with which the most diabolical temptation, the urge to commit suicide, could be explained as both the Devil's own work and a consequence of natural disease," *Mystical Bedlam*, 169.
57. Casaubon, *A Treatise Concerning Enthusiasme*, 42–43.
58. Casaubon, *A Treatise Concerning Enthusiasme*, 58.
59. Martin Heidegger, *The Principle of Reason*, trans. Reginald Lilly (Bloomington and Indianapolis: Indiana University Press, 1996), 11–12. Referring to the rule, *nihil est sine causa*, Heidegger points to the following dilemma: "Something most odd would follow, namely that precisely the principle of reason—and it alone—would fall outside its own jurisdiction; the principle of reason would remain without reason." On the other hand, supposing that the principle of reason is itself the supreme reason, "What are we getting ourselves into if we take the principle of reason at its word and move towards the reason of reasons? Does not the reason of reasons press forward beyond itself to the reason of reason of reasons? If we persist in this sort of questioning, where can we find a respite and a perspective on reason? If thinking takes this path to reason, then surely it can't help but fall intractably into groundlessness." While Heidegger makes these comments with specific reference to Leibniz, they seem applicable to Leibniz's near contemporary as well.
60. Henry More, *Enthusiasmus Triumphatus; or, A Brief Discourse of the Nature, Causes, Kinds, and Cure of Enthusiasm*, Augustan Reprints Society Texts, no. 118 (Los Angeles: William Andrews Clark Memorial Library, 1966).
61. More, *Enthusiasmus Triumphatus*, 8
62. More, *Enthusiasmus Triumphatus*, 8.
63. More, *Enthusiasmus Triumphatus*, 18.
64. More, *Enthusiasmus Triumphatus*, 19.

65. Williamson, "Restoration Revolt," 588.
66. Smith, *Perfection Proclaimed*, 23–72; 23–24: "Customarily the conversion narrative, or 'confession of experience,' is regarded as separate from the prophetic outpourings which typified the worship and pamphlets of sectarians. This is partly because confessional narratives have been seen as a precursor of autobiography proper. But within the contemporary understanding of prophecy, both categories were defined as examples of divine inspiration."
67. Smith, *Perfection Proclaimed*, 34.

NOTES TO CHAPTER SEVEN

1. John Milton, *Complete Poems and Major Prose*, ed. Merritt Y. Hughes (New York: Macmillan Publishing Company, 1957), Introduction. Subsequent citations from *Samson Agonistes*, which appear parenthetically, refer to this edition.
2. On this topic, see Joseph Wittreich, *Interpreting Samson Agonistes* (Princeton: Princeton University Press, 1986); Christopher Hill, *The Experience of Defeat* (New York: Penguin Books, 1984). Wittreich notes Thomas Newton's Variorum commentary, 5:"Where Milton is regularly beheld 'in the person of Samson' and where, repeatedly, Milton's dramatic poem is regarded in its political aspect as a reproach to his countrymen, and in its religious aspect as 'a concealed attack on the church of England' whose 'opulent Clergy . . . he tacitly compares with the lords and priests of the idol Dagon.' . . . Milton, while brooding over 'the trials and sufferings of his party after the Restoration,' is thought also to focus upon his own situation, and probably that of Sir Henry Vane, and then to describe through the sufferings of Samson his own grief and misery, his own melancholy." By contrast, Hill refuses to read *Samson* either as a quietist play or as an ode to the utter futility of struggle against one's oppressors, 317: "Only one thing could possible be more 'heroic and exemplary' than the life and death of Christ: ending the apostasy which had frustrated the achievements of the Son of God. Milton and his like believed this had happened during the Revolution. The restoration of Charles II and bishops brought back the apostasy, as Samson had been imprisoned and degraded after his first victories. But what had once been overthrown could be overthrown again."
3. Sharon Achinstein, "*Samson Agonistes* and the Drama of Dissent," *Milton Studies* 33 (1996): 133–58. See also David Lowenstein, *Representing Revolution in Milton and His Contemporaries* (Cambridge: Cambridge University Press, 2001), 269–81.
4. Barbara K. Lewalski, *The Life of Milton* (Oxford: Blackwell Publishing, 2000), 378, cites chaplain Matthew Griffith, who represented the returning Charles II as "an avenging Samson about to wreak sudden destruction on

everyone . . . who had been guilty of sedition against the Lord's anointed." David Loewenstein, *Representing Revolution in Milton and his Contemporaries: Religion, Politics, and Polemics in Radical Puritanism*. Cambridge: Cambridge University Press, 2001, notes the extensive of Samson imagery among radical writers following that same Charles' coronation.
5. Don Cameron Allen, *The Harmonious Vision* (Baltimore: Johns Hopkins University Press, 1954), 71–94, 83.
6. Irene Samuel, "*Samson Agonistes* as Tragedy," *Calm of Mind*, 235–57. John Donne knew well enough not to assert too definitively what Samson's own reasons may have been; nevertheless, rarely can it be said that a person commits such an act out of serenity, no matter how much of a hero that person is taken to be.
7. Daniel T. Lochman, "'Seeking Just Occasion': Law, Reason, and Justice at Samson's Peripety," *Milton Studies* 26 (1990): 271–88; 272; Henry McDonald, "A Long Day's Dying: Tragic Ambiguity in *Samson Agonistes*," *Milton Studies* 27 (1991): 263–83; 267; John T. Shawcross, "Irony as Tragic Effect: *Samson Agonistes* and the Tragedy of Hope," *Calm of Mind*, 289–306.
8. Mary Ann Radzinowicz, *Toward Samson Agonistes: The Growth of Milton's Mind* (Princeton: Princeton University Press, 1978), 87–89; Anthony Low, *The Blaze of Noon: A Reading of Samson Agonistes* (New York and London: Columbia University Press, 1974): 64–71.
9. Stanley Fish, *How Milton Works* (Cambridge and London: Harvard University Press, 2001). Chapters 12 and 13 consist of updated versions of earlier essays: "Question and Answer in *Samson Agonistes*," *Critical Inquiry* 11 (1969): 237–64; "Spectacle and Evidence in *Samson Agonistes*," *Critical Inquiry* 15 (1989): 556–86.
10. Karen Edwards, "Inspiration and Melancholy in *Samson Agonistes*," in *Milton and the Ends of Time,* ed. Juliet Cummins (Cambridge: Cambridge University Press, 2003), 224–40.
11. Wittreich devotes the entire first chapter of his book-length study—the first of two—toward navigating the history of *Samson* debates. Lewalski, *Life of Milton*, offers a more concise (and more updated) account.
12. The question of dating Milton's text does not pertain here; any of the proposed dates fall well within the period when the cultural significance of melancholy was undergoing changes.
13. Edwards, "Inspiration and Melancholy," 229–30.
14. John Milton, *The Complete Prose Works of John Milton*, 8 volumes, eds. Don M. Wolfe et al. (New Haven, CT: Yale University Press, 1953–82): vol. 8, 4. Subsequent citations from "Of True Religion," which appear parenthetically, refer to this edition.
15. To some extent, my argument follows Michael Lieb's extensive analysis of the role of fear in *Samson Agonistes*. Michael Lieb, "'Our Living Dread': The god of *Samson Agonistes*," *Milton Studies* 33 (1996): 3–25.

16. In making this argument, I follow the claims of John Shawcross, who argues that the tragedy of *Samson Agonistes* consists in the Israelites' willingness to let Samson struggle for them. See John T. Shawcross, *The Uncertain World of Samson Agonistes,* Studies in Renaissance Literature, (Cambridge: D.S. Brewer, 2001).
17. Lewalski, *Life of Milton,* 237. See also Lewalski "Milton and Idolatry," SEL *Studies in English Literature 1500–1900* 43.1 (2003) 213–232.
18. See, for instance, Mark Houlahan, "Spin Controlling Apocalypse in *Samson Agonistes,*" *Studies in English Literature 1500–1900* 31 (1994): 3–22. As he argues, 5: "For Samson narrating and interpreting his selves, backsliding and then returning to grace, is an integral part of realizing his vocation, at least within the confines of the Greek tragic form Milton self-consciously uses, in which Samson, the Chorus, and their visitors have little to do but discuss and report events unfolding elsewhere."
19. John Milton, "A Defence of the English People," *The Complete Prose Works of John Milton,* eds. Don Wolfe et al., vol. 4 (New Haven, CT: Yale University Press, 1953–82), 402.

Bibliography

PRIMARY SOURCES

Abbott, George. "Archbishop Abbot's Letter Regarding Preaching." In *Records of the Old Archdeaconry of St. Albans: A Calendar of Papers* A.D. *1575 to* A.D. *1637.* Ed. H. R. Wilton Hall. St. Albans, 1908, 150–52.

Allen, W. *The Danger of Enthusiasm Discovered, in an Epistle to the Quakers: In which 'Tis Endeavoured, to convince them of being guilty of Changing God's Method of bringing men to Salvation.* London, 1674.

Amyas, Richard. *An antidote against melancholy. Or, A treasury of 53. rare secrets & arts Discovered.* London, 1659.

An Account of the causes of some particular rebellious distempers. London, 1670.

Articles Agreed Upon by the Archbishops and Bishops of Both Provinces and the whole Cleargie. London, 1628.

Bacon, Sir Francis. "The Essays or Counsels, Civill and Morall." *The Oxford Francis Bacon.* Vol. 15. Ed. Michael Kiernan. Oxford: Clarendon Press, 1985.

Baxter, Richard. *Gods goodness vindicated.* London, 1671.

Bray, Thomas. *A New Sect of Religion Descryed, Called Adamites.* London, 1641.

Breton, Nicholas. *Breton's Melancholike Humours.* Johnson and Warwick, 1815.

———. *The Good and the Badde, or Descriptions of the Worthies and Vnworthies of this Age. Where the Best may see their Graces, and the Worst discerne their Baseness.* The English Experience, No. 853. Norwood, New Jersey: Walter J. Johnson, Inc., 1977.

———. *Machivells Dogge.* London, 1617.

———. *Pasquils Mad-Cap. And his Message.* The English Experience, its Record in Early Printed Books Published in Facsimile, no. 200. New York: Da Capo Press, 1969.

Bridges, Walter. *Ioabs Counsell and King Davids Seasonable Hearing it. Delivered in a Sermone Before the Honorable House of Commons. At their late solemne Fast, Feb. 22.* London, 1643.

Bright, Timothy. *A Treatise: Wherein is declared the sufficience of English Medicines, for cure of all diseases, cured with Medicine.* London, 1580.

———. *A Treatise of Melancholie.* 1586. The English Experience: Its Record in Early Printed Books, Published in Facsimile, no. 212. New York: Da Capo Press, 1969.

———. *Characterie, an Arte of Shorte, Swifte, and Secrete Writing by Character.* Inuented by Timothe Bright, Doctor of Phisike. London, 1588.

Burton, Robert. *The Anatomy of Melancholy.* Eds. Nicholas K. Kiessling, Thomas C. Faulkner and Rhonda L. Blair. Oxford: Clarendon Press, 1990.

———. *The Anatomy of Melancholy.* Ed. Holbrook Jackson. New York: New York Review of Books, 2001.

Caesar and Pompey, or, Caesar's Revenge. In *Narrative and Dramatic Sources of Shakespeare,* vol. 5. Ed. Geoffrey Bullough. New York: Columbia University Press, 1964.

Casaubon, Meric. *A Treatise Concerning Enthusiasme, As it is an Effect of Nature: but is mistaken by many for either Divine Inspiration, or Diabolicall Possession.* A Facsimile Reproduction of the Second Edition of 1656. Ed. Paul J. Korshin. Gainesville, FL: Scholars' Facsimiles & Reprints, 1970.

Cogan, Thomas. *The Haven of Health: Chiefly Made for the Comfort of Students, and Consequently for All Those that Have a Care of Their Health.* London, 1589.

Comber, Thomas. *Christianity no Enthusiasm: Or, The Several Kinds of Inspirations and Revelations Pretended to by the Quakers Tried, and Found Destructive to Holy Scripture and True Religion: In Answer to Thomas Ellwood's Defence thereof; in his Tract, Miscalled Truth Prevailing, &c.* London, 1678.

Crofts, Robert. *Paradise Within us: Or, The Happy Mind.* London, 1640.

Donne, John. *The Complete English Poems.* Ed. A. J. Smith. New York: Penguin Books, 1971.

———. *Biathanatos.* Ed. Ernest W. Sullivan II. Newark: University of Delaware Press, 1984.

———. *Devotions Upon Emergent Occasions, Together With Death's Duel.* Ann Arbor: University of Michigan Press, 1959.

———. *Letters to Severall Persons of Honour: A Facsimile Reproduction.* Delmar, New York: Scholars' Facsimiles & Reprints, 1977.

———. *Pseudo-Martyr.* Ed. Anthony Raspa. Montreal and Kingston: McGill-Queens, University Press, 1993.

———. *The Sermons of John Donne.* Eds. George R. Potter and Evelyn M. Simpson. Berkeley and Los Angeles: University of California Press, 1962.

Du Laurens, Andre. *A Discourse of the Preservation of the Sight: Of Melancholike Diseases; of Rheumes, and of Old Age.* 1599. Trans. Richard Surphlet. London: Oxford University Press, 1938.

Earle, John. *Micro-Cosmographie Or, a peece of the world discovered.* London, 1628. STC, 1727.

Elyot, Sir Thomas. *The Castel of Helth.* 1541. New York: Scholars' Facsimiles and Reprints, 1937.
Englands Mad Petition to the Right Honourable, The, &c. London, 1647.
The Factious Citizen, or, The Melancholy Visioner. A Comedy, As it was Acted at the Duke's Theatre. London, 1685.
Ficino, Marsilio. *The Book of Life.* Trans. Charles Boer. Woodstock, CT: Spring Publications, 1980.
Forset, Edward *The Body Natural and Politique.* The English Experience, its Record in Early Printed Books Published in Facsimile, no. 520. New York: Da Capo Press, 1973.
Fountaine, Edward. *Melancholys bane: or, Choice, pleasant, and profitable recreations.* London, 1654.
Foure Deliberate, and Solid Queries of State, Resolved to the three Kingdomes. London, 1647.
G. B. *Rarities: Or the Incomparable Possibilities in Secret Writing* (London, 1665).
Gregory, Edmund. *An historical anatomy of Christian melancholy.* London: 1646.
Harvey, William. *The Anatomical Exercises.* Ed. Geoffrey Keynes. New York: Dover Publications, 1995.
Hibernicus, Mercurius-Mastix. *A muzzle for Cerberus, and his three vvhelps Mercurius Elencticus, Bellicus, and Melancholicus.* London, 1648.
Hickes, George. *The Spirit of Enthusiasm Exorcised: in a Sermon Preached before the University of Oxford, On Act-Sunday, July 11, 1680.* London, 1680.
Higginson, Francis. *Irreligion of the Quakers.* London, 1678.
Hill, John. *Hypochondriasis, A Practical Treatise.* The Augustan Reprint Society, No. 135. Los Angeles: William Andrews Clark Memorial Library, 1969.
Hobbes, Thomas. *Behemoth, or The Long Parliament.* Chicago and London: The University of Chicago Press, 1990.
"A Homily Against Disobedience and Wylfull Rebellion." In *Divine Right and Democracy: An Anthology of Political Writing in Stuart England.* London: Penguin Books, 1986, 94–98.
Hooker, Richard. *Ecclesiastical Polity: Selections.* Ed. Arthur Pollard. Manchester: Carcanet, 1990.
Huarte, John. *The Examination of mens Wits. In which, by dicouering the varietie of natures, is shewed for what profession each one is apt, and how far he shall profit therein.* The English Experience, No. 126. New York: Da Capo Press, 1969.
Hume, David. *A Treatise of Human Nature.* Ed. L. A. Selby-Bigge. Oxford: Clarendon Press, 1978.
Humfrey, John. *A Brief receipt moral & Christian, against the passion of the heart, or sore of the mind, incident to most, and very grievous to many, in the trouble of enemies. Being one single sermon by I. H. Minister of Froome. Published at this rate by itself, that any who need it, and have it. For the ease and benefit especially of the more tender, weak*

and melancholy; who feel these arrows stick in their spirits, but know not the way of plucking them out, or aswaging the pain of them. London, 1655.

James I. *Political Writings*. Cambridge Texts in the History of Political Thought. Cambridge: Cambridge University Press, 1994.

Jonson, Ben. *The Complete Plays of Ben Jonson*. Four volumes. Ed. G. A. Wilkes. Oxford: Oxford University Press, 1981.

Joviall Crew, The: Or, the Devil Turn'd Ranter. London, 1650.

Knox, John. *On Rebellion*. Cambridge Texts in the History of Political Thought. Cambridge: Cambridge University Press, 1994.

Laurence, Leonard. *A Small Treatise betwixt Arnalte and Lucenda Entituled The Evill-intreated Lover, or The Melancholy Knight*. London, 1639.

Locke, John. *An Essay Concerning Human Understanding*. New York: Prometheus Books, 1995.

Lodge, Thomas. *The Wounds of Civil War*. Regents Renaissance Drama. Ed. Joseph W. Houpert. Lincoln: University of Nebraska Press, 1969.

Marriott, John. *The English mountebank: or, a physical dispensatory, wherein is prescribed, many strange and excellent receits of Mr. Marriot*. London, 1652.

Mascall, William. *A new and true mercurius: or, Mercurius metricus*. London, 1661.

Melancholicus, Mercurius. *The armies letanie, imploring the blessing of God on the present proceedings of the armie*. London, 1647.

———. *Craftie Cromwell: or, Oliver ordering our new state*. London, 1648.

———. *The cuckoo's-nest a [sic] Westminster, or the Parlement between two lady-birds*. London, 1648.

———. *Ding dong, or Sr. Pitifull Parliament, on his death-bed*. London, 1648.

———. *Mistris Parliament brought to bed of a monstrous childe of reformation*. London, 1648.

———. *Mrs. Parliament, her invitation of Mrs. London, to a Thanksgiving dinner*. London, 1648.

———. *A nose-gay for the House of Commons*. London, 1648.

———. *The Parliament arraigned, convicted, wants nothing but execution*. London, 1648.

———. *The Parliaments thanks to the Citie*. London, 1648.

———. *The second part of Crafty Crvmwell, or, Oliver in his glory as king*. London, 1648.

The Melancholy Complaint of D. Otes, of the Black Ingratitude of this Present Age Towards him, and the Evil Rewards he has Receiv'd for his Numberless Services Done for the Nation. London, 1684.

Mennes, Sir John. *Recreation for ingenious head-peeces, or, A pleasant grove for their wits to walk in*. London, 1654.

Merry-Man, Doctor. *The pennilesse parliament of threed-bare poets: or, The merry fortune-teller, wherein all persons of the four severall complexions may finde their fortunes. Composed by Doctor Merry-man: not onely to purge melancholy: but also to procure tittering and laughing. Full of witty mirth, and delightfull recreation, for the content of the reader.* London, 1649.

Milton, John. *Complete Poems and Major Prose.* Ed. Merrit Y. Hughes. New York: MacMillan Publishing Company, 1957.

———. *Complete Prose Works of John Milton.* Ed. Don Wolfe, et al. New Haven, CT: Yale University Press, 1953–1982.

Mirandola, Giovanni Pico. *Oration on the Dignity of Man.* Trans. A. Robert Caponigri. Washington, D.C: Regnery Gateway, 1956.

Montaigne, Michel de. "The Apology for Raymond Sebond." In *The Complete Essays.* Trans. Donald M. Frame. Stanford: Stanford University Press, 1957: 318–457.

Moore, John, Lord Bishop of Ely. *Of Religious Melancholy. A Sermon Preach'd before the Queen at White-Hall, March 6, 1691.* London, 1708.

More, Henry. *Enthusiasmus Triumphatus: or, A Brief Discourse of the Nature, Causes, Kinds, and Cure of Enthusiasm.* Augustan Reprint Society, no. 118. Los Angeles: William Andrews Clark Memorial Library, 1966.

Nashe, Thomas. "Terrors of the Night." In *The Unfortunate Traveller and Other Works.* New York: Penguin Books, 1971.

North, Sir Thomas. *Plutarch's 'Lives.'* In *Narrative and Dramatic Sources of Shakespeare,* vol. 5. Ed. Geoffrey Bullough. New York: Columbia University Press, 1964.

Paracelsus. *Four Treatises.* Ed. Henry E. Sigerist. Baltimore and London: Johns Hopkins University Press, 1941.

Pascal, Blaise. *Pensées.* Trans. Honor Levi. Oxford: Oxford University Press, 1995.

Petrarca, Francesco. *The Revolution of Cola di Rienzo.* Ed. Mario Emilio Cosenza. New York: Italica Press, 1996.

Phanatiques Creed, The, or a Door of Safety. London, 1655.

Ponet, John. *A Short Treatise of politique power; and of the true obedience which subjects owe to Kings, and other civill governours.* London, 1556.

Powell, Thomas. *A salve for soul-sores.* London, 1679.

The Rebells Warning-Piece; Being Certain Rules and Instructions left by Alderman Hoyle (a Member of Parliament) being a Burgesse for York-shire, who hanged himself Ianuary 30. Within half an hour after that day twelve-moneth he and his Sectarian Brethren had murthered their KING. Printed for the Good of the State, 1649.

Retrogradus, Mercurius. *Welcome, Most Welcome Newes.* London, 1647.

Reynolds, Edward. *Evgenia's Teares for Great Brittaynes Distractions or, Some slender observations reflecting on those sad Times.* London, 1642.

———. *Treatise of the Passions and Faculties of the Soule of Man.* London, 1656.

Rogers, Timothy. *A Discourse Concerning Trouble of Mind, And the Discourse of Melancholly.* London, 1691.

Rowlands, Samuel. *The melancholy cavalier. Or, Fancy's master-piece. A poem by J.C.* London, 1654.

Scogan, John. *Scogin's jests.* London, 1680.

Sedgwick, Joseph. *A Sermon, preached at St. Marie's in the University of Cambridge May 1ˢᵗ, 1653. Or, An essay to the discovery of the spirit of enthusiasme and pretended inspiration, that disturbs and strikes at the Universities.* London, 1653.

Shakespeare, William. *As You Like It.* The Arden Shakespeare Second Series. Ed. Agnes Latham. London: Arden Shakespeare, 1975.

———.*Hamlet.* The Arden Shakespeare Second Series. Ed. Harold Jenkins. London and New York: Routledge, 1982.

———. *Julius Caesar.* The Arden Shakespeare Third Series. Ed. David Daniell. London: Thomas Nelson, 1998.

———. *The Merchant of Venice.* The Arden Shakespeare Second Series. Ed. John Russell Brown. London and New York: Routledge, 1985.

Spencer, John. *A discourse of divers petitions of high concernment, and great consequence.* London: printed by H. Dudley, 1641.

———. "The Elizabethan Malcontent." In *Joseph Quincy Adams Memorial Studies.* Ed. James G, McManaway. Washington, D.C.: Folger Shakespeare Library, 1948, 523–35.

Spenser, Edmund. *The Faerie Queene.* In *The Works of Edmund Spenser: A Variorum Edition*, vol. 2. Eds. Edwin Greenlaw, Charles Grosvenor Osgood, Frederick Morgan Padelford, Ray Heffner. Baltimore: Johns Hopkins University Press, 1947.

———. *The Faerie Queene.* Ed. A. C. Hamilton. New York and London: Longman, 1977.

———. *The Shorter Poems of Edmund Spenser.* New Haven & London: Yale University Press, 1989.

Taylor, John. *A Medicine for the Times. Or, an Antidote against Faction.* London, 1641.

———. *The Diseases of the Times Or, The Distempers of the Common-wealth.* London, 1642.

———. *Mad Fashions, Od Fashions, All out of Fashions, or, The Emblems of these Distracted times.* London, 1643.

Underhill, Thomas. *Hell Broke Loose: or An History of the Quakers Both Old and New.* London, 1660.

Walton, Isaak. *Lives.* London: Falcon Educational Books, 1951.

Wakefield, Robert. *On The Three Languages.* Medieval and Renaissance Texts and Studies. Ed. and Trans. G. Lloyd Jones. Binghamton, NY: Suny Press at Binghamton, 1989.

Warmstry, Thomas. *An Answer To Certaine Observations of W. Bridges, concerning the present warre against His Majestie. Whereby hee pretends to justifie it against that Hexapla of considerations. Viz. Theologicall, Historicall, Legall, Criticall, Melancholy, and Foolish; wherein, as he saith, it is look't upon by the squint-eyed multitude.* London, 1643.

Whitehead, George. *Enthusiasm Above Atheism: or, Divine Inspiration and Immediate Illumination [by God Himself] Asserted. And the Children of Light Vindicate: In Answer to a Book, entituled,* The Danger of *Enthusiasm Discovered.* London, 1674.

Winstanley, William. *The delectable history of Poor Robin the merry sadler of Walden.* London, 1680.

Wright, Thomas. *The Passions of the Minde in Generall: a Reprint Based on the 1604 Edition.* Urbana: University of Illinois Press, 1971.

Younge, Richard. *A Christian library, or, A pleasant and plentiful paradise of practical Divinity.* London, 1655.

———. *The Prevention of Poverty, Together with the Cure of Melancholy, Alias Discontent. Or the best and surest way to Wealth and Hapiness: being Subjects very seasonable for these Times; wherein all are Poor, or not pleased, or both; when they need be neither.* London, 1655.

SECONDARY SOURCES

Achinstein, Sharon. "*Samson Agonistes* and the Drama of Dissent," *Milton Studies* 33 (1996): 133–58.

Adelman, Janet. *Suffocating Mothers: Fantasies of Maternal Origin in Shakespeare's Plays, "Hamlet" to "The Tempest."* London and New York: Routledge, 1992.

Agamben, Giorgio. *Infancy & History: Essays on the Destruction of Experience.* Trans. Liz Heron. London: Verso, 1993.

———. *Stanzas: Word and Phantasm in Western Culture.* Theory and History of Literature, vol. 69. Trans. Ronald L. Martinez. Minneapolis: University of Minnesota Press, 1993.

———. *The Open: Man and Animal.* Trans. Kevin Attell. Stanford: Stanford University Press, 2004.

Allen, Don Cameron. *The Harmonious Vision.* Baltimore: Johns Hopkins University Press, 1954.

Alulis, Joseph. "Fathers and Children: Matter, Mirth, and Melancholy in *As You Like It.*" In *Shakespeare's Political Pageant: Essays in Literature and Politics.* Eds. Joseph Alulis and Vickie Sullivan. London: Rowman & Littlefield Publishers, Inc., 1996: 37–60.

Anderson, Judith H. *Words that Matter: Linguistic Perception in Renaissance English.* Stanford: Stanford University Press, 1996.

Andreasen, N. J. C. "Donne's *Devotions* and the Psychology of Assent." *Modern Philology* 63 (1965): 207–18.

Anson, John. "*Julius Caesar*: The Politics of the Hardened Heart." *Shakespeare Studies* 2 (1967): 11–33.

Appelbaum, Robert. *Literature and Utopian Politics in Seventeenth-Century England.* Cambridge and New York: Cambridge University Press, 2002.

Aristotle. *De Interpretatione.* The Loeb Classical Library. Trans. H. P. Cooke and Hugh Tredennick. Cambridge, Massachusetts: Harvard University Press, 1938.

Arshagouni, Mary. "Politics of John Donne's *Devotions Upon Emergent Occasions:* or, New Questions on the New Historicism." *Renaissance and Reformation/Renaissance et Reforme* 27 (1991): 233–48.

Babb, Lawrence. *The Elizabethan Malady: A Study of Melancholia in English Literature from 1580 to 1642.* East Lansing: Michigan State University Press, 1951.

——. *Sanity in Bedlam: A Study of Robert Burton's "Anatomy of Melancholy."* East Lansing: Michigan State University Press, 1959.

Bald, R. C. *John Donne: A Life.* Oxford: Clarendon Press, 1970.

Barber, C. L. *Shakespeare's Festive Comedy: A study of Dramatic Form and its Relation to Social Custom.* Princeton: Princeton University Press, 1959.

Barker, Francis. *The Tremulous Private Body: Essays on Subjection.* Ann Arbor: University of Michigan Press, 1995.

Bellamy, Elizabeth J. *Translations of Power: Narcissism and the Unconscious in Epic History.* Ithaca and London: Cornell University Press, 1992.

Benjamin, Walter. *The Origin of German Tragic Drama.* Trans. John Osborne. London: Verso, 1977.

——. "On Language as Such and on the Language of Man." In *Selected Writings: Volume One, 1913–1926.* Eds. Marcus Bullock and Michael W. Jennings. Cambridge, MA: Harvard University Press, 1996.

Berger, Harry. *The Allegorical Temper: Vision and Reality in Book II of Spenser's "Faerie Queene."* Handon, CT: Archon Books, 1967.

Berman, Ronald. "A Note on the Motives of Marcus Brutus," *Shakespeare Quarterly* 23 (1972): 197–200.

Biester, James. *Lyric Wonder: Rhetoric and Wit in English Renaissance Poetry.* Ithaca: Cornell University Press, 1997.

Blank, Paula. "The Dialect of *The Shepheardes Calender.*" *Spenser Studies* 10 (1992): 71–94.

——. *Broken English: Dialects and the Politics of Language in Renaissance Writings.* London and New York: Routledge, 1996.

Bowden, William. "The Mind of Brutus." *Shakespeare Quarterly* 17(1966): 57–67.

Bradley, A. C. *Shakespearean Tragedy.* 3d edition. London: Macmillan Press, 1992.

Breitenberg, Mark. *Anxious Masculinity in Early Modern England.* Cambridge Studies in Renaissance Literature and Culture, no. 10. Cambridge: Cambridge University Press, 1996.

Brown, Richard Danson. *'The New Poet': Novelty and Tradition in Spenser's Complaints.* Liverpool: Liverpool University Press, 1999.

Burkhardt, Sigurd. *Shakespearean Meanings.* Princeton: Princeton University Press, 1968.

Bushnell, Rebecca. *Tragedies of Tyrants: Political Thought and Theater in the English Renaissance.* Ithaca: Cornell University Press, 1990.

Bynum, W. F., Roy Porter, and Michael Shepherd, eds. *The Anatomy of Madness: Essays in the History of Psychiatry in Three Volumes.* New York and London: Tavistock Publications, 1985.

Cain, Thomas H. "Spenser and the Renaissance Orpheus." *University of Toronto Quarterly.* 41 (1971): 24–47.

———. *Praise in "The Faerie Queene."* Lincoln: University of Nebraska Press, 1978.

Campbell, Lily. *Shakespeare's Tragic Heroes: Slaves of Passion.* London: University Paperbacks, 1930.

Canavan, Thomas L. "Robert Burton, Jonathan Swift and the Tradition of Anti-Puritan Invective." *Journal of the History of Ideas* 34 (1973): 227–42.

Canguilhem, Georges. *The Normal and the Pathological.* Trans. Carolyn R. Fawcett in collaboration with Robert S. Cohen. New York: Zone Books, 1989.

Carey, John. *John Donne: Life Mind and Art.* London and Boston: Faber and Faber, 1981.

Carlton, William J. *Timothe Bright, Doctor of Phisicke: A Memoir of "The Father of Modern Shorthand."* London: Elliot Stock 62, 1911.

Cheney, Patrick. *Spenser's Famous Flight: A Renaissance Idea of a Literary Career.* Toronto: University of Toronto Press, 1993.

Coffey, John, "Pacifist, Quietist, or Patient Militant? John Milton and the Restoration," *Milton Studies* 42 (2002): 149–74.

Cogswell, Thomas. *The Blessed Revolution: English Politics and the Coming of War, 1621–1624.* Cambridge: Cambridge University Press, 1989.

Colie, Rosalie L. *Paradoxica Epidemica: The Renaissance Tradition of Paradox.* Princeton: Princeton University Press, 1966.

Collinson, Patrick. *The Religion of Protestants: The Church in English Society 1559–1625.* Oxford: Clarendon Press, 1982.

Cooper, Robert M. "The Political Implications of Donne's *Devotions.*" In *New Essays on Donne.* Ed. Gary A. Stringer. Salzburg: Institut für Englische Sprache und Literatur, 1977: 192–210.

Craig, Martha. "The Secret Wit of Spenser's Language." In *Essential Articles for the Study of Edmund Spenser.* Ed. A. C. Hamilton. Hamden, CT: Archon Books, 1972, 313–33.

Cressy, David and Lori Anne Ferrell, eds. *Religion & Society in Early Modern England: A Sourcebook.* London and New York: Routledge, 1996.

Curtis, Mark H. "The Alienated Intellectuals of Early Stuart England." In *Crisis in Europe 1560–1660: Essays from Past and Present.* Ed. Trevor Aston. London: Routledge and Kegan Paul, 1965: 295–316.

Curtius, Ernst Robert. *European Literature and the Latin Middle Ages.* Trans. Willard R. Trask. Bolingen Series no. 36. Princeton: Princeton University Press, 1953.

Cust, Richard. "News and Politics in Early Seventeenth Century England," *Past and Present* 112 (1986): 60–90.
Davis, J. C. *Fear, Myth and History: The Ranters and the Historians*. Cambridge: Cambridge University Press, 1986.
Dollimore, Jonathan. *Radical Tragedy: Religion, Ideology and Power in the Drama of Shakespeare and his Contemporaries*. Durham: Duke University Press, 1993.
Dorner, Klaus. *Madmen and the Bourgeoisie: A Social History of Insanity and Psychiatry*. Oxford: Oxford University Press, 1981.
Drakakis, John. "Fashion it Thus: *Julius Caesar* and the Politics of Theatrical Representation." In *Shakespeare's Tragedies: Contemporary Critical Essays*. Susan Zimmerman, ed. New York: St. Martin's Press, 1998.
Duncan-Jones, Katherine. *Ungentle Shakespeare: Scenes From His Life*. London: Arden Shakespeare, 2001.
Edwards, Karen L. "Inspiration and melancholy in *Samson Agonistes*." In *Milton and the Ends of Time*. Ed. Juliet Cummins. Cambridge: Cambridge University Press, 2003: 224–40.
Engel, William E. *Mapping Mortality: The Persistence of Memory and Melancholy in Early Modern England*. Amherst: University of Massachusetts Press, 1995.
Enterline, Lynn. *Tears of Narcissus: Melancholia and Masculinity in Early Modern Writing*. Stanford: Stanford University Press, 1995.
Ferry, Anne. *The "Inward" Language: Sonnets of Wyatt, Sidney, Shakespeare, Donne*. Chicago: The University of Chicago Press, 1983.
Fichter, Andrew. "'And nought of *Rome* in *Rome* perceiu'st at all': Spenser's *Ruins of Rome*." *Spenser Studies* 2 (1981): 183–92.
Fish, Stanley E. "Question and Answer in *Samson Agonistes*." *Critical Inquiry* 11 (1969): 237–64.
——. *Self-Consuming Artifacts: The Experience of Seventeenth Century Literature*. Berkeley: University of California Press, 1972.
——. "Spectacle and Evidence in *Samson Agonistes*." *Critical Inquiry* 15 (1989): 556–86.
——. *How Milton Works*. Cambridge and London: Harvard University Press, 2001.
Fletcher, Angus. *The Prophetic Moment: An Essay on Spenser*. Chicago: University of Chicago Press, 1971.
Foucault, Michel. *Madness and Civilization: A History of Insanity in the Age of Reason*. Trans. Richard Howard. New York: Vintage Books, 1965.
——. *The Order of Things: An Archaeology of the Human Sciences*. New York: Vintage Books, 1970.
——. *The Birth of the Clinic: An Archaeology of Medical Perception*. Trans. A. M. Sheridan Smith. New York: Vintage Books, 1973.

Fouke, Daniel. *The Enthusiastical Concerns of Dr. Henry More: Religious Meaning and the Psychology of Delusion.* Leiden, New York: E. J. Brill, 1997.

Fox, Ruth A. *The Tangled Chain: The Structure of Disorder in the "Anatomy of Melancholy."* Berkeley: University of California Press, 1976.

Freist, Dagmar. *Governed by Opinion: Politics, Religion and the Dynamics of Communication in Stuart London, 1637–1645.* London and New York: Tauris Academic Studies, 1997: 177–238.

Freud, Sigmund. *The Interpretation of Dreams. The Standard Edition of the Complete Psychological Works of Sigmund Freud,* vol. 4. Ed. and trans. James Strachey in collaboration with Anna Freud. London: The Hogarth Press and the Institute of Psychoanalysis, 1957.

———. *Totem and Taboo: Some Points of Agreement Between the Mental Lives of Savages and Neurotics.* Ed. and trans. James Strachey. New York and London: W. W. Norton & Company, 1950.

———. "Mourning and Melancholia." *The Standard Edition of the Complete Psychological Works of Sigmund Freud,* vol. 14. Ed. and trans. James Strachey in collaboration with Anna Freud. London: The Hogarth Press and the Institute of Psychoanalysis, 1957.

Fudge, Erica. *Perceiving Animals: Humans and Beasts in Early Modern English Culture.* New York: St. Martin's Press, 2000.

Gidding, George (Lord Byron). *The Life, Letters, and Journals of Lord Byron.* Ed. Thomas Moore. London, 1901.

Gilman, Ernest. "A Theatre for Voluptuous Worldlings (1569) and the Origins of Spenser's Iconoclastic Imagination." In *Imagination on a Long Rein: English Literature Illustrated.* Ed. Joachim Moller. Marburg: Jonas Verlag, 1998, 45–55.

Giustiniani, Vito R. "Homo, Humanus, and the Meanings of 'Humanism.'" In *Renaissance Essays II.* Ed. William J. Connell. Rochester: University of Rochester Press, 1993.

Godlee, Fiona. "Aspects of Non-Conformity: Quakers and the Lunatic Fringe." In *The Anatomy of Madness: Essays in the History of Psychiatry in Three Volumes,* vol. 2. Eds. W. F. Bynum, Roy Porter and Michael Shepherd. London and New York: Tavistock Publications, 1985, 73–85.

Goldberg, Jonathan. *Voice Terminal Echo: Postmodernism and English Renaissance Texts.* New York and London: Methuen, 1986.

———. *James I and the Politics of Literature: Jonson, Shakespeare, Donne, and Their Contemporaries.* Stanford: Stanford University Press, 1989.

Gravelle, Sarah Stever. "The Latin-Vernacular Question and Humanist Theory of Language and Culture." In *Renaissance Essays II.* Ed. William J. Connell. Rochester: University of Rochester Press, 1993.

Gray, Dave and Jeanne Shami. "Political Advice in Donne's *Devotions.*" *Modern Language Quarterly* 50 (1989): 337–56.

Greene, Gail. "'The power of speech to stir men's blood': The Language of Tragedy in Shakespeare's *Julius Caesar.*" *Renaissance Drama* 11 (1980): 67–93.

Greene, Thomas M. *The Light in Troy: Imitation and Discovery in Renaissance Poetry.* New Haven and London: Yale University Press, 1982.

Gross, Kenneth. *Spenserian Poetics: Idolatry, Iconoclasm and Magic.* Ithaca: Cornell University Press, 1985.

Guibbory, Acshah. *Ceremony and Community from Herbert to Milton: Literature, Religion, and Cultural Conflict in Seventeenth-Century England.* Cambridge: Cambridge University Press, 1998.

———. "Donne's Religion: Montagu, Arminianism and Donne's Sermons, 1624–1630." *English Literary Renaissance* 31 (2001): 412–39.

Guillory, John. *Poetic Authority: Spenser, Milton, and Literary History.* New York: Columbia University Press, 1983.

Gurr, Andrew. *The Shakespearean Stage 1574–1642.* Cambridge: Cambridge University Press, 1980.

Hadfield, Andrew. "Was Spenser a Republican?" *English: The Journal of the English Association* 47 (1998): 169–82.

Hale, David G. *The Body Politic: A Political Metaphor in Renaissance English Literature.* The Hague: Mouton, 1971.

Hallett, Charles and Elaine. *The Revenger's Madness: A Study of Revenge Tragedy Motifs.* Lincoln and London: University of Nebraska Press, 1980.

Hammill, Graham. "'The thing/Which never was': Republicanism and *The Ruines of Time,*" *Spenser Studies* 18 (2003): 165–83.

Harris, Jonathan Gil. *Foreign Bodies and the Body Politic: Discourses of Social Pathology in Early Modern England.* Cambridge Studies in Renaissance Literature and Culture, no. 25. Cambridge: Cambridge University Press, 1998.

Hassoun, Jacques. *The Cruelty of Depression: On Melancholy.* Trans. David Jacobson. Foreword by Michael Vincent Miller. Reading, MA: Addison-Wesley Longman Inc., 1997.

Hawes, Clement. *Mania and Literary Style: The Rhetoric of Enthusiasm from the Ranters to Christopher Smart.* Cambridge: Cambridge University Press, 1996.

Hawkes, David. *Idols of the Marketplace: Idolatry and Commodity Fetishism in English Literature, 1500–1680.* New York: Palgrave, 2001.

Haynes, Jonathan. *The Social Relations of Jonson's Theater.* Cambridge: Cambridge University Press, 1992.

Healy, Thomas and Jonathan Sawday, eds. *Literature and the English Civil War.* Cambridge and New York: Cambridge University Press, 1990.

Heidegger, Martin. *The Principle of Reason.* Trans. Reginald Lilly. Bloomington and Indianapolis: Indiana University Press, 1996.

Helgerson, Richard. *Forms of Nationhood: The Elizabethan Writing of England.* Chicago: The University of Chicago Press, 1992.

Herman, Peter. *Squitter-wits and Muse-haters: Sidney, Spenser, Milton and Renaissance Antipoetic Sentiment.* Detroit: Wayne State University Press, 1996.
Heyd, Michael. "Robert Burton's Sources on Enthusiasm and Melancholy: From a Medical Tradition to Religious Controversy." *History of European Ideas* 5 (1984): 17–44.
Hill, Christopher. *The World Turned Upside Down: Radical Ideas During the English Revolution.* New York: Penguin Books, 1975.
———. *The Experience of Defeat: Milton and Some Contemporaries.* New York: Penguin Books, 1984.
———. *Puritanism and Revolution: Studies in Interpretation of the English Revolution of the 17th Century.* New York: St. Martins Press, 1997.
Hirst, Derek. *England in Conflict, 1603–1660: Kingdom, Community, Commonwealth.* London: Arnold Publishers, 1999.
Hodges, Devon L. *Renaissance Fictions of Anatomy.* Amherst: University of Massachusetts Press, 1985.
Houlahan, Mark. "Spin Controlling Apocalypse in *Samson Agonistes*.": *Studies in English Literature 1500–1900* 31 (1994): 3–22.
Hume, Anthea. *Edmund Spenser: Protestant Poet.* Cambridge: Cambridge University Press, 1984.
Hyde, Thomas. "Vision, Poetry, and Authority in Spenser." *English Literary Renaissance* 13 (1983): 127–45.
Hyman, Lawrence. *The Quarrel Within: Art and Morality in Milton's Poetry.* Port Washington, NY: Kennikat Press, 1972.
Jenkins, Harold. "As You Like It." In *Shakespeare: Modern Essays in Criticism.* Revised. Ed. Leonard F. Dean. London: Oxford University Press, 1967.
Jenner, Mark S. R. "The Great Dog Massacre," In *Fear in Early Modern Society.* Eds. William G. Naphy and Penny Roberts. Manchester and New York: Manchester University Press, 1997: 44–61.
Johnson, Jeffrey. *The Theology of John Donne.* Cambridge: D. S. Brewer, 1999.
Judson, Alexander C. *The Life of Edmund Spenser.* In *The Works of Edmund Spenser: A Variorum Edition,* vol. 11. Baltimore: Johns Hopkins University Press, 1947.
Kahn, Coppélia. *Roman Shakespeare: Warriors, Wounds, and Women.* London and New York: Routledge, 1997.
Kane, Sean. *Spenser's Moral Allegory.* Toronto: University of Toronto Press, 1989.
Kerrigan, William. *The Prophetic Milton.* Charlottesville: University Press of Virginia, 1974.
King, Bruce. *Seventeenth-Century English Literature.* New York: Schocken, 1982.
King, John N. *English Reformation Literature: The Tudor Origins of the Protestant Tradition.* Princeton: Princeton University Press, 1982.
———. *Spenser's Poetry and the Reformation Tradition.* Princeton: Princeton University Press, 1990.

Kinsman, Robert. "Folly, Melancholy, and Madness: A Study in Shifting Styles of Medical Analysis and Treatment, 1470–1675." In *The Darker Vision of the Renaissance*. Berkeley: University of California Press, 1974.

Kitzes, Adam H. "Paradoxical Donne: *Biathanatos* and the Problems with Political Assimilation." *Prose Studies* 24 (2001): 1–17.

Klein, Melanie. "A Contribution to the Psychogenesis of Manic-Depressive States." In *The Selected Melanie Klein*. Ed. Juliet Mitchell. New York: The Free Press, 1986.

Klibansky, Raymond, Erwin Panofsky, and Fritz Saxl. *Saturn and Melancholy: Studies in the History of Natural Philosophy, Religion and Art*. New York: Basic Books, 1964.

Knight, W. Nicholas. "Brutus' Motivation and Melancholy." *The Upstart Crow* 5 (1984): 108–24.

Knights, L. C. *Drama and Society in the Age of Jonson*. London: Chatto and Windus, 1937.

Kristeva, Julia. *Black Sun: Depression and Melancholia*. Trans. Leon S. Roudiez. New York: Columbia University Press, 1989.

Lacan, Jacques. *Écrits: A Selection*. Trans. Alan Sheridan. New York: W. W. Norton & Co., 1977.

Lange, Marjory E. "Humourous Grief: Donne and Burton Read Melancholy." In *Speaking Grief in English Literary Culture: Shakespeare to Milton*. Eds. Margo Swiss and David A. Kent,. Pittsburgh: Duquesne University Press, 2002: 69–97.

Leinwand, Theodore. "Shakespeare and the Middling Sort." *Shakespeare Quarterly* 44(1993): 284–303.

Levy-Navarro, Elena. "John Donne's Fear of Rumours in the *Devotions upon Emergent Occasions* and the Death of John King." *Notes & Queries* 245 (December 2000): 481–83.

Lepenies, Wolf. *Melancholy and Society*. Trans. Jeremy Gaines and Doris Jones. Cambridge, MA: Harvard University Press, 1992.

Lewalski, Barbara K. *The Life of Milton*. Oxford: Blackwell Publishing, 2000.

———. "Milton and Idolatry.": *Studies in English Literature 1500–1900* 43 (2003): 213–232.

Lieb, Michael. *Milton and the Culture of Violence*. Ithaca: Cornell University Press, 1994.

———. "'Our Living Dread': The God of *Samson Agonistes*,' *Milton Studies* 33 (1996): 3–25.

Liebler, Naomi Conn. *Shakespeare's Festive Tragedy: The Ritual Foundations of Genre*. London and New York: Routledge, 1995.

Lindley, Keith, ed. *The English Civil War and Revolution: A Sourcebook*. London and New York: Routledge, 1998.

Lochman, Daniel T. "'Seeking Just Occasion': Law, Reason, and Justice at Samson's Peripety." *Milton Studies* 26 (1990): 217–88.

Loewenstein, David. *Milton and the Drama of History: Historical Vision, Iconoclasm, and the Literary Imagination.* Cambridge: Cambridge University Press, 1990.

———. *Representing Revolution in Milton and his Contemporaries: Religion, Politics, and Polemics in Radical Puritanism.* Cambridge: Cambridge University Press, 2001.

Low, Anthony. *The Blaze of Noon: A Reading of "Samson Agonistes."* New York and London: Columbia University Press, 1974.

Lukacher, Ned. *Daemonic Figures: Shakespeare and the Question of Conscience.* Ithaca and London: Cornell University Press, 1994.

Lyons, Bridget Gellert. *Voices of Melancholy: Studies in Literary Treatments of Melancholy in Renaissance England.* Ideas and Forms in English Literature. London: Routledge & Kegan Paul, 1971.

MacDonald, Michael. *Mystical Bedlam: Madness, Anxiety and Healing in Seventeenth-Century England.* Cambridge History of Medicine. Cambridge: Cambridge University Press, 1981.

Maley, Willy. "Spenser's Languages: Writing in the Ruins of English." In *The Cambridge Companion to Edmund Spenser.* Ed. Andrew Hadfield. Cambridge: Cambridge University Press, 2001.

Maravall, José Antonio. *Culture of the Baroque: Analysis of a Historical Structure.* Trans. Terry Cochran. Theory and History of Literature, vol. 25. Minneapolis: University of Minnesota Press, 1986.

Marotti, Arthur F. *John Donne: Coterie Poet.* Madison: The University of Wisconsin Press, 1986.

Martz, Louis. *The Poetry of Meditation.* New Haven and London: Yale University Press, 1954.

Maus, Katherine Eisaman. *Inwardness and Theater in the English Renaissance.* Chicago: University of Chicago Press, 1995.

McAlindon, Thomas. *Shakespeare's Tragic Cosmos.* Cambridge: Cambridge University Press, 1991.

McCullough, Peter. "Donne as Preacher at Court: Precarious 'Inthronization.'" In *John Donne's Professional Lives.* Ed. David Colclough. Cambridge: D. S. Brewer, 2003: 179–202.

McDonald, Henry. "A Long Day's Dying: Tragic Ambiguity in *Samson Agonistes.*" *Milton Studies* 27 (1991): 263–83.

McDowell, Nicholas. *The English Radical Imagination: Culture, Religion, and Revolution, 1630–1660.* Oxford: Oxford University Press, 2003.

McGregor, J. F. and B. Reay, eds. *Radical Religion in the English Revolution.* Oxford: Oxford University Press, 1984.

McKeon, Michael. *Origins of the English Novel, 1600–1740.* Baltimore: Johns Hopkins University Press, 1987.

Miller, David Lee. "Spenser's Vocation, Spenser's Career." *English Literary History* 50 (1983): 197–231.

———. *The Poem's Two Bodies*. Princeton: Princeton University Press, 1988.
Miola, Robert. "*Julius Caesar* and the Tyrannicide Debate." *Renaissance Quarterly* 38 (1985): 271–89.
Montrose, Louis. "Of Gentlemen and Shepherds: The Politics of Elizabethan Pastoral Form." *English Literary History* 50 (1983): 415–59.
Mueller, Martin. "Plutarch's 'Life of Brutus' and the Play of Its Repetitions in Shakespearean Drama." *Renaissance Drama* 22 (1991): 47–93.
Mueller, William R. "Robert Burton's Economic and Political Views." *The Huntington Library Quarterly* 11 (1948): 341–59.
———. *The Anatomy of Robert Burton's England*. University of California Publications, English Studies 2. Berkeley and Los Angeles: University of California Press, 1952.
———. *John Donne: Preacher*. Princeton: Princeton University Press, 1962.
Neely, Carol Thomas. *Distracted Subjects: Madness and Gender in Shakespeare and Early Modern Culture*. Ithaca and London: Cornell University Press, 2004.
Nietzsche, Friedrich. "The Utility and Liability of History." In *Unfashionable Observations*. The Complete Works of Friedrich Nietzsche. Volume two. Stanford: Stanford University Press, 1995.
Nohrnberg, James. *The Analogy of "The Faerie Queene."* Princeton: Princeton University Press, 1980.
Norbrook, David. *Poetry and Politics in the English Renaissance*. London: Routledge & Kegan Paul, 1984.
———. *Writing the English Republic: Poetry, Rhetoric and Politics, 1627–1660*. Cambridge: Cambridge University Press, 1999.
O'Dair, Sharon. "Social Role and the Making of Identity in *Julius Caesar*." *Studies in English Literature 1500–1900* 33 (1993): 289–307.
Oliver, P. M. *Donne's Religious Writing: A Discourse of Feigned Devotion*. London & New York: Longman, 1997.
Ostovich, Helen M. "'So Sudden and Strange a Cure': A Rudimentary Masque in *Every Man Out of His Humour*." *English Literary Renaissance* 22 (1992): 315–32.
Palmer, D. J. "Tragic Error in *Julius Caesar*." *Shakespeare Quarterly* 21 (1970): 399–409.
Panofsky, Erwin. *The Life and Art of Albrecht Dürer*. Princeton: Princeton University Press, 1943.
Paster, Gail Kern. *The Body Embarrassed: Drama and the Disciplines of Shame in Early Modern England*. Ithaca: Cornell University Press, 1993.
———. "Melancholy Cats, Lugged Bears, and Early Modern Cosmology: Reading Shakespeare's Psychological Materialism Across the Species Barrier." In *Reading the Early Modern Passions: Essays in the Cultural History of Emotion*, eds. Gail Kern Paster, Katherine Rowe, and Mary Floyd-Wilson. Philadelphia: University of Pennsylvania Press, 2004: 113–29.
Patrick, J. Max. "Robert Burton's Utopianism." *Philological Quarterly* 27 (1948): 345–58.

Patterson, Annabel. *Censorship and Interpretation.* Madison: University of Wisconsin Press, 1984.

——. "Quod oportet *versus* quod convenit: *John Donne, Kingsman?* In *Critical Essays on John Donne.* Ed. Arthur Marotti. New York: G. K. Hall & Co., 1994.

Piccolomini, Manfredi. *The Brutus Revival: Patricide and Tyrannicide During the Renaissance.* Carbondale and Edwardsville: Southern Illinois University Press, 1991.

Pocock, J. G. A. *The Machiavellian Moment: Florentine Political Thought and the Atlantic Republican Tradition.* Princeton: Princeton University Press, 1975.

Poole, Kristen. *Radical Religion from Shakespeare to Milton: Figures of Nonconformity in Early Modern England.* Cambridge: Cambridge University Press, 2000.

Prescott, Anne Lake. "Spenser (Re)Reading du Bellay: Chronology and Literary Response." In *Spenser's Life and the Subject of Biography.* Eds. Judith H. Anderson, Donald Cheney and David A. Richardson. Amherst: University of Massachusetts Press, 1996: 131–45.

Provost, Foster. "Treatments of Theme and Allegory in Twentieth-Century Criticism of *The Faerie Queene.*" In *Contemporary Thought on Edmund Spenser.* Eds. Richard C. Frushell and Bernard J. Vondersmith.Carbondale: Southern Illinois University Press, 1975.

Radzinowicz, Mary Ann. *Toward "Samson Agonistes": The Growth of Milton's Mind.* Princeton: Princeton University Press, 1978.

Radden, Jennifer, ed. *The Nature of Melancholy: From Aristotle to Kristeva.* Oxford: Oxford University Press, 2000.

Read, David. *Temperate Conquests: Spenser and the Spanish New Worlds.* Detroit: Wayne State University Press, 2000.

Rebhorn, Wayne. "The Crisis of the Aristocracy in *Julius Caesar.*" *Renaissance Quarterly* 43 (1990): 75–111.

Renaker, David. "Robert Burton's Palinodes." *Studies in Philology* 76 (1979): 162–81.

Roberts, Donald Ramsay. "The Death Wish of John Donne." *Publications of the Modern Language Association of America* 62 (1947): 958–76.

Rossky, William. "Imagination in the English Renaissance: Psychology and Poetic." *Studies in the Renaissance* 5 (1958): 49–73.

Rothstein, Eric. "Et in Acedia Ego." *Madness, Melancholy, and the Limits of the Self.* Graven Images: Studies in Culture, Law, and the Sacred, vol. 3 Eds. Andrew D. Weiner and Leonard Kaplan. Madison: University of Wisconsin Law School, 1996, 65–91.

Russel, Conrad. *The Causes of the English Civil War.* Oxford: Clarendon Press, 1990.

Salkeld, Duncan. *Madness and Drama in the Age of Shakespeare.* Manchester and New York: Manchester University Press, 1993.

Samuel, Irene. "*Samson Agonistes* as Tragedy." In *Calm of Mind: Tercentary Essays on "Paradise Regained" and "Samson Agonistes" in Honor of John S. Diekhoff.* Ed.

Joseph A. Wittreich. Cleveland and London: The Press of Case Western Reserve University, 1971.

Sawday, Jonathan. *The Body Emblazoned: Dissection and the Human Body in Renaissance Culture.* London: Routledge & Kegan Paul, 1995.

———. "Shapeless Elegance: Robert Burton's Anatomy of Knowledge." In *English Renaissance Prose: History, Language, and Politics.* Neil Rhodes, ed. Tempe, Arizona: Medieval & Renaissance Texts & Studies, 1997, 173–202.

Schiesari, Juliana. *The Gendering of Melancholia: Feminism, Psychoanalysis, and the Symbolics of Loss in Renaissance Literature.* Ithaca and London: Cornell University Press, 1992.

Schleiner, Winfried. *The Imagery of John Donne's Sermons.* Providence: Brown University Press, 1970.

———. *Melancholy, Genius, and Utopia in the Renaissance.* Wiesbaden, 1991.

Schoenfeldt, Michael. *Bodies and Selves in Early Modern England: Physiology and Inwardness in Spenser, Shakespeare, Herbert, and Milton.* Cambridge Studies in Literature and Culture, no. 34. Cambridge: Cambridge University Press, 2000.

Scott, William Ingis Dunn. *Shakespeare's Melancholics.* London: Mills & Boon, 1962.

Screech, M. A. "Good Madness in Christendom." In *The Anatomy of Madness: Essays in the History of Psychiatry in Three Volumes.* Eds. W. F. Bynum, Roy Porter, and Michael Shepherd. London and New York: Tavistock Publications, 1985.

Seelig, Sharon Cadman. *Generating Texts: The Progeny of Seventeenth-Century Prose.* Charlottesville and London: University Press of Virginia, 1996.

Sena, John. "Melancholy Madness and the Puritans." *Harvard Theological Review* 66 (1973): 293–309.

Shami, Jeanne. "Kings and Desperate Men: John Donne Preaches at Court." *John Donne Journal: Studies in the Age of Donne* 6 (1987): 9–23.

———. "Donnes Sermons and the Absolute Politics of Quotation." in John Donne's Religious Imagination: Essays in Honor of John to Slovcross. Eds. Frances Mapezzi and Renford Joan Fronte. Conway. AR: University of Central Arizona Press, 1995.

———. "Labels, Controversy, and the Language of Inclusion in Donne's Sermons." In *John Donne's Professional Lives.* Ed. David Colclough. Cambridge: D. S. Brewer, 2003: 135–57.

Sharpe, Kevin. *Remapping Early Modern England: The Culture of Seventeenth-Century Politics.* Cambridge: Cambridge University Press, 2000.

Shawcross, John T. "Irony as Tragic Effect: *Samson Agonistes* and the Tragedy of Hope." In *Calm of Mind: Tercentary Essays on "Paradise Regained" and "Samson Agonistes" in Honor of John S. Diekhoff.* Ed. Joseph A. Wittreich. Cleveland and London: The Press of Case Western Reserve University, 1971.

Shawcross, John T. *The Uncertain World of Samson Agonistes,* Studies in Renaissance Literature. Cambridge: D.S. Brewer, 2001.

Shuger, Debora Kuller. *Habits of Thought in the English Renaissance: Religion, Politics, and the Dominant Culture.* Renaissance Society of America Reprint Texts 6. Toronto: University of Toronto Press, 1997.

Siemens, R. G. "'I haue often such a sickly inclination': Biography and the Critical Interpretation of Donne's Suicide Tract, *Biathanatos.*" *Early Modern Literary Studies* 7 (2000).

Simpson, Evelyn. *A Study of the Prose Works of John Donne.* Oxford: Clarendon Press, 1948.

Smith, Nigel, ed. *A Collection of Ranter Writings.* London: Junction Books, 1983.

———. *Perfection Proclaimed: Language and Literature in English Radical Religion 1640–1660.* Oxford: Clarendon Press, 1989.

———. *Literature & Revolution in England, 1640–1660.* New Haven and London: Yale University Press, 1994.

Somerville, J. P. *Royalists & Patriots: Politics and Ideology in England, 1603–1640.* 2d. ed. London and New York: Longman, 1999.

Spencer, Theodore, ed. *Shakespeare's Plutarch.* New York: Penguin Books, 1964.

Stachniewski, John. "John Donne: The Despair of the 'Holy Sonnets,'" *English Literary History* 48 (1981): 677–705.

———. *The Persecutory Imagination: English Puritanism and the Literature of Religious Despair.* New York: Oxford University Press, 1991.

Steadman, John. *Moral Fiction in Milton and Spenser.* Columbia and London: University of Missouri Press, 1995.

Stein, Arnold. *Heroic Knowledge: An Interpretation of "Paradise Regained" and "Samson Agonistes"* Minneapolis: University of Minnesota Press, 1957.

Stone, Lawrence. *The Causes of the English Revolution, 1529–1642.* London and New York: Routledge, 1972.

Strier, Richard. "Radical Donne: Satire III." *English Literary History* 60 (1993): 283–322.

———. "Donne and the Politics of Devotion." In *Religion, Literature, Politics and Post-Reformation England, 1540–1688.* Eds. Donna B. Hamilton and Richard Strier Cambridge: Cambridge University Press, 1996, 93–114.

Sutherland, John and Cedric Watts. "The Watch on the Centurion's Wrist." In *Henry V, War Criminal? & Other Shakespearean Puzzles.* Oxford: Oxford University Press, 2000.

Targoff, Ramie. *Common Prayer: The Language of Public Devotion in Early Modern England.* Chicago: University of Chicago Press, 2001.

Taylor, Myron. "Shakespeare's *Julius Caesar* and the Irony of History." *Shakespeare Quarterly* 24(1973): 301–08.

Tellenbach, Hubertus. *Melancholy: History of the Problem, Endogeneity, Typology Pathogenesis, Clinical Considerations.* Trans. Erling Eng. Pittsburgh: Duquesne University Press, 1980.

Trevor, Douglas. "John Donne and Scholarly Melancholy." *Studies in English Literature 1500–1900* 40 (2000): 81–102.

———. *The Poetics of Melancholy in Early Modern England.* Cambridge: Cambridge University Press, 2004.

Trevor-Roper, Hugh. *Renaissance Essays.* Chicago: The University of Chicago Press, 1985.

Van Es, Bart. "Priuie to his Counsell and Secret Meaning: Spenser and Political Prophecy." *English Literary Renaissance* 30 (2000): 3–31.

Vicari, Patricia E. "The Triumph of Art, the Triumph of Death: Orpheus in Spenser and Milton." In *Orpheus: The Metamorphosis of a Myth,* ed. John Warden. Toronto: University of Toronto Press, 1982: 207–30.

———. *The View From Minerva's Tower: Learning and Imagination in "The Anatomy of Melancholy."* Toronto: University of Toronto Press, 1989.

Waddington, Raymond B. "Melancholy Against Melancholy: *Samson Agonistes* as Renaissance Tragedy." In *Calm of Mind: Tercentary Essays on "Paradise Regained" and "Samson Agonistes" in Honor of John S. Diekhoff.* Ed. Joseph A. Wittreich. Cleveland and London: The Press of Case Western Reserve University, 1971.

Wall, John N. *Transformations of the Word: Spenser, Herbert, Vaughn.* Athens, GA: University of Georgia Press, 1988.

Watson, Robert N. *The Rest is Silence: Death as Annihilation in the English Renaissance.* Berkeley and Los Angeles: University of California Press, 1994.

———. "As You Liken It: Simile in the Wilderness," *Shakespeare Survey* 56 (2003): 79–92.

Webber, Joan. *The Eloquent "I": Style and Self in Seventeenth Century Prose.* Madison: University of Wisconsin Press, 1968.

Weiner, Andrew D. and Leonard V. Kaplan, eds. *Madness, Melancholy, and the Limits of the Self.* Vol. 3 of *Graven Images: Studies in Culture, Law, and the Sacred.* Madison: University of Wisconsin Law School, 1996.

Wenzel, Siegfried. *The Sin of Sloth: Acedia in Medieval Thought and Literature.* Chapel Hill: The University of North Carolina Press, 1967.

Wiggins, Peter DeSa. *Donne, Castiglione, and the Poetry of Courtliness.* Bloomington and Indianapolis: Indiana University Press, 2000.

Williams, Kathleen. "Vision and Rhetoric: The Poet's Voice in *The Faerie Queene*," *English Literary History* 36 (1969): 131–44.

———. "Spenser and the Metaphor of Sight." In *Renaissance Studies in Honor of Carol Camden.* J.A. Ward, ed. Rice University Studies 60, ii. Houston: Rice University Press, 1974.

Williamson, George. "The Restoration Revolt Against Enthusiasm." *Studies in Philology* 30 (1933): 571–603.

———. "Mutability, Decay, and Seventeenth-Century Melancholy." *English Literary History* 2 (1935): 121–50.

Wilson, Richard. "'Is This a Holiday?': Shakespeare's Roman Carnival." *English Literary History* 54 (1987): 31–44.

———. "A Brute Part: *Julius Caesar* and the Rites of Violence." *Cahiers Elisabethans: Late Medieval and Renaissance English Studies* 50 (1996): 19–32.

Wittkower, Rudolf and Margot. *Born Under Saturn: The Character and Conduct of Artists: A Documented History from Antiquity to the French Revolution.* New York and London: W. W. Norton & Company, 1963.

Wittreich, Joseph. *Interpreting Samson Agonistes.* Princeton: Princeton University Press, 1986.

Wofford, Susanne Lindgren. *The Choice of Achilles: The Ideology of Figure in the Epic.* Stanford: Stanford University Press, 1992.

Wong, Samuel. "Encyclopedism in the *Anatomy of Melancholy.*" *Renaissance and Reformation/Renaissance et Reformation* 22 (1998): 5–22.

Woodbridge, Linda. *The Scythe of Saturn: Shakespeare and Magical Thinking.* Urbana and Chicago: University of Illinois Press, 1994.

Wooton, David, ed. *Divine Right and Democracy: An Anthology of Political Writing in Stuart England.* New York: Penguin Books, 1986.

Index

A

A New Sect of Religion Descryed, Called Adamites (Bray), melancholy malcontents and religious sects, 167
Abbott, Archbishop, religious enthusiasm, 157
Africa, 153
Agamben, Giorgio, 67, 159
Age of Enthusiasm, 19, 155–156
Age of Reason, 19, 155–156
alienation, melancholy and, 15, 55, 61–62
Allen, W.
    "New Notions and new affected Modes and Phrases," 165
Anatomy of Melancholy (Burton), 123–150, 138–150, 147
    Anabaptists, 142, 147
    ancient Egypt and, 135–136
    Anglican church, 142
    Arminianism, 145
    Ars Poetica (Horace), 137
    Articles Agreed upon by the Archbishops and Bishops of Both Provinces and the whole Cleargie, 146
    artisan classes and, 148
    as asymmetrical, 138–150
    Bedlam hospital, 147–148
    Brownists, 142, 147
    Calvinism, 142, 145, 146
    Catholics, 139, 142
    Church of England, 145, 146, 147
    conflicting loyalties and, 149
    Democritus Jr. as persona, 129, 140
    "Democritus Jr. to the Reader," 18, 124, 127, 129–138, 139
    ecclesiastical doctrine, 145
    ecclesiastical institutions and, 144
    economics and, 135, 136
    ekphrasis, 125
    encyclopedic method, 127
    England's public troubles in, 134
    England's theological problems, 140
    Erasmus, reference to, 145–146
    Familists, 147
    governments and, 134
    Heraclitus, 140, 150
    Hercules, 137, 138, 144, 145
    heroic figures, 135
    idolatry and, 141
    illiterates and, 143–144, 149
    illness and, 139
    kingdoms and horticulture, 134
    Laud, William, Archbishop of Canterbury, 128, 146
    as literature, 126, 127
    Luther, Martin, 143, 144
    Lutherans, 142
    madness and, 125, 138, 139
    madness and desire to be Christ-like, 148
    madness of the prophet, 149
    madness of the world and, 124, 137
    medical literature on melancholy and religious polemics, 156
    melancholy, 124, 150

melancholy and language, 128, 131, 132, 149
melancholy and madness, 124
melancholy and society, 132, 133, 139, 162
melancholy and the world, 124, 125, 137
messianism and, 135, 144, 148
mimetic character of false religion, 141
motivation for writing, 129
New Atlantis in, 139
"On Religious Melancholy," 127
physical and psychological defects of the nation's governors, 124
poetic commonwealth, 138, 147
poetic language, 137, 138
poetry and, 139
political reform, 124, 128, 136, 142, 145
political troubles and melancholy, 124
politics and, 126, 127, 136, 144
as post-mortem examination, 124
pre-Roman England and, 134
"Preface," 134, 139, 144
pseudo prophets, 148, 149
psychosis and, 148
Puritans, 139
reform and, 135, 137
reformed English Church, 139
religious controversies, 124, 125, 140, 142
religious enthusiasm, 126, 139, 147, 148, 149
"Religious Melancholy," 18
religious melancholy, 126, 127–128, 138–150, 139, 140, 141
religious practices, 141, 143, 144
religious reform, 124
Rome and, 134
skepticism in, 147
social reform, 126
social structure and, 148, 150
superstition and, 139, 141
Swift and, 156
Terra Australis Incognita, 139
true church, history of, 143
true religion, 142
tyranny, 139, 140, 145–147, 149
utopia and, 128, 137, 138
water imagery, 140, 150

writing and, 150
Anglican propagandists, 163
animals
  imagery of, 68
  in Jonson, 59–84, 76
  in Shakespeare, 59–84, 76
  on stage, 68
Arabia, English medicine and, 32
Aristotle, 29, 169, 171
  catharsis, 175
Arminianism, prohibited by Parliament on grounds of treason, 145
ars moriendi tradition, 108
Ars Poetica (Horace), 137
Art of Logic (Milton), 181
Articles Agreed upon by the Archbishops and Bishops of Both Provinces and the whole Cleargie, 146
  doctrine of double predestination, 146
  "Preface to the Articles," 145, 146
As You Like It (Shakespeare)
  Adam (servant), 80, 82, 83
  animal rights in, 77, 77–78
  animals and, 68, 76, 77–78, 78, 79, 80, 81, 82
  anthropocentric basis for political associations in, 77
  authenticity and theatricality in, 84
  authority and, 76
  community in, 83
  Corin and Silver as shepherds in, 82
  dogs and, 68
  Duke, 76, 77, 79, 82, 83
  Duke Senior, 76, 78, 80, 81
  as forest comedy, 75
  Ganymede, 76
  Hymen, 84
  Jacques' "Seven Ages of Man" speech in, 83
  Jaques, 68, 69, 75, 78, 79, 82, 84
  Jaques and melancholy, 12, 76–80, 83–84
  Jaques as melancholy malcontent in, 75, 77, 80, 85
  Jaques on-stage interaction with animals, 64
  Jaques view of animals in, 76
  melancholy in, 77, 80, 85, 87

Index

natural rights in, 76
Oliver, 81
Orlando, 81, 82, 83, 84, 87
Orlando as lovesick, 76, 80
reference to Adam in, 79
Robin Hood, 76
Rosalind, 76, 84
wedding in, 83
Asia, English medicine and, 37
assassination, as justifiable remedy for social ills, 90

B

Bacchus, 43–45
Bacon, Francis, 139
  essay on sedition, 90
  modern science and, 159
  rebellion and, 90
  state responsibility for removing causes of discontent, 90
Basilikon Doron (King James)
  governance and, 106
  king as physician in, 97, 106
  rumor as sickness in, 112
Bedlam hospital, 19, 140, 148
Biathanatos (John Donne)
  defense of Christian Martyrs in Roman Empire, 106
  defense of suicide and, 105
  suicide and the will of God, 115
Blasphemy Act of 1650, Ranters and, 164
body-politic, the, 5, 92
  in Bacon, Francis 90, 91
  The Body Natural and Politique (Forset, Edward), 89–90
  crisis of, 88–93
  disease and, 55, 160
  in Donne, *Devotions*, 107, 114
  ideologies of, 87–88, 92, 98
  imagery in the Renaissance, 91
  in John Ponet, 91
  in *Julius Caesar* (Shakespeare), 87, 92, 95, 97–98
  late Elizabethan period and, 88
  in Parsons, Roger, 91
  the political body and, 93–101
  rebellion as disease and, 88

revolt and, 92
Roman, 96
in Spenser, Edmund, 48–49, 55
Boehme, Jacob, 119
Book of Judges, 194
  Samson, 191
Bray, Thomas, *A New Sect of Religion Descryed, Called Adamites*, 167
Bridges, Walter, Sermon of Six false reasons for civil war, 162
Bright, Timothy, 16, 28, 28–57, 29, 30, 31
  allusions to Cicero and Cato, 34
  Characterie an Arte of Shorte, Swifte, and Secrete Writing by Character, 33, 37
  commonwealth and, 35
  diseases and cures in ethnographic context, 56
  Elizabethan monarchy and, 32, 33
  English language and, 32, 34, 36, 56
  humors and, 32
  languages and, 34, 37
  Latin and, 35
  linguistics and, 33, 37
  medicine and, 31, 32, 33, 37, 38
  melancholy and, 36, 56, 59
  melancholy vs. despair in, 37, 59–60
  nationalism and, 33, 38, 56, 59
  physical ailments and afflictions of the soul, 36
  physiological model as ethnologically inflected, 32, 37
  political terminology and physical health, 48
  racial typing in, 37
  Reformation biases and, 32
  Shorthand and, 33, 34, 35
  Spenser and, 56
  Treatise of Melancholie, 27, 31, 35, 37, 59
  A Treatise: Wherin is declared the sufficience of English Medicines, for cure of all diseases, cured with Medicine, 32
Bruno, Giordano, 6
  melancholy and pseudo-prophecy, 157
Brutus
  Caesar's rise to power and, 86
  as defender of liberty, 85

melancholy and, 86
Plutarch and, 95
rebellion and, 86
Burton, Robert, 123–150, 131, 158, 179.
  see also individual works
  Anatomy of Melancholy, 5, 17, 18, 123–150
  anti-enthusiasm, 164
  authority and, 18, 128
  ceremonial practices and, 147
  Church of England, 157
  conservatism and, 149
  criticism of public institutions as melancholy madness, 18
  Democritus Jr., 12, 18, 124, 127, 129, 139–140, 171
  fictionalized vantage point of, 125
  Laudian church, 128
  melancholy and, 18, 130, 132, 171
  melancholy and government, 18, 133
  "Melancholy and the Question of Government," 17
  "New Atlantis," 128, 137, 139
  Orphic fantasies, 128
  pictorial terminology, 125
  political reform and, 18, 133
  political reform as medicine, 134
  political troubles and illness, 133
  problem of writing, 127
  religion and, 126
  religious enthusiasm, 18, 155, 157, 158
  religious melancholy and, 18
  social maladies and, 133
  utopia and, 133, 136
  writing and, 126, 127, 130, 131

C

Caesar, assassination of, 85, 86
Calvin, John, 175
Calvinism, 146
Cambridge Platonists, 155, 158, 172, 179
Casaubon, Meric, 19, 156, 158, 171, 172, 179
  ancient languages and, 169
  contemporary histories of enthusiasm, 168
  divination and, 169
  divine inspiration and, 172–173
  enthusiasm and rationality, 170
  humours and, 169
  Logos, 155
  melancholy and inspiration, 168
  natural and supernatural causes, 170
  prophecy and, 168
  religious enthusiasm, 127, 155
  religious enthusiasm as melancholy madness, 172
Catholicism
  England and, 181
  fear and, 126
Cato, 33
Chaucer, 41
  "Knight's Tale," 27
Christianity no Enthusiasm (Comber), melancholy and religious enthusiasm, 164
Church, early Roman, 106
Church of England, 15, 18, 146
  dissenters and, 157
church reform, 16
Cicero, 33
civil dissension
  malcontents and, 85–102
  melancholy, 85–102
civil war, 7, 153–174
  madness and, 7, 19, 153
  revolution and, 19
  Samson imagery popular in, 177
Colloquies (Erasmus), preface, 145
Comber, Thomas, *Christianity no Enthusiasm*, 164
Commonwealth and Government of Venice, The, 46
  Lewis Lewkenor translation into English and, 46
  Spenser's dedicatory sonnet and, 46
commonwealth, physical body and, 49, 55, 89, 92, 114, 121, 124, 163
compilatio, Renaissance textual tradition of, 127
Copernicus, 62
Croft, Thomas, *Paradise Within us: Or, The happie Mind*, 161

D

deconstruction, 12

Index

Democritus, 140, 150
  as model for Burton's *Anatomy of Melancholy,* 129
"Democritus Jr. to the Reader," as Burton's epistle to the reader, 129–138
demonology, 164
depression as physiological disorder, 21
Devotions Upon Emergent Occasions (Donne), 103–150, 108
  authority and, 110, 121
  body politic, the, 107
  disease and, 121
  "Expostulations and Prayers," 109
  Fama as allegorical figure, 120
  gossip and, 108
  hermeneutic difficulties of, 109
  illness and, 107, 113
  illness and politics, 107, 115, 116
  Jacobean policies and, 109
  King James and, 110
  melancholy and sin, 115
  political imagery in, 109, 116
  politics and, 18, 108–109, 110
  Prince Charles and, 108–109
  public discourse and, 121
  publication date and, 108
  role of the will, 117
  royalist positions in, 114
  rumor and, 108, 110, 110–111, 112–113
  rumor and illness, 112–113
  rumor and the state, 111, 118
  sin and, 110, 115
  suicide, 115, 118
  twelfth meditation and, 116
  vapors and rumor, 116, 118
disease, ideologies of, 153–174
Dissenters, 163
"The Distractions of the Times," 7
distractions of the times, 151–175
Dollimore, Jonathan, 60, 62–63
Don John, as melancholy character in Shakespeare, 85
Donne, John, 5, 17, 20. *see also* individual works
  anxiety of, 110
  Arminianism, 119
  Biathanatos, 105
  Christianity and, 106
  commonwealth and physical body in, 114
  commonwealth and suicide, 114
  Dean of St. Paul's, 123
  death and, 105
  Devotions Upon Emergent Occasions, 17, 18, 105–122
  disease and rebellion, 107
  ethics of suicide martyrdom, 115
  exile at Mitcham, 105
  The Faerie Queen, 7
  fashionable melancholy of early years, 107
  Freud and, 105
  Holy Sonnets, 105
  Iago and, 111
  idolatry and, 119
  illness as rebellion and, 113
  Jacobean ideology of absolute monarch, 113
  Jews and, 119
  Laudianism and, 119
  Lothian portrait and, 20, 107
  melancholy and, 10, 11, 17, 105, 117, 123
  melancholy and rebellion against institutional norms, 107
  melancholy and religious rebellion, 106
  melancholy and sickness, 107
  melancholy as a pose, 107
  melancholy as rebellion and, 17
  obedience to the state and, 114
  political dissidents and, 114
  preaching before King Charles and, 106
  print and accessibility of public discourse, 111
  Pseudo-Martyr, 115
  public persona and, 112
  rebellion and, 113
  rebellion as melancholy, 106
  rebellion as sickness, 106
  return to health and, 120
  rumor and, 18, 110, 112, 120–121
  rumor and rebellion, 121
  self-reproach for his past, 107
  sermon at St. Paul's, 106
  Sermon at Whitehall, 105

sin and rebellion as signs of political disease, 121
suggestion that King as physician of the state take action against rumor, 112
suicidal depression during exile at Mitcham estate, 107
suicide, 105, 115
suicide and the state, 115
textual authority and, 105–122
Du Bellay, Joachim, tower of Babel and, 39, 40
du Laurens, Andre (Laurentius)
discourse on melancholy, 27–29
melancholy and pseudo-prophecy, 157
Duchess of Malfi, The, 84
Durer, Albrecht, 8, 28
Melancholia I, 10

E

Eikon Basilike, as counterfeit autobiography, 189
Elizabethan period, 86
concept of nationhood and, 31
Elyot, Thomas, *Castel of Helth,* 27
England
madness and, 160
melancholy and, 4, 160
national religion and, 60
suicide and, 160
England, 16th century, 2
cheap print in, 111
newsy culture of, 111
pamphleteers, 112
political discourse and circulation of news, 112
poverty and, 61
unemployment and, 61
England, 17th century, 2
England, early modern, 5, 6, 8
mental disorder in, 31–33, 153
Englands Mad Petition to the Right Honourable, The, etc., (anonymous pamphlet), satirical request for expansion of Bedlam hospital, 161
English church, reformed, 6

English culture, shift from Latin-based to vernacular idiom, 35
English language, 30, 34, 38–39
the *Bible* and, 35
Book of Common Prayer and, 35
English national identity, post-Reformation, 16
English satire, 40
enthusiasm, 39, 42–43
as anti-authoritarian, 158–159
contemporary histories of, 168
debates over, 159
demystification of, 168
divine inspiration, 168
illness and, 19
in jest, 168–173
madness and, 158, 168
melancholy and, 158, 168
Reason and, 156
religious, 2
revolt against, 19
secularization of, 158
skepticism towards, 163–164
Enthusiasmus Triumphatus (More), critique of religious enthusiasm, 179
Erasmus, *Colloquies,* 145
Eurydice, 38, 45
Every Man Out of His Humour (Jonson)
animal imagery in, 69
Asper, 68, 69
Asper and "humor," 68
Asper and melancholy, 68
Buffone, 70, 72, 75
conventions of comedy and, 72
Cordatus, 74
dogs in, 68, 71, 72–73, 74, 75
Fastidious, 70
Macilente, 68, 72, 73, 75
Macilente as melancholy malcontent in, 71
Mitus as minor character in, 74
Puntarvolo, 68, 75
Puntarvolo and his dog in, 71, 72
Puntarvolo as melancholy in, 70, 72, 75
Sordido's suicide in, 74

F

Faerie Queene, The (Spenser), 54

Index

Acrasia as evil character in, 48
alienation in, 55
Alma as character in, 50
Arthur as representing grace in, 52
Book II, Guyon and Arthur, 47
castle and language in, 55–56
castle as public government and, 55
castle as Tower of Babel in, 56
Castle of Alma episode in, 47, 48, 51, 54
disruption of language in, 53
Eumenestes in, 54
Eumnestes' authority usurped in, 52
Guyon and Arthur as characters in, 50, 52, 55
King Nine (Ninus, Nimrod), 54
language as threat to the castle in, 55
language in, 54
Maleger, 51, 53, 55
Maleger as melancholy in, 52, 55
Maleger as original sin in, 52
Maleger defeated in, 48
Maleger's troups in, 52, 53
Mammon as evil character in, 48
melancholy in, 52, 53, 86
melancholy Phantastes in, 47, 49, 50, 51, 53
narrator in, 53
Phaedria as evil character in, 48
Phantastes, 56, 89
rebellions in, 53
revolt as symbol of madness, 51
revolt in, 47
revolt of Maleger's troops, 47
temperance in, 48, 54
Tower of Babel in, 53–54
feminism, 12
Ficino, Marsilio, 6, 8, 9, 10, 16, 28, 30, 126
Problems and, 4
Fifth Monarchists, 19
Fish, Stanley, 127, 178
Floyd, Thomas, *The picture of a perfit common wealth*, 92
Forset, Edward, 90
The Body Natural and Politique, 89
temporality and, 92

Foucault, Michel
genealogical studies and, 21
political terminology and physical health, 49
French civil wars, 147
Freud, Sigmund, 4
death drive and, 105
melancholy and, 13
"Mourning and Melancholia," 13
psychologists and, 154
Sophocles and, 105
Fudge, Erica, 63

G

Gift of Tongues, Acts of the Apostles, 39
Gilpin, John
Anabaptists, 166
the devil and, 166
melancholy despair, 166
Quakers and enthusiasm, 165
Godlee, Fiona, 8, 154
government
melancholy and, 103–150
rumor and illness as interruptions of well-ordered body-politic, 113

H

Hamlet (Shakespeare)
Hamlet and time in, 93
Hamlet as melancholy, 85
melancholy and revenge in, 84
Harris, Joanathan Gil, 52, 91
Harvey, Gabriel, 30
Hawes, Clement, 8, 156
Heidegger, Martin, 170
Heraclitus, 12, 140, 150
Hercules, 136, 144
Higginson, Francis, *Irreligion of the Quakers*, 164
Hippocratic medicine, 2
humors and, 2
Homily Against Wylfull Disobedience and Rebellion, 5, 90
Hooker, Richard
false prophets and, 148
melancholy and, 157

Huarte, John, *Examination of Men's Wits,* 5
human beings
    animals and, 63, 64, 67, 67–68, 69, 73, 74, 77
    bestial aspects of behavior, 63
    as chameleons, 64–69, 66
    definition of, 63, 65
    mimesis and, 65, 76
    as political animals, 69
    status of, 64
    as talking beasts, 64–69
    theatricality and, 82
    as unique creatures, 64
humanism, 64
humanitas, 64, 69
Hume, David, 130
humors
    black, 1–24
    Bright and, 32
    Galen and, 21
    Hippocrates, 21
    Hippocratic medicine and, 2
    Julius Caesar (Shakespeare) and, 100
    melancholy and, 2, 20, 21, 176
    Milton and, 176
    in Renaissance, 177
    in *Samson Agonistes* (Milton), 176
"Humour" plays, 68
    animals in, 59–84
    of Jonson, 59–84
    malcontents in, 59–84
    of Shakespeare, 59–84

I

"Il Penseroso" (Milton), 180, 181, 182
    contemplative genius and, 176
illness
    political vulnerability and, 116
    social conditions and, 133
India, English medicine and, 32
interregnum, 7, 153–174
    madness and, 19, 153
    melancholy and, 8
    texts, 2
Irish rebellions, 15
Irreligion of the Quakers (Higginson), heresy and blasphemy, 164

J

Jack Cade uprising, 134
Jacobean "decentering of man," 62
Jesuit infiltration of England during 1580s, 15
Jonson, Ben, 17. *see also Every Man Out of His Humour*
    animals and, 69
    animals on stage and, 64, 72–73
    character types and, 73
    comedies of, 61, 62
    human beings and animals in, 74, 75, 84
    "humour" plays of, 59–84
    melancholy and, 107
    Puttenham's treatise and, 28
    Theophrastus and, 73
"The Joviall Crew, or, The Devill turn'd RANTER," charges of madness and demon worship in, 167
Julius Caesar (Shakespeare), 85–101, 93
    anachronism of clocks in, 98
    assassination of Caesar in, 87
    the body politic in, 87, 88, 92, 95, 97–98, 98, 101
    Brutus, 87, 93, 95, 97
    Brutus and body politic imagery, 92, 95, 96
    Brutus and melancholy in, 86
    Brutus as delirious in, 98–99
    Brutus as political malcontent, 86, 88, 99
    Brutus as purger, 97
    Brutus' conflict in, 100
    Brutus' radical disorientation in, 100
    Brutus vs. other theatrical malcontents, 99
    Caesar, 87, 95, 98
    Caesar's power and, 94, 101
    Caska and, 99
    Cassius, 87, 95
    Cassius as malcontent, 99
    Cassius' farewell to Brutus in, 93–94
    Cicero, 93, 99, 100
    civil war in, 87
    enthusiastic rhapsodies of the prophets in, 100
    grief and the state in, 84

Index

humors and, 100
malcontents and, 85, 87, 93
melancholy and, 87, 88, 92, 100, 101
melancholy as radical uncertainty in, 88
melancholy discontent and, 86, 87
melancholy in speech by Messala in, 100–101
Messala, 87
political troubles as disease in, 87
politics and, 100
Portia, 86, 87
prophecy and, 100
Rome and, 87, 94
Rome and madness, 99
Rome as melancholy in, 87, 100
soothsayer's warning to Caesar, 100
time in, 93
tyrannicide in, 87–88

K

Keats, Odes, 21
king, as physician, 113
King Charles, 121
   Donne's sermons and, 106
King Charles I, execution of, 189
King Henry VIII, 40
King James, 5
   Basilikon Doron, 97, 106, 112
   comparison to physician, 88
   death of, 108
   dissolution of Parliament, 113
   liberty and, 86
   obedience to the state and, 114
   rumor and, 110
   scandals and, 111
   Spanish affair, 113
   "The Trew Law of Free Monarchies," 86
King Lear (Shakespeare), 62
   Edmund, 60
   melancholy and revenge in, 84
   melancholy as performance, 60
Klein, Melanie, psychoanalytic theory and, 13
Kristeva, Julia
   language and melancholy, 21
   psychoanalytic theory and, 13

L

"L'Allegro" (Milton), 181
   companion lyrics, 176
language
   as corrupt, 47
   and health of political institutions, 47
   and mental dispositions, 36
   modern vernacular, 46
Laud, William, Archbishop of Canterbury, 121, 146
Laudian church
   polarization with Puritan ministers, 147
   policy, 119, 128–129, 146
Laurentius, *see also* du Laurens
Leibniz, G. W., 170
Leveller army, defeat at Burford, 19
Lewalksi, Barbara, 184
"Life of Brutus" (Plutarch), 95–96
Life of Sister Katharine of Jesus, Nunne of the Order of our Lady, etc. The,
   Casaubon and, 168
Linnaeus, human beings and animals, 67–68
Locke, John, 156
   melancholy as source of enthusiasm, 156
Logos, 155
London
   Elizabethan, disorientation of, 61
   melancholy malcontents and, 61
Lyly, John, melancholy and, 23

M

"Mad Fashions Od Fashions, Alls out of Fashion" (Taylor), madness and the times, 160
madness, 164
   17th century, 158
   Augustan conception of, 155
   early modern, 19
   enthusiasm and, 158
   feigned, 154
   holy Christian, 154
   ideologies of, 8, 153–174
   marginalization and, 8
   politics and, 154, 160, 161
   religion and, 161
   religious enthusiasm and, 153
   rhetoric of, 163

social order and, 8, 154, 160
social reform and, 154
versions of, 153–154
vocabulary for in 17th century, 160
Maenads, Bacchus worship and, 45
malcontents. *see also* melancholy malcontents
civil dissension and, 85–101
defenders of liberty against tyranny, 85
toleration of, 91
martyrdom
biblical narratives and, 195
England and, 195
medical treateses on melancholy
classic concept of melancholy, 27
literary implications and, 27
melancholy and discourse, 27
medicine
poetic discourse and, 30
poetic practice and, 28
melancholy, 1, 12, 49, 158, 164, 171
aggression and, 13–14
alienation and, 15
animals and, 70
authentic vs. inauthentic, 68
Bright and, 27–58, 60
Burton and, 123–151
character and, 123
civil war and, 3
conservatism and, 158
cultural tradition and, 28, 179
defining, 11
delusion and, 164
depression and, 2, 4, 14, 21, 22
despair and, 36
discontent and, 16
discourse and, 25–27
disruption and, 2, 4
Donne and, 106
dual nature of, 157
in Elizabethan England, 14–15, 16, 27, 30, 60
as "Elizabethan Malady," 30
England and, 14, 15
English vernacular and, 30
enthusiasm and, 157, 168
error and, 101

in *The Faerie Queen* (Spenser), 52, 53, 86
fashionable, 6, 15
Freud and, 4
"genial," 10, 28
genius and, 8, 10, 15, 22, 28, 157
government and, 103–150
grace and, 106
grief and, 4, 14
history and, 8, 21
humors and, 2, 20, 21, 176
iconography and, 11, 15
ideology and, 8
justice and, 12
language and, 15, 22, 40, 56, 123–151
literary research and, 20, 28
literature and, 8, 28
madness and, 157
malcontents, 7, 11, 60
medicine and, 27, 28, 59
medieval attitudes towards, 10
Milton and, 175–196
misconduct and, 3
nationhood and, 16–17, 19, 27–58
pamphleteers and, 19
physiology and, 2, 17, 30
poetry and, 2, 28, 59
political discontent and, 15, 17, 20
political oppression and, 85
political reform and, 127
political turmoil and, 3, 5, 7, 12, 13, 19
politics and, 2, 4, 6, 14, 16, 23, 60
popular version in public playhouses, 60
prophecy and, 4
pseudo-Aristotelian doctrine of, 15
psychology and, 2
Quakers and, 164
rebellion and, 3, 6, 17
religion and, 2, 3, 123, 167
religious enthusiasm and, 3, 4, 20
religious radicalism and, 8
religious rebellion, 106
religious reform and, 127
remedies for, 33
Renaissance and, 8, 22
revenge and, 84
ridicule of on stage, 123
ruling classes and, 22

Index 265

    Satan and, 167
    self-loathing and, 13
    Shakespeare and, 28
    Sidney and, 28
    sin and, 123
    Spenser and, 27–58, 31, 56, 60
    stereotype of, 123
    study of, 27
    as "The Elizabethan Malady," 27
    theories of, 8, 20, 21
    travel and, 16
    turmoil and, 3
    types of, 6, 59
    unspeakable, 180–184
    violence and, 3
melancholy discontent, 123
melancholy malcontents, 60, 68. *see also* malcontents
    animals and, 59–84, 63
    continental philosophy, 60
    as Elizabethan stock figures, 60
    in Jonson's plays, 64, 68, 84
    on-stage interactions with animals, 64
    as outsiders, 60, 62
    political discontent and, 84
    Renaissance humanist principles and, 62
    revenge tragedies and, 84
    Roman catholicism, 60
    Rome, 60
    Shakespeare's Hamlet as, 61
    in Shakespeare's plays, 64, 68, 84
    theater and, 62
    travel and, 60
    as urban, 61
"The Melancholy Visioner, Or The Factious Citizen"
    Dr. Cauis in, 3
    Quakers and, 3.
Merchant of Venice, The (Shakespeare), 28
Michalangelo, melancholy and, 10
Midsummer Night's Dream, A (Shakespeare), 73
    dogs in, 73
    "Pyramus and Thisbe" in, 73
    Starveling as character in, 73
Milton, John, 173–197. *see also* individual works
    allegorical poetry and, 177
    Art of Logic, 181
    Catholicism and, 181, 183
    delusion as punishment for idol worship, 184
    enthusiasm, 184
    execution of Charles I and, 189
    humors and, 176
    madness and, 173–197
    melancholy and, 175–196, 180, 183, 195
    melancholy and inspiration, 181
    melancholy and public conduct, 180
    melancholy and religious toleration, 181
    melancholy ecstacies and, 182
    as pamphleteer, 181
    Paradise Lost, 173
    prophetic inspiration and, 182
    prophets and, 179, 195
    public debates and, 181
    public worship and, 180
    religious enthusiasm, 195
    religious melancholy, 184
    religious tolerance and, 181, 183
    Restoration and, 181
    Samson Agonistes, 19, 173
    Samson and political defeat, 177
    Samson as melancholy, 11
    Scripture and, 183
    Thessalonians, 184
    tragedy and, 175
    True Religion, 185
Montaigne, Michel de, 66–68
    "Apology for Raymond Sebond," 66
    humans and animals in, 66
    language and, 67
    reason in animals, 66
More, Henry, 1, 19, 156, 158, 171, 172, 180
    attack on Quakers, 172
    contemporary histories of enthusiasm, 168
    Democritus Jr. reference, 171
    divine inspiration, 173
    enthusiasm as pathological, 172
    Enthusiasmus Triumphatus: Or, A Brief Discourse of The Nature, Causes, Kinds, and Cure of Enthusiasm, 1, 170–172, 179

invectives against religious enthusiasm, 127
melancholy and enthusiasm, 170
prophecy and, 168
religious enthusiasm, 155, 172
religious sects as pathology, 172

N

nationality, 59
  health and illness, 31
  medicine and, 31–33, 37–38
New Atlantis, 128, 137, 139
new historicism, 12
"New Notions and new affected Modes and Phrases" (Allen), enthusiasm and, 165
Nietzsche, melancholy and, 4

O

Oaths of Supremacy and Allegiance, 16
Orpheus, 38, 42, 140
  in Burton, 12
  Christian Gift of Tongues and, 39
  "enthusiasmos" and, 39
  Joachim du Bellay and, 39
  Julius Caesar and, 12
  in Puttenhman, 38
  quasi-divine language and, 39
  Samson Agonistes and, 12
  in Sidney, 38
  in Spenser, 12, 38–39, 41, 42, 44–45
  transformation of beasts into human beings and, 38

P

pamphleteers, 7
  humor theory and, 19
  melancholy and political unrest, 19
  political language and madness in, 160
  religious turmoil and, 167
pamphlets, 2, 111, 153
  ideological functions of madness in, 160
  as illness, 112
  melancholy and, 27
  Ranters as Satan Worshipers, 167
Panofsky, Erwin, 9–10
Paradise Lost (Milton), 173
  Michael and Adam (Book11), 176

Paradise Within us: Or, The happie Mind (Croft)
  public ramifications of diseases, 162
  theories of the humors and, 161
Parliament
  Charles and, 109
  dissension and, 7, 181
  James and, 113–114
  madness and, 181
  prohibition of Arminianism, 145
Parsons, Roger, 95
  the body politic in, 91
Pascal, Blaise, 99
Paster, Gail Kern, 63
Petition of Twelve, 163
Petrarch, 11, 39
  ancient Roman republic and, 20
  love poetry of, 15, 139
physicians, English, 30
Pico, 62–66, 68
  fable of, 65, 66
  human dignity and, 66
  Oration on the Dignity of Man, 62, 64
picture of a perfit common wealth, The (Thomas Floyd), political treatise on commonwealth and, 92
Plato, *Republic*, 5
Plutarch, 33
  "Life of Brutus," 95–96
poetic diction, shifts in from Edwardian to Elizabethan periods, 20
poetry, 30
  ability to reshape the world, 18, 42, 127–129, 136–138, 139, 167
  English, 38
  as force that could subdue animals, 45
  lyric, 11
  political, 38
  theories of, 28–31
political conflict
  madness and, 7, 160, 161
  melancholy and, 5, 7
political "health," 6
political oppression, melancholy and, 85
political radicalism, 154
  as pathological, 154
political reform

Index

madness and invalidation of, 154
melancholy and, 127
political theorists, 5
Ponet, John, 95
  the body politic in, 91
  Short Treatise of Politike Power, 90
Porter, Roy, 8
Prince Charles
  diplomatic fiasco of Jacobean court, 108
  journey to Madrid and, 108
  marriage to the Infanta of Spain, 109
problematic status of human beings, 64, 64–69, 65
Problems, 28, 29
  Aristotle and, 4, 161
  Theophrastus and, 4
prophecy, 4, 8, 19, 28, 30, 39–40, 44, 49–50, 127–127, 146–149, 155–159
  authority of, 173
  experience and, 173
Protectorate, 2
  silencing of radical religious sects during, 126
Pseudo-Martyr (John Donne), human will and, 115
psychoanalysis
  aggression and self-reproach, 13
  Freud and, 105
  melancholy and aggression, 13
  revival of melancholy, 21
  theory of, 12
  twentieth century, 14
psychology
  early modern, 160
  models and, 21
Puritans, 121, 173
  Samson story and, 177
  uprisings, 126
Puttenham, *Arte of English Poesie*, 28, 38

Q

Quakers, 8, 19, 154–155, 159, 163
  as danger to the Commonwealth, 165
  devil and, 165
  enthusiasm and, 165
  melancholy and, 164, 172
  Satan's influence and, 166
Queen Elizabeth, 15
  ability to withstand discontent, 16
  challenges to authority of, 15
Quibus, Dr. Caius, *The Factious Citizen, or, The Melancholy Visioner*, 1, 3

R

radical sects, 163
  arguments against in 17th century, 164
  disruptive behavior in England, 179
  rhetorically violent lay prophecies and, 179
Ranters, 19, 163, 164
  Satan and, 166, 167
  writings of, 173
Ranters Bible (Roulston), Ranters as blasphemous in, 167
Raphael, melancholy and, 10
raptures, 160–168
rebellion, 89
  comparisons with illness, 106
  disease and, 88
rebellion as melancholy, in John Donne, 106
religion, madness and, 161
religious enthusiasm
  Burton, Robert, 155
  Casaubon, Meric, 155
  change in status of, 155
  disenchantment with, 158
  divine inspiration, 158
  as divine rapture, 155
  invective against, 126, 157
  madness and, 153, 154, 157
  melancholy and, 158
  melancholy madness and, 154
  More, Henry, 155
  as pathological, 126, 155, 158
religious enthusiasm, melancholy and, 3, 4, 20
religious radicalism, public perception of, 19
religious rebellion, melancholy and, 106
religious reform, melancholy and, 127
religious sects, 19
  melancholy and, 167
Renaissance, humors in, 177
Restoration

melancholy and, 168, 175
silencing of radical religious sects during, 126
texts, 2
Revengers Tragedy The, melancholy and revenge in, 84
revolution, madness and, 153
rivalry between Jonson and Shakespeare, "War of the Theaters" and, 63
Roman civil wars, humors and, 7
Rome, 15, 85
"Roots and Branches" petition, abolition of ecclesiastical government, 162
Roulston, Gilbert, *Ranters Bible,* 167
Roundhead, 163
Royalists, Samson story and, 177
rumor
    John Donne and, 105–122
    Fama, relation to, 44, 120
    as melancholy vapor and, 18
    politics and, 18

S

Samson Agonistes (Milton), 175–196
    Bacchanalian orgy and, 194
    chorus and, 186, 187
    chorus and madness at the public level, 194
    chorus exultation over Samson's death in, 185
    controversies about, 179
    Dalila, 188, 189, 193, 194
    despair and, 173
    divine proclamations in, 188
    dramatic conflict in, 186
    fish-god Dagon and, 177
    humors in, 176, 177
    idol worship in, 194
    inspiration and, 173, 178
    Israelites and, 185, 186, 188, 190, 192, 194
    madness and, 194
    Manoa, 176, 187–188, 190, 191–192, 193, 194
    melancholy and, 173, 176, 181, 195
    melancholy in Restoration, 175
    Philistines and, 177, 194
    public language in, 188, 190
    redemption in, 194
    religion and, 179
    religious enthusiasm and, 19, 179
    religious melancholy and, 179
    religious prophecy and, 19
    Samson, 173, 176, 179, 192, 193
    Samson and divine inspiration, 173, 195
    Samson and language in, 187–188
    Samson and madness, 173, 195
    Samson and melancholy, 173, 176, 177, 180
    Samson and melancholy discontent, 195
    Samson and providence, 179, 186
    Samson and vengeance, 195
    Samson as Phoenix in, 194
    Samson as political allegory, 177
    Samson's conflict in, 185, 189
    Samson's death in, 186, 191
    Samson's iconoclasm, 173
    Samson's self-destructive violence in, 177, 178
    Samson's strength in, 190, 194
    "shameful garrulity" in, 184–195
    superstition and idolatry in, 185
    uncertainty in, 195
Schleiner, Winfried, *Melancholy, Genius, and Utopia,* 8
Schoenfeldt, Michael, 54–55
Scripture, interpretation of, 154–155
Sedgwick, Joseph
    prophecy and authority, 159
    sermon about prophecy and authority, 159
Seneca, 33, 130, 132
Shakespeare, William, 68. *see also* individual works
    animals on stage and, 64
    Brutus and melancholy in, 11, 86
    Hamlet and melancholy, 12
    "humour" plays of, 59–84
    melancholy and, 10
    melancholy characters in, 85
Shelley, Mary, 90
shepherd
    prophetic style of poetry and, 40
    radical reformist poets and, 40

Index

Shepheardes Calendar (Spenser), 38–45
    Colin Clout in, 40, 41
    Dido, Queen of Shepherds, 40
    divine fury in, 43
    EK, 42, 43, 44
    English language and, 38
    English poetry and, 39
    the Galimaufrey and hodgepodge of language, and, 38–45
    "October" Eclogue, 41–45
    "The New Poet," 38
Sidney, Sir Phillip
    Apology, 28
    Defense of Poesie, 29
    poetry of, 28
Skelton, John, 40
Sophocles, 105
Spain, English medicine and, 32
Spanish war, 15
Speech of Lord Digby's to the House of Commons, image of ruler as physician in, 163
Spenser, Edmund, 15, 16, 28–57, 30, 43, 59. *see also* individual works
    "Called the English Poete," 42
    Colin Clout as fictional persona of, 40
    Colin Clout as melancholy love-sick lyricist, 20
    commonwealth and, 56
    English Poet, 28, 29
    the *Faerie Queene, Book II*, 47
    interest in ek-static poetry, 38
    Irish and, 55
    Joachim du Bellay and, 39, 40
    John van der Noot and, 39
    language and, 40, 45, 56, 59
    letter to Gabriel Harvey, 38
    linguistic reform and, 38
    as lyricist, 50
    melancholy and, 56, 59
    melancholy and human inability to comprehend, 57
    melancholy vs. despair in, 59–60
    misrule and, 49
    nationhood and, 59
    Ninus and, 56
    Orpheus and, 18, 38, 41
    Petrarch and, 39
    physiological health and, 55
    poetic authority and, 42
    poetic prophecies and political instability, 56
    poetics of enthusiasm and, 45
    poetry and politics in, 40
    poetry and prophesy, 40
    poetry of, 17, 19, 28
    political affiliations of, 46
    political institutions and, 59
    political terminology and physical health, 48–49
    politics and limited human comprehension, 57
    prophesy and madness, 50
    prophetic and visionary poetry, 40
    prophetic language and, 50
    reading and, 56
    revolt of Malager's troop in *The Faerie Queene*, 47
    Timothy Bright and, 56
    Tower of Babel and, 40, 45–56, 46, 47, 59
    translation of Du Bellay's "Complaints," 7
    translation of visionary poetry, 39
    vernacular languages and, 39, 40
    View of the Present State of Ireland, 55
state
    compared to body, 5, 116
    dissolution of, 116
subjectivity, 23
suicide, 103–150
    Christianity and, 106
    John Donne and, 105–122
    and madness, 106
    as resistance to Roman Empire, 106
    Samson Agonistes and, 177
Swift, Jonathan
    invectives against the Puritans, 127
    religious enthusiasm, 155
    A Tale of a Tub, 155

T

Tasso, melancholy and, 10
Taylor, John, 163

"Mad Fashions Od Fashions, Alls out of
  Fashion," 160
the Royal Society, 168
"The Terrors of the Night" (Thomas Nashe),
  melancholy apparitions and, 87
Theophrastus, 4, 62
  "Characters," 73
  importance in 17th century London,
    73
theories of poetic genius, physiologic disorder and, 28
Thessalonians, 184
Thomas Nashe, "The Terrors of the Night,"
  87
Tower of Babel, 39, 42, 45
  Hittites and, 54
  physiological repercussions of, 45
  as political model, 46
  political repercussions of, 45
True Religion (Milton), superstition and
  idolatry in, 185

U

Underhill, Thomas
  Quakerism as madness in, 166
  Satan's influence on the Quaker sect, 166

V

Venice, 46
  futility of political ambitions and, 47
  problematic nature of government of, 46
Vindiciae Contra Tyrannos (Stephanus Junius
  Brutus), 85
Virgil, rumor and, 121

W

Wakefield, Robert, as English linguist, 36
Warburg critics, the, 9–11
Whitehead, George
  defense of Quakerism, 159
  "Divine Inspiration and Immediate Illu-
    mination {by God Himself}
    Asserted," 159
witchcraft, 164
Wright, Thomas, *Passions of the Minde in
  Generall*, 5, 90

Y

Younge, Richard
  poverty and discontent, 2
  *The Prevention of Poverty, Together with
    the Cure of Melancholy, Alias
    Discontent*, 1